W9-ASG-788

The Catholic Marriage Manual

The Catholic Marriage Manual

Reverend George A. Kelly

Random House  NEW YORK

FOURTH PRINTING

Manufactured in the United States of America by Kingsport Press, Inc.

Library of Congress Catalog Card Number: 58–10953

NIHIL OBSTAT

John A. Goodwine, J.C.D.
Censor Librorum

IMPRIMATUR

Francis Cardinal Spellman
Archbishop of New York

The nihil obstat *and* imprimatur *are official declarations that a book or pamphlet is free of doctrinal or moral error. No implication is contained therein that those who have granted the* nihil obstat *and* imprimatur *agree with the contents, opinions or statements expressed.*

August 3, 1958

Dedicated to the Memory of
My Late Devoted Father
CHARLES WILLIAM KELLY
and to my Beloved Mother
BRIDGET FITZGERALD KELLY
whose six living children
will always remember how they
spent themselves for our
welfare, and whose combined
piety will live to influence
the formation of their great-
great-grandchildren.

ACKNOWLEDGMENTS

The writer wishes to convey his sincere thanks to all those who had a share in the writing and publication of this book. The friendly interest and foreword provided by my Archbishop, His Eminence, Francis Cardinal Spellman, is particularly appreciated. The Reverend Stephen J. Kelleher, J. C. D., pro-Synodal Judge of the New York Matrimonial Curia and Paul Lapolla of Random House were especially helpful with their comments and criticisms. I am indebted to Mr. Paul Gallico for permission to quote from an article of his, which appeared in the *Reader's Digest;* to Doubleday and Company for the use of material drawn from Father John A. O'Brien's *Happy Marriage;* and to the Cana Conference of Chicago for an excerpt from *The New Cana Manual.*

Special words of gratitude are due John Springer of Scarsdale, New York, who through the year of writing was so helpful with his research and who collaborated with the writer in determining the subject matter covered by this book. Whatever value THE CATHOLIC MARRIAGE MANUAL has for readers is due in great part to his generous and intelligent assistance.

CONTENTS

FOREWORD

By His Eminence, Francis Cardinal Spellman, Archbishop of New York

The apostolate of fostering the integrity and sanctity of Christian marriage is one of the most important missions of the Church, especially in our day when diabolical forces are at work to undermine the most fundamental of all human societies, the family.

The Church has constantly proclaimed that a man's family is a kingly treasure and his home truly a castle—the place to which God looks, as He did to Bethlehem, for the beginning of mortal lives which are also eternal, for the beginning of the lives of tiny citizens of two worlds: of earth and heaven.

When Christian family life flourishes, the civilized world benefits. It is important, therefore, that all married couples comprehend the deepest meaning of their calling—collaboration with God Himself in the work of creation and redemption—and that they approach the married state with the full realization of their holy vocation.

Since ignorance of any one of the many areas of married life can be harmful to parents and children, men and women entering marriage, as well as those already married, should seek the guidance not only of learned human sciences but the wise counsel of Holy Mother the Church.

The Catholic Marriage Manual is intended to fulfill this need by giving an insight into the beauty of sacramental marriage, as well as by demonstrating the practical steps by which Christian couples can perfect their own marital union and fulfill the requirements of Catholic parenthood.

My fervent prayer is that God may continue to bless the valiant efforts of the Church to sanctify marriage and that an ever increasing number of sons and daughters will come from these holy families to labor in the vineyard of the Master.

The Catholic Marriage Manual

1

Marriage Is a Sacred Vocation

As a married man or woman, you have one of the greatest gifts—and one of the greatest opportunities to do good—that it is possible for human beings to possess on earth. In your sacrament of marriage, you have a vocation from God—a special call by Him to you and your mate—to serve Him together in a holy sacrament until death. He does not expect you to do it alone. On your wedding day He walked away from the altar with you and promises you even now all the help you need from Him to fulfill your role. And as if the satisfactions of heartwarming companionship for life and parenthood were not enough, He assures you, as the Church states in her marriage ritual, "the greatest measure of earthly happiness that may be allotted to man in this vale of tears," as well as happiness with each other and your children in heaven forever.

If you understand these simple facts about your marriage, you will gain a new and revealing insight into the marvelous potentialities of your state. You will find new spiritual beauty in your life together. You will welcome the privileges of parenthood with new, inspired zest. You will learn to accept life's gifts and to bear its trials with a serenity you perhaps never thought possible.

Marriage is your vocation . . . One of life's great puzzles is that so few married couples regard their state in life as a vocation. If your brother or sister planned to become a priest or a nun, you would not doubt that he or she had been called to a special way of life by God. Should they change their minds and marry, you would accept as explanation that they had lost their vocation. Yet your vocation as a married man or woman is just as much a call by God as that to the religious life. You are asked to do a different work: to become parents and to make each other happy, the while working for the salvation of all the souls entrusted to your care. And this sacred trust, since God has called you to it, is the best possible vocation for you. Your marriage is not to be belittled as some second-rate way of life. This is where God wants you to be. Matrimony is the state God from all eternity summoned you to. He arranged the order of events and permitted you so to organize your life that providentially you and your mate would meet, attract each other, marry, and set up your own unique Christian home.

This way of life to which you were directed by God's inspiration, therefore, is a holy and exalted state. As the priest shares God's redemptive power through Holy Orders, you share His creative power through matrimony. The priest is elated with the sublimity of his vocation because he teaches, rules, sanctifies, and administers the sacraments in the name of Jesus Christ. Why should you not be equally elated because you are His instrument, His tool in the work of creation? You are the one He calls upon to initiate a precious human being, to teach it, to develop its soul, mind, character, and to guide it along the path toward a good life here and eternal life hereafter. By His own will, He chose to depend on you. Consider that fact carefully—and you will regard your marriage as a truly noble state.

How noble that married life of yours is can be measured by the realization that God has created for you a unique human relationship. The Kingdom of God on earth is like a mosaic. Its beauty and value are determined by the diversity of the myriad separate settings. Your marriage is different from anyone else's in this world. God wanted it so. He wanted you to develop your virtues in a way possible to no one else. He wanted your children to look and to be only as the two of you could make them look and be. While this Divine dictate imposes a grave responsibility, it is also a special privilege and a source of unique satisfaction. You know that you can answer His call in a very personal way and that your work in His behalf will never be compared to anyone else's, because only you could have done it.

A calling to a man and a woman . . . God could have worked out His purposes of creation in many ways. To His infinite mind, "increase and multiply" did not *have* to mean an Eve by the side of Adam. In the plant and animal world He uses many devices. However, for perpetuating the human race, He chose to create a man and a woman; moreover, He decided that these two should complement each other, that the weaknesses of the one should be offset by the strengths of the other. Every man, therefore, is made different from every woman, and every woman, different from every man. These differences are emotional as well as physical; they are reflected in the different approach to many questions which arise in marriage. These differences were created because God expects the man and the woman to perform different functions in marriage. He intended man to be the head and woman the heart of the home.

Few statements can trigger a hotter discussion than the assertion that man in marriage should be the head of the family. Even when the American wife finds a great deal of satisfaction in doing what comes naturally—clinging to her husband, depending on him, and deriving much comfort from his strength—she is still likely to reject his leadership if only in the name of Susan B. Anthony. It is well to remember, also, that the American male, while flattered by the suggestion of marital pre-eminence, is too often frightened by its responsibility and quite willing to have the little woman take over.

Yet if God made man and woman different so that they could play complementary roles in marriage, common sense would seem to suggest that family life would be better where the partners performed the functions for which each is best suited. And apart from anything God has to say explicitly about the matter, any study of male and female will teach us that man is best suited by nature to be the head, and woman especially fitted to be the heart of the home. One is not inferior to the other; each simply complements the other.

Young couples echoing the clichés of popular magazines may say that marriage is a fifty-fifty proposition, whatever that may mean. Actually, marriage, if anything, is a hundred-hundred proposition—the union of a hundred-per-cent man and a hundred-per-cent woman. St. Paul was only passing on traditional doctrine when he said, "Man is the head of the woman as Christ is the head of the Church." (Ephesians 23:5) All of man's natural aggressiveness, his masculine brawn, his logical mind, make being head easy for him. What is more, nothing gives a man greater satisfaction and sense of fulfillment than a realized sense of importance. Men want recognition. They thrive on it. And their natural instinct in marriage is to be head. If they abdicate the masculine role in the family, they feel guilty; if they are denied it, they are resentful.

Nothing like this is natural to the woman. If she is aggressive or domineering it is because she has been made so, and that is not good. Two egotists do not easily make a harmonious pair. By virtue of her natural endowments the woman provides the devotion, the self-sacrifice, the tenderness in the family. No man can be as dedicated to human beings, even his own flesh and blood, as his wife. Her contentment comes from giving herself to husband and children, not in bossing them. Mrs. Dwight Eisenhower stated the gentle woman's viewpoint: "Is it worth it to have my own way about this? What am I gaining anyway if Ike would rather have it some other way?"

St. Paul was wiser than many people realize when he summed up the whole question in a few words: "Wives, obey your husbands; husbands, love your wives." What does a man want more than respect and recognition? What does a woman want more than love? And yet in counseling obedience and love to the married, St. Paul was directing each to give the other what is most difficult for each to give. The wife, being human, resists obedience; the man, being masculine, does not love easily.

Of course, in our day the mention of authority conjures up images of despots. The fact that God intends man to represent authority in the home does not mean that God put him there as a tyrant, or that the obedience of the wife is the obedience of a slave to a master, of an inferior to a superior, of a minor incapable of decision to an adult. His headship in no way detracts from her dignity as wife, mother, and companion.

The role of the husband is to promote greater harmony and greater love in the home. No divided house can long stand. No body can have two heads. Unless this question had been decided by God, there would be perpetual conflict over the power of final decision, as there is, unfortunately, in many a modern home today. Much of the conflict in modern marriage would disappear if men would assume their responsibilities and women would be content to be heart and homemaker.

In homes where people love each other and are considerate, there is open discussion of all major matters and agreement on what or what not to do. In some cases the wife will have a powerful influence on her husband, which is as it should be. Where he is a weakling or neglectful, it falls to her to take his place in directing the family. The husband's position has significance mainly when some important decision has to be made (for example, a move to a new house) and there is no immediate agreement. If the decision cannot be postponed until there is harmony of viewpoint, then the responsible husband will make the decision, and the loving wife will cheerfully acquiesce in the decision with humility. The husband, more than she, symbolizes law, authority, order, and any attempt to belittle him or deny his headship in such matters will certainly incur his wrath and destroy before the children the image of God's fatherhood that man was chosen to exemplify.

To serve Him . . . Volumes of texts from Scripture, teachings of the early Fathers of the Church and the logical arguments of the theologians could be adduced to prove that in creating man and woman God mainly intended to insure the perpetuation of mankind. His first commandment to Adam and Eve was to increase and multiply. St. Paul said that a woman shall be saved by childbearing, and his statement applies with equal force to men. The very name of matrimony derives from two words—*matris* and *munus*—meaning the office and function of motherhood.

The whole success of your marriage depends, therefore, upon your recognition of the fact that its purpose is the bearing and rearing of children. Once you make this purpose your own, you accept one of the greatest of God's gifts—a share in His creative and redemptive power. When you bear a child you are likely to accept the wonderful event unthinkingly. And yet when the first rays of the sun dispelled the clouds of the sky or the first wave of the ocean rolled up against the land and Adam and Eve were raised from the slime of the earth, all the heavens applauded God's power. If heaven still applauds the birth of your new son, why not you? You are permitted to share in the magnificent act of creation each time you take the step by which a new human life may be formed. And every child born to you is given you to be treated as Christ would have you treat it. You are the infant's first teacher and its sanctifier, and your home is a little church.

The task which God asks you to perform in marriage is so holy that every Catholic should be eager to fulfill it, just as the priest is eager to fulfill the work prescribed by Holy Orders.

Every Catholic has a high regard for the priestly vocation and treats a priest with respect. Some priestly duties might appeal less to the candidate for Holy Orders than others; yet, of course, he accepts all as a part of his calling. Suppose, however, that hearing confessions was not to his liking and that after ordination he refused to perform that aspect of his calling. You would be properly shocked. You would comment that such a man lacks the ideals essential to the priestly state in life. He is making reservations in his priesthood; he has not completely accepted in daily life the ideals of Christ. He is entering his vocation lacking a true willingness to shoulder his responsibilities, and his state of mind would result in tragedy for himself and disadvantage to the Church and the faithful.

Should not the same conclusion be reached about the man and woman who approach the sacrament of matrimony having already decided that they may have one child after a few years, or that they will limit their family to two or three children? Or who, within themselves, agree to accept marriage so long as the problems are few, so long as the husband behaves himself, so long as the wife remains attractive—the alternative in their minds being separation or divorce? They too are hedging; they seek to rewrite God's laws to avoid their duties while they accept their privileges. The success of marriage depends upon the capacity to make sacrifices for the ideals of the calling. That priest is happiest who devotes himself completely and exclusively, without equivocation, to the work of Holy Orders. That marriage is happiest in which husband and wife are similarly dedicated not only to each other but to the business of matrimony. What will it profit a couple if they enjoy conjugal companionship if by their own selfish will they contribute little to God's Kingdom or to humanity?

In a sacrament . . . According to some secular approaches to marriage, the union of husband and wife is either ridiculed outright or is presented as a life of burden. You are bound to one man or woman for the rest of your life. You are overwhelmed by bills the first of every month and your major problem is to balance your budget. You are weighed down with bearing and caring for children. People who view marriage in this light cannot help but regard it as a grim business which requires a cold-blooded outlook.

The Catholic looks at marriage in a marvelously different way. He views it as an institution with a truly wonderful vision. Here is an opportunity for him to enjoy life in the fullest, most inspirational degree possible on earth, and to enjoy an eternity with God in heaven. He views marriage not only as the union of man and woman for the purposes of procreation. It is more. It is a partnership with God; a union with Him to do His work of creation and redemption and sanctification upon earth. And as a partner, God will help every Christian couple. The very fact that He elevated marriage to the dignity of a sacrament is proof that He will do so.

How many couples, complaining about their own difficulties in marriage, see friends of theirs or neighbors who seem to thrive on the very conditions of life so overwhelming to them? These others bear children frequently; sickness only augments their love; poor economic circumstances do not crush them. They live with the realization that Christ joined them at the altar rail and is walking with them every step of their way through life together. Whenever they need His help, He is there supporting them with His grace. Everything they do in marriage, beginning with sharing an apartment, is related to heaven and is a guarantee of their happiness. And because so many Catholic couples produce these "miracles," their more worldly neighbors become afraid. The seculars do not understand, so in envy or guilt they scoff. They do not realize that with God's help even they are capable of the Christian vision of marriage.

When God joined you in sacramental wedlock, He realized in you the living example of Christ's union with His Church. Your family became Christ's Kingdom in miniature, the father assuming the role of Christ, the mother symbolizing the Church. So much of God's love and God's grace henceforth was to be poured to His creatures through you. Your children were not only to be born of flesh but through you to become sons of God. Their eyes were to look not only upon the faces of their parents but, in the fullness of time, on the face of God Himself. Sanctity and holiness were to be the normal effect of your life together. As the housewife once prayed: "Since I have no time to be a saint by storming heaven's gates, make me a saint by getting meals and washing up the plates." If you live marriage as God created it, and as Christ elevated it, you are saints. You will have developed, through your love of marriage and each other, qualities of your own goodness which perhaps you never realized you possessed. We see this happening all the time among Catholic couples. By earthly standards a particular husband and wife may appear unfitted for life together. We wonder how they can meet their responsibilities, adjust to conflicting temperaments and viewpoints, and overcome their pronounced character weaknesses. Yet thirty or forty years elapse, and we discover that they have lived fine lives together—lives that are models of sanctification and the envy of their less religious neighbors. How did they do it? They were able to elevate themselves and to meet their responsibilities by partaking of the aids of sanctifying grace which God made available to them in marriage. The sacrament was truly their salvation.

Consider what the sacrament of matrimony means to you in connection with your vocation. No nun, no matter how holy, has received a sacrament of nunhood. Religious brothers and monks have not had the privilege of a sacrament when they entered their state in life. The fact that you received a sacrament while these holy people did not is visible proof of the importance of your vocation. Because of your sacrament, Christ resides in your home as He does in the Church. Of course, our Blessed Lord is in the Eucharist and the Church is the temple of Christ, and you must go to the altar to make contact with Him. However, wherever you find a sacrament you also find Christ. You will find Him in your own home because the Christian home is a dwelling place for Christ.

The bond of marriage, therefore, is an important cornerstone of the House of God. Christ has ordained you to a common life which has vitally important supernatural purposes. Its chief purpose is to build up the Mystical Body of Christ. And since you are living with Christ, as well as with each other, you must have religious aspirations just as the priest does. In practice Catholic marriage involves not mere companionship but personal identity with each other and with Christ; not mere parenthood but the enlargement of God's heavenly Kingdom; not only developing character in the children but their training for sanctity; happiness on earth certainly, but even more, beatitude with God forever. The Catholic home is more than an isolated family life. It involves working for Christ and His Kingdom with other couples in the Church.

Priests are aware of this power of sacramental grace. Often a new priest doubts his ability to perform the duties of his vocation in the manner expected of him. But the hand of God steers him in such a way that the priest reaches heights that he never thought he was capable of reaching. And what he achieves is mysteriously in the interest of his own salvation, as well as the salvation of the souls for whom he has been given some degree of responsibility.

Because your soul is encased in a body, it is sometimes difficult for you to recognize this sacramental basis of your marriage. We all become so engrossed at times in the mechanics of living that we forget our supernatural existence. Yet your faith can be such that you believe that God is with you and will help you in every aspect of your marriage. Thus every act of your state—

the preparing of a meal, the repairing of a faucet, the painting of a wall, the marriage act itself—can be the means by which you grow in sanctity.

When you do come to realize that your marriage is a sacrament, a special work of God, you will be filled with enthusiasm for your vocation. The confidence that you acquire from leaning on Christ will inspire the diligence, maturity, and skill that parenthood requires. This confidence, of course, does not absolve you from making efforts to develop your own natural talents for marriage; but now you will have not only your virtues, but God helping you to cultivate them.

Together until death . . . Marriage is a permanent union. The man called to the vocation of the priesthood gets only one chance; you who are called to the vocation of marriage likewise have but one chance. Consequently, you must learn to live together harmoniously.

The husband and wife who leave the altar rail after receiving the priest's blessing are beginning a new life. Before they can grow in marriage, they must learn. They must learn as much as they can about each other. They must learn to adapt themselves to the realities and not attempt to force marriage to adapt to them, just as the child must adapt to much of life as he finds it without kicking uselessly against the common lot.

There must of necessity be a long period of adjustment in marriage. Even if you are married seventy-five years, you will still perceive areas in your relationship which you could improve. You cannot expect perfect adjustment, perfect understanding, and perfect happiness within the first six months, even within the first ten years. Marriage is a process of growth. But if you bring to it the proper ideals of heart and mind, a willingness to understand and to sacrifice, your adjustment will improve with every year.

You must recognize that your marriage is something greater than even both of you put together. It is possible for you to have an ideal marriage even though husband and wife are but ordinary people. Each of you may acquire qualities that were not found in either prior to marriage, and both come to the pleasant realization that the whole is *greater* than the sum of its parts.

Married couples need *prudence, justice, fortitude* and *temperance.* The prudent husband and wife make good practical judgments about what are the important things in marriage. Furthermore, they develop the knack of knowing how to get what they need most, and what they want, without trampling on the rights of each other, their children, or their neighbors. A sense of justice contributes to marital harmony because it encourages respect for the other members of the family. Honorable people never gain their own satisfactions at someone else's expense. There will be times when any member of the family may threaten the peace of the household by his unbridled ambition, anger, passion, or pride. The more he tempers and controls his own basic impulses, the better will be the opportunities for happiness among the remaining members of the household. And since a certain amount of pain or anguish is inevitably associated with human living, patience and fortitude are necessary characteristics of a struggling couple. When heroism is called for, husbands and wives should have the capacity to be heroes.

These four natural virtues alone, however, no matter in what abundance they are present, will prove inadequate to a sacramental state of life which requires, above all, the virtues of *faith, hope,* and *charity.*

The first step that you will take on your road to sanctity is faith in the sacramental qualities of your marriage. If you reread the Gospels with the specific intention of finding passages relating to the importance of faith, you will be astonished to note how often Christ emphasized the importance of this quality in our spiritual development. Jesus spoke of faith that moves mountains when the woman touched the hem of His garment, begging to be healed. He turned to her, saying, "Go, woman, thy faith has made thee whole."

Christian faith will give you the ability to view life as Christ views it and the humility to organize your marriage according to His Will. Insofar, too, as the innumerable details of married life today lead to worry and a fruitless chase after the illusion of security, you must live with the hope and expectation that God is with you. Did not Christ say: "Why are you anxious about what you shall eat?" The most consoling mandate He ever gave Christians was: "Seek ye first the Kingdom of God and His justice and all other things will be added besides." Families that trust in God generally display more diligence, thrift, and ingenuity than those which regard marriage as solely a challenge to human efficiency.

It is love inspired of God, however, that is most important to your marriage. Christ realized, better than anyone else, the difficulties associated with married love. So in order to purify the love of a married couple for each other he gave them the grace of a sacrament. Love as it is commonly conceived of by many today consists of the sensual attraction of husband to wife. But when the grace of God enters, the man does not look upon his wife merely as a sex partner; he regards her in an idealistic way—as his partner in parenthood and married sanctity. Therefore, the grace of God will purify human love and make it the exalted thing it should be. Thanks to grace, sex becomes an instrument of love—not an end or objective of it.

The grace of God also makes you capable of greater love than you ever thought possible. When the average young bride and bridegroom come to the altar, they are full of themselves—self-centered. They have not learned to purify their love by giving of themselves, except, perhaps, in small ways. Yet they soon rise to levels of self-sacrifice beyond their dreams. For example, a typical expectant bride probably spends hours each day on personal adornment. She expects much for herself and is prepared to give little. Two years later, she no longer fancies herself a beauty as she spends sleepless nights over the bed of her sick infant. The gay party-loving young girl has been changed into the serious, responsible, self-sacrificing mother by one thing—the grace of Almighty God.

You realize, of course, that the priest did not marry you when you stood before the altar on your wedding day. You married each other. You administered the sacrament; you gave Christ to each other. Thus you must strive to use in marriage the grace to which your participation in the sacrament entitles you. This is the real goal in marriage: to purify that love which began on your wedding day on a natural plane, into the supernatural thing that Christ wants it to be. Love, of course, is not merely a matter of feeling. Real loving is willing. When you truly love, regardless of how you feel, you *will* to do for your husband or wife only that which is good.

Love is all-embracing. When you love, you realize that every personality is made up of certain strengths and corresponding weaknesses and that you must love the weakness as well as the strength. To do this requires the act of the will. At times a husband may be tempted to retract his love, or a wife faces her husband's weaknesses and wishes that she could withdraw her commitments, but they do not. He loves her not only because of her virtues, but because she is his partner in Christ and because he loves Christ. She loves him because she loves her marriage as an instrument of Christ's will.

When set in this sacred framework, sex can be an instrument of your growing love for each other. For the physical act should be merely a sign of your interior love. It is an act of giving: the husband gives himself completely with every vestige of his corporal being and his wife receives him with the same complete abandonment. If the physical act is intellectually sterile, devoid of any spiritual meaning, it becomes a kind of prostitution of marriage. But if it springs from the thought of good, it will be a source of greater love. This pure kind of love can raise you to undreamed-of heights.

The mysterious gift of God's grace also transforms your approach to parenthood. When you are aware of this grace, you look upon your child not only as a gift from the Creator but as something more: a human being you will return to God. You come to believe that God has permitted you to share in His process of creation, that He has given you the opportunity to fill up His Kingdom with your flesh and blood.

St. Augustine, in addressing fathers, often called them "my fellow Bishops." He conveyed the idea that they were the heads of their families much as the Bishop is the head of the Church. For in his home, the father has the same functions that the Church has on a universal scale: he has the obligation to teach, to rule, and to sanctify.

Probably few couples realize the good they can do simply by leading sanctified lives in marriage. For example, assume that a husband and wife have five children. Within twenty-five years, those five children will have the responsibility for the upbringing of perhaps twenty-five more children. Assuming the same average, when three generations have gone by, one couple will have been responsible for more than one hundred and fifty-five lives. If your example has been a good one, most—if not all—will be magnificent human beings and wonderful Christians; and the tradition of sanctity you bequeath to them will continue for generations more. When you go to God, and He asks what kind of a married couple you were, you need only point to the world you left behind. On the other hand, what harm even one bad couple can do by example! Through their failure to educate for Christ, within sixty years they can leave behind them the seeds of sinfulness, infidelity, heresy, apostasy—the seeds of all that is evil in the world.

With God's grace, your home is the center of education and of worship. You have the privilege of teaching your children to look at life from a supernatural point of view at an early age, and of encouraging them to accept the facts of life with greater grace. For example, the young girl who sees her mother accept motherhood with cheerfulness and love will herself grow up with a proper attitude toward the joys of childbearing and child rearing. Your home is also a center of apostolic activity on behalf of Christ, for in learning to love your husband or wife and your children, you also learn to love all people. And the greater this love becomes, the greater becomes your love for family. For love feeds upon love just as hate feeds upon hate.

The married couples who wish to go even further, to perfect their life and their work for God, will practice the same virtues which are at the very heart of the religious life—*poverty, chastity,* and *obedience.* If you live in the spirit of these virtues, your home will be especially blessed with happiness that comes from heaven.

The spirit of poverty that should characterize your way of life does not mean that you must live without necessities or decent comforts, even luxury. It simply means that you can do without things when you have to without complaining. Our Blessed Lord had a respectable home, warm clothing, wholesome food. Yet not having more did not upset Him. He was detached enough from things so that His happiness did not depend on them. Compare His attitude with that of some married couples whose happiness depends on their getting everything they want and getting it now. This is not an age that sees Christ in the poor or that awaits God's good time for providing. Too many people are unhappy with their earnings, even though they can buy more goods than were ever before available to ordinary workers. We do not recommend that Catholic husbands and wives go out of their way to embrace poverty, but they must be prepared, if they live marriage as they should, to have poverty embrace them and not be embarrassed or ashamed to be poor.

Many modern couples falsely believe also that marriage puts an end to the need for chastity. Nothing could be more wrong. Even the sexual appetites of the married are subject to God's Will. You must realize that from time to time, out of love for your spouse, you must regulate your desires, even to the point of abstinence. Obedience also can be practiced by husband and wife when each seeks to do what the other wants. If one of the parties is a rebel by training and has never acquired the capacity to conform easily to someone else's demands, then conflict is the inevitable result. Even though the husband is the head of the house, the home will run much more smoothly if both partners learn to obey each other.

What must you do to gain the fullest measure of God's grace for your marriage? The first necessity is your willingness to cooperate with each other—to work together in harmony. From the moment you leave the altar on your wedding day, your growth in love, and much of your sacramental life, depends on the closeness of your union. Working together as a team involves the subordination of your own ego, your own pride, and sometimes even your own needs.

The trouble with many marriages is that people have lived together for ten, twenty, or thirty years, and have never united —except physically. But the greatest union that can exist in marriage is the total union of soul, mind, and body. That union comes only with the ability of the husband and wife to make known to each other their wants and their needs, and with the willingness of the other partner to satisfy those wants and needs once they are aware of their existence. Thus the whole essence of marriage is a common life. There is no such thing as independent living. You must give yourself—and give yourself gladly—if your marriage is to succeed.

The second necessary consideration is commitment. You must commit yourself completely to each other and commit your union to Christ—in brief, you must make a total commitment. When you do so, you cease to have a "private life" outside of your marriage. The husband's interests are his wife's interests; her friends are his friends; her hopes and fears are his hopes and fears. Your commitment is not only to your mate but also to your children. You cannot hold back on the loving care and attention you give them. You accept the responsibility for their upbringing in its entirety.

Finally, the partners who walk in the fullness of grace are consecrated to serve the glory of God. The consecrated husband and wife are idealists. They walk through life with their eyes on the skies and take their burdens in stride. They know that no matter what earthly troubles come their way, God is by their side. They see God in each other and in their children, and they seize the chance to serve God in many ordinary ways throughout each day. They have consecrated themselves to the Eternal God.

2

The Keys to Mutual Love

TO SUCCEED at any vocation, you must have patience, a determination to learn, a willingness to put aside momentary desires for the sake of final success. The vocation of marriage is no exception. It requires hard work. In fact, it is probably the hardest job of all. For example, consider what a wife and mother must be. She must be an inspiring companion to her husband. She must be a housekeeper who has some skill in cooking, sewing and cleaning. She must be something of an economist, able to handle her household budget and to shop efficiently for food, furnishings and clothing. She must be proficient in the feeding and physical care of her children. She must be a nurse. She must be a teacher with a working knowledge of child psychology to discipline her youngsters properly. In addition to the actual skills needed for the successful performance of these jobs, she requires spiritual and emotional qualities —patience, tolerance, understanding, kindness, gentility, fortitude, prudence.

The successful husband and father needs similar qualities. To inspire respect for his leadership he should be reasonably competent as a man: he must be the head of the family; he must be a provider for his wife and children. He must be a source of inspiration to his wife, encouraging her to fulfill her duties as wife and mother. He, too, must be a teacher, for his example will probably be the most important influence in the development of his son's personality. He also requires insights into the spiritual and emotional needs of his wife and children. He requires high resolutions and a strong sense of duty to meet those needs.

Since it is obvious that a man and woman need so many qualities to succeed as husband and wife and as father and mother, why do so many take the marriage vows without really knowing what will be expected of them? Even couples who have lived together for years sometimes fail to realize how many adjustments they must make and how much self-discipline they must impose if their marriage is to weather future difficulties successfully.

Listen to the dreamy popular songs on the radio, read the romantic novels in many magazines, and view the love stories portrayed on television or in the movies. Seldom will you find even a vague suggestion that the vocation of marriage requires unremitting hard work by both partners. Problems that arise in marriage as portrayed on television are almost always solved in time for the final commercial. Popular songs convey a constant impression that personality conflicts can be washed away in the sea of sex. Even articles on marriage in popular magazines and books, seriously intended to help couples achieve better adjustment, often introduce a typical problem and, a few sentences later, report how the couple, by performing a magic act like visiting a marriage counselor, correct all past difficulties and live happily thereafter.

Few publications emphasize that mutual sacrifice is essential to marital success. In that magnificent little volume *The Imitation of Christ,* compiled by Thomas Kempis in the fifteenth century, it is written: "Unless thou deny thyself, thou shalt not have perfect liberty." Those words might be studied by every married person. Unless you practice severe self-discipline and subjugate your own desires, striving instead to fulfill the needs of your spouse and children, you cannot gain the full happiness of marriage. Despite what the movies say, no one "finds" happiness. If you obtain it at all, you must earn it.

And it will be earned only by what the Catholic marriage ritual calls "the great principle of self-sacrifice." On your wedding day you surrendered your individual lives in the interest of a deeper and wider common life. From that day forward you belonged to each other. You were expected to become one in mind, one in heart, and one in affections. And as the ritual counseled: "Whatever sacrifices you may hereafter be required to make to preserve this common life, always make them generously."

Does this mean that we must picture married life in grim, terrifying colors? Not a bit! Sacrifice is difficult and irksome only in the absence of love. Love makes it easy, and the more perfect the love, the more joy in the sacrifice.

When two people learn to bear patiently with marriage and with each other, marital harmony is the result. And this meeting of minds is the greatest source of happiness humans can obtain on earth. No earthly pleasure can match that which the loving husband gives his wife, the wife gives her husband, or children give their parents. Very few people indeed appreciate that it is the warm and living union of two persons which alone gives life its full meaning.

Three pillars of happiness: To be a good wife, you must first *understand* your husband, recognizing the fundamental aspects of his character and how his personality differs from your own. Secondly, you must *accept* him—accept him not only as a man, but as a man with an individuality unlike that of any other man on earth. Finally, you must *inspire* him to achieve the fullest spiritual and emotional growth of which he is capable. The good husband must also *understand, accept,* and *inspire* his wife so that she can achieve her full potentiality as a woman.

Let us examine these three requirements in detail.

Understanding: Probably everyone over the age of six knows that men and women are different. Few of us understand the full extent of that difference. Their fundamental life interests are different; they think in a different way; they react differently to various emotional and physical stimuli. The man who expects his wife to handle household affairs as he handles his affairs in the office, therefore, is expecting the impossible. The woman who expects her husband to react as she does to the cry of a child overlooks the fundamental differences between the sexes. Men are men, made with personality characteristics designed to help them do their work of providing leadership. Women are given endowments to enable them to perform their functions as bearers and educators of children.

As a result, a woman generally is more idealistic. She sees things in a more romantic, more emotional way. Her husband prefers to think of himself as more logical. Faced with his wife's statement that she dislikes one of his friends, he may demand to know why, appealing to her sense of logic. Because she thinks in a more intuitive way, she may not answer logically. "I can't tell exactly why I dislike him," she may say. "I just don't feel he is a good influence."

A man tends to be quick in his decisions. A woman tends to be slower and more deliberate. Observe how men and women shop at a department store. Before he enters the shop, the male has a fairly clear idea of what he wishes to buy. He goes directly to the appropriate counter, examines two or three samples, and makes his purchase. In a few minutes he is out of the store and about other business. On the other hand, his wife usually will have no clear picture of what she intends to purchase. As she walks to the counter, she debates whether she should get one particular brand—or something else. She examines not three samples, but half a score, sometimes even as many as the clerk has in stock. And even as she walks away with the package under her arm, she is not sure that she bought the right thing. She may still change her mind the next day and ask the shop to exchange the merchandise.

In his role as provider, the man must usually make decisions and act upon them quickly, and he generally cannot afford the luxury of worrying about them once they are made. Such emotions as he may have are pushed down deeply because of his continuing need to be decisive. On the other hand, God has designed woman to be emotional. She could be no other way and still fulfill her goal of motherhood. The newborn infant and the young child need demonstrated affection, kissing and manifestations of love, just as they need food and clothing. A woman lacking the ability to give that love would be poorly equipped for her role.

A woman usually is less confident of herself—her attractiveness, her qualities as wife and mother—than her husband would admit to being about himself. She wants to know that she is needed and loved, that her husband and children value her services. Her husband needs love just as desperately, but generally will not admit it openly. He seeks recognition of his masculinity. He must know that he is a satisfactory lover, that he is professionally competent, that he has personal charm.

Being direct, the typical man has no time for the subtleties characteristic of women's thinking. If he says to his wife, "Let's go out to dinner tonight," he usually means just that. Her reaction is likely to be, "Does he say that because he dislikes my cooking? Has he done something he is trying to hide? Is it because of that cute waitress?"

If you try to understand your mate's nature, you will be able to deal competently with problems that result from it. Here are two examples:

A husband usually returned home from work each evening in a highly irritable mood. His wife had learned through tearful experience to keep the youngsters from his sight at these times. Not until he finished dinner was it safe to bring them out. What caused his meanness? Simply the physical fact that he worked at a fast pace all afternoon and by evening he was hungry and his energy was at a low point. Many men are cranky under such circumstances. When his wife recognized that his mean disposition had a physical basis, she made it a habit to have a large glass of fruit juice standing ready in the refrigerator. When she saw him turn into the driveway, she ran to the refrigerator and greeted him at the front door, juice in hand. After she learned that one basic fact about her husband's nature, there were fewer tearful episodes in the household.

A wife was extremely tense on certain days and cheerful on others. Her husband did not realize that her moods were partly beyond her control until she casually remarked that she always felt low on the day or days preceding menstruation. It has been scientifically verified that millions of women suffer from a condition known as premenstrual tension which affects their personalities adversely. When the husband recognized this fact, he began to make allowance for it. He went out of his way to avoid irritating his wife on those days, and he tried to ease her depression with patience and the assurance that she was passing through a temporary condition.

If you make an honest effort to understand your mate's personality, the general characteristics of the sex as well as personal idiosyncrasies, you will help yourself to live with them harmoniously. Often they are conditions you cannot easily change. It is simpler to adjust to them as best you can.

There would be little conflict in marriage arising from misunderstanding if spouses talked with each other gently but honestly. You cannot understand, let alone accept, what you do not know. And since husbands and wives are *not* mind readers, understanding can only begin in conversation. John Warren Hill, Presiding Justice of the New York Domestic Relations Court, has expressed it this way: "If you have a real or imaginary grievance, complaint, or suspicion against your mate, *talk it out.* If you are becoming more and more irritated by a persistent action or habit, *talk it out.* If you are unhappy about something that is or is not being done, *talk it out.*" Most of the time talking will remove the grievance and where it does not, the satisfaction of getting the complaint off your chest will be its own reward.

Often one may see a married couple go through a meal in a public restaurant with hardly a word to say to each other. They are not angry. They simply find it difficult to make conversation. Not all couples are so mute in each other's presence, but many husbands and wives, particularly after the children are born, get out of the habit of exchanging pleasantries and confidences. When differences of opinion or resentments crop up, the tendency then is to bottle them within, except insofar as the local bartender and Mother are allowed to become confidants. And yet how can two people be one in mind and heart if they are not each the other's best confidant? The wife before whom the husband stands revealed loves him the more. The husband to whom the wife goes for attention or direction is magnified thereby, even when she is complaining about him.

Early in marriage a young couple should learn the art of communication. Learn to tell your mate all about your defeats as well as your victories. Usually your spouse will not be offended even by criticism—that is tactful, especially when it is not petty nagging. It is better for the husband to indicate to his wife that he is displeased with her housekeeping or her cooking than to bear the wrongs impatiently. If the other realizes that love, not ridicule, motivates the criticism, there will perhaps be wounded pride, but no real anger.

Acceptance: When you as a husband recognize that your wife needs to express herself emotionally and intuitively, you take a long step toward accepting her for what she is—a woman. When you as a wife recognize your husband's need to express himself forcefully and sometimes boisterously, you accept him for what he is—a man. Many troubles encountered by modern couples result from a husband's unwillingness to encourage his wife to be a woman, and from the wife's unwillingness to let her man fulfill the masculine role assigned to him by God. Let us therefore consider what your acceptance of your mate really involves.

A woman by nature is generally warm, tender, understanding and loving. These are qualities she should have as mother, homemaker, and custodian of affection and love in the family. Women are not by natural disposition aggressive, authoritative, coldly analytical.

A woman also wants to be dominated by her husband. As a rule, only when he fails to recognize his responsibilities or discourages his wife from developing her womanly characteristics does the woman assume the dominant role.

Social commentators declare that despite her innate wishes, Mother has become the real boss in millions of homes. She often has the final word in the choice of the car. She selects the furniture, often even her husband's clothes. She may choose the movies she and her husband will see, may decide whom they will entertain, and often casts the deciding vote on where they will spend their vacation. She often disciplines the children, handles the bank account and pays all the bills.

Her rise to domestic power can be explained in many ways. In great part the failure of the husband to assert his own authority is responsible. But regardless of the explanation, the change in roles has helped diminish that femininity of the woman which is so conducive to marital happiness.

But no woman truly wants a submissive husband, nor does she wish to take his place. She may often try to dominate; this is merely experimentation. No one is more disappointed than she if her husband weakly permits her to make an inroad. When she challenges her husband to assert his leadership, she will be pleased to submit if he asserts himself. Let him refuse the challenge, however, and she will take over, even if reluctantly. She will pay a high price for her seeming victory.

It is not surprising, therefore, that surveys of women's aspirations almost unfailingly conclude that they want to be women in the traditional role of their sex. For example, in a survey of hundreds of women by Cornell University researchers, not one expressed a preference for a husband less intelligent than herself. Other researchers have asked women what they would do if somehow they found themselves married to men less intelligent than they. Answers seldom varied. They would try never to emphasize their superiority; they would try never to let their husbands feel inferior. Why? Because to do so would deny the male his traditional role of leadership, and the female her traditional role of dependence.

A wife must allow her husband to assume his full prerogatives as the male; a husband must encourage his wife to be feminine. In no other way can two persons achieve their maximum potentiality in marriage.

Acceptance of a mate, like understanding, must also be based upon individual characteristics. Another word for acceptance is loyalty. Your mate deserves your loyalty at all times.

Some wives habitually compare their husband's positions with those of relatives or neighbors. Often a wife nags her spouse because he does not earn as much as her brother or the man across the street. In such cases she is saying, in effect, that her husband is not competent. She is failing to accept him for what he is. He may be a thoughtful husband, excellent father, considerate lover. By emphasizing one quality in which he does not compare favorably with another, she is expressing her failure to accept him as a husband and as a man. She, therefore, is failing to provide the most important attribute for a happy marriage. She is failing to inspire her husband.

Inspiration: Father Leo J. Kinsella spent many years as a judge in the matrimonial court of the Chicago Archdiocese. During that time, he had the opportunity to explore intimately the factors that led to difficulties in many hundreds of marriages. In his excellent inspirational book, *The Wife Desired,* he declared:

"I have no recollection of a single broken marriage wherein the wife was primarily to blame and at the same time an inspiration to her husband. Failure and inspiration do not mix well. The ability to inspire her husband is the wife's best guarantee of success in marriage. Only if she fails to inspire need she be fearful for their love and the future of their marriage. . . .

"Take it from me, ladies, inspiration is your love potion. Men wander through the cold world seeking the warm eyes of inspiration like a thirsty deer standing at a fountain of water. Not having it, they are lost souls. On finding it, they leap for joy, and the very mountain breaks forth into singing. So, be kind, ladies, lest men die of hunger and thirst. Give hope and encouragement to carry on. It is so easy for you; just be as God made you, his loveliest creatures."

A national magazine has adopted the slogan, "Never underestimate the power of a woman." This reminder actually is more necessary for women than for men. It is especially necessary for wives. Most of them vastly underestimate their ability to inspire their husbands. Some do not even know that they possess this power. Others are but dimly aware of it. Yet the fact remains that in most marriages, the wife who inspires can lead her husband to undreamed-of heights, or by neglecting her ability to inspire, can drag him down to dreary depths.

Every husband desires his wife to be a step above him, leading him upward. His wife must never descend from the level that her Creator, her sex, and even her husband expect of her. It is she who must keep the spiritual standards of a family high. Despite all obstacles, it is she who must, by example and prayer, inspire him to do better.

Occasionally wives not only underestimate their ability but also their obligation to inspire their husbands spiritually. The wife who keeps herself modest, pure and above suspicion, by that very fact contributes to her husband's inspiration and to his spiritual enrichment.

Nor should a wife underestimate her ability to inspire her husband emotionally. By nature, men become discouraged easily. Those in the business world literally go to battle every day. They constantly struggle with others for promotion, for competitive advantages, for financial advancement. They often suffer disappointments and frustrations. And when they return to lick their wounds after a depressing day in the "business jungle," it is their wives—and they alone—who can heal the wounds and restore the spirit. A wife must strive to let her husband know that she has faith in him, that she is cheering for him in his battles, and that his wounds, defeats and triumphs are her wounds, defeats and triumphs.

Inspiring your husband to carry on in adversity may often be difficult. Sometimes he will welcome words of encouragement and will accept advice. Sometimes he will confide in you fully. At other times, he will be visibly disturbed but unwilling to discuss his defeats. He may reject your efforts to cheer him. Suggest how he might handle his problem more successfully, and he may accuse you of trying to run his affairs. The wife who takes her duty to inspire seriously will accept these rebuffs patiently. She will not forget that the basic purpose of inspiration is to make her husband realize that he is a better person with greater capabilities than he himself realizes.

Praise—a continuing stream of it, in both direct and subtle forms—is the main tool of the wife who inspires.

"But my husband is conceited enough," many wives reply at this point. "All he talks about is how good he is. His virtues are his favorite subject, and I doubt that I could get a word in even to agree with him." Wives who make a comment of this type are revealing why their husbands are so conceited—the men get so little inspiration at home that they find it necessary to bolster their egos by constantly reminding themselves and others of their superior qualities. The man who is frequently complimented for his capabilities does not have to remind others of them. Only when his wife or others fail to provide praise does he resort to "do-it-yourself" compliments. Except in rare pathological cases when no amount of inspiration will suffice, the average man will reduce his own boasting almost in direct proportion to the quantity of praise heaped upon him by his mate.

Of course, inspiration is not a one-way street. Wives need it too. In fact, most need more of it than their husbands.

Someone once suggested that an ideal way to make man and wife appreciate each other would be for him to take care of the children and the housework for a week, while she went to business and struggled through his daily problems. This suggestion has merits. The typical male has only the vaguest conception of his wife's duties and problems at home with the children all day long—and of the admirable way in which she handles them.

Almost without exception, young mothers feel a need for adult companionship. Throughout the day, they talk to their children in simple language and discuss simple subjects. The man who goes to business and talks to grownups does not know of his wife's lonely days. Rarely does he realize the added loneliness she feels when after conversing with infants or children in one-syllable words from dawn to dusk, she then faces a mate who does not care to talk to her at night.

A mother becomes discouraged, too. At times, her discouragement can exceed that of her husband. She needs to be told that her children are making progress and that she is doing a superb job of raising them. The husband should remember his wife's needs along with his own.

Know how to compliment! To be an inspiring husband or wife, you should learn the art of paying a compliment. As simple a comment as, "You sure have a way with pies" will bring a pleased smile to her face—and pie to your plate more often. A compliment to your husband when he's well turned-out—"My, isn't Daddy handsome!"—will do far more to keep him out of those disreputable slacks than caustic comments ever will. You will find that the course of your married life will run more smoothly if you learn to say the pleasant word.

Husbands and wives who have been married for a long time sometimes take each other so for granted that the paying of compliments falls into disuse. Some partners even reach the point at which they confess that they cannot find qualities to praise in the other.

Of course, everyone has virtues. It should be easiest for you to recognize these virtues in your mate, because these characteristics attracted you in the first place. Learn to spend time each day dwelling on your mate's good qualities. As you consider them, you may realize that you have more to be thankful for in your partner than you have realized. Moreover, looking at the positive side is a certain antidote to one of the great blemishes on modern marriage: the urge to indulge in self-pity. Self-pity is the major device of people who feel that the world has given them a bad deal. It is particularly prevalent among men and women who are prone to dwell upon their mates' defects—and not upon their virtues.

A final caution to wives: While you should accept fully your obligation to inspire your husband, carefully draw a distinction between inspiring him so that he will grow in a spiritual and emotional way, and inspiring him solely for the sake of material success.

We live in an age when success is measured by the better home, the bigger car, the more fashionable fur coat. But money can never substitute for the true love of a husband and father, and the wife who encourages her husband to get ahead in business at the sacrifice of spiritual values often later regrets it, because her constant spurring may cause him to put material goals above all others. Of course, some husbands become obsessed with material goals on their own; then their wives should strive to make them realize that growth of the spirit is of far greater importance than growth of a bank balance.

3

A Catholic Doctor Looks at Marriage

BY BERNARD J. PISANI, M.D.
ST. VINCENT'S HOSPITAL, N. Y.

AS WE have seen, spiritual and psychological communion is essential for true enjoyment of the marital act. While the physical aspects of sex are overstressed in our society—one who listens to popular songs or views popular movies sometimes gets the impression that only physical aspects matter—nevertheless, it is equally wrong to minimize the importance of physical love in marriage.

The act of sex for married people has a high place in God's plans. It is a creation of God. He intended it to be used, for He gave mankind no other method of bringing life into the world and of cementing the marriage bond. In fact, the first recorded word of God speaking to man is His Divine instruction to use the organs of reproduction which He created. In the first book of Genesis, it is recorded that after God created Adam, "He left him, saying, 'increase and multiply.'"

Since sex is God's creation, it is presumptuous for any creature to call it "dirty" or "vulgar." Yet misunderstanding of the goodness of sex when its use conforms with God's law is the cause of many difficulties in marriage. These problems stem from the prevailing point of view of a century ago that the sex act was not "nice" under any circumstances. Sex was something shameful—a necessary evil that should be kept hidden from children as long as possible. Remnants of that puritanical point of view remain. Often a woman in her twenties, who is ready to enter matrimony, has the fixed notion taught by her parents that the act of physical love is an animal function which should be tolerated when necessary but never enjoyed. She has been warned since adolescence about the evils of sexual intercourse. Because of their own misunderstanding her parents were unable to draw the necessary distinction between the improper use of sex outside of marriage and its proper role inside marriage. They regard God's creation as a necessary evil at best.

Such false ideas can endanger a marriage. They prevent the true communion between husband and wife which is the essence of married love. Sometimes the ideas are imbedded so deeply that the couple is not even aware of their existence, but they may express themselves in the form of revulsion when a partner is seen unclothed or when contact is made between various parts of the body. Couples married many years may still hold this puritanical view of sex, for attitudes implanted and held over a period of years can be changed only with great difficulty. If you cannot bring yourself to accept the truth that the union of bodies in marriage should sublimely manifest the union of heart, mind and soul, it may help you to reflect that the marital act was the means God ordained for the creation of every human life—of every saint in history, of your own parents and loved ones. Viewed in this perspective it will be easier for you to recognize that the marital act is a sacred act which induces grace in the souls of the married couple when it is performed in harmony with God's will.

In rejecting the puritanical view that sex is bad, we must also avoid the opposite extreme commonly held by modernists—that sexual indulgence has no limits or responsibilities. When the marriage act is thus regarded, it is considered as a personal privilege for self-gratification and not as a unifying act of love.

Men who hold this un-Christian view then tend to seek intercourse chiefly for their own satisfaction, and their wives submit out of a sense of duty instead of love. Under these circumstances the husband selfishly exploits his wife, and she loses her rightful dignity. To avoid this danger, the Catholic husband and wife should not primarily seek their own personal enjoyment in performing the marriage act, but should seek to give pleasure to the partner.

Once we accept the truth that the marital act unites soul, heart and mind as well as body, we realize that overemphasizing the physical aspects obscures its true purpose. This danger is especially acute when couples seek to follow the blueprints set down by some marriage manuals. You do not need a diagram to tell you how to perform the act. Instead, you should bring your partner a feeling of spontaneity—of love engendered by spiritual and emotional harmony. You cannot be spontaneous when you are thinking of different ways to achieve new thrills, or when your main concern is to experiment with positions. The best way for you to achieve mutual satisfaction is to inform yourself of the physical aspects of the act and to apply that knowledge in your own relaxed and spontaneous way, keeping foremost in mind the emotional and physical needs of your partner.

Differences in approach to the act: Husbands and wives often fail to understand that by their very natures they approach the sex act differently. The man is more easily aroused. He requires little direct stimulation to create an interest in the sex union. In fact, he may feel desire as a result of the very sight of his wife or the smell of her perfume, of a toss of her head or even a glance that is warm and affectionate. His wife responds more slowly, and is affected by a different type of stimulus. Tenderness, gentleness of touch, and consideration by her husband are of paramount importance. Whereas his arousal is most often achieved by physical stimuli, hers is achieved by emotional ones as well.

A husband generally may be stimulated to desire intercourse at any time of day, week, or month, even at times when he is ill. His wife's desire, on the other hand, tends to be affected by cycles. Her responses depend to some extent upon the balance or interplay of hormones in her system. As these vary at different stages of her menstrual cycle, her desire rises and falls accordingly. Many women have a more powerful sex urge on the day preceding menstruation than at other times; others reach a maximum intensity of desire immediately after menstruation; still others desire marital relations most keenly during their period of ovulation—about midway in the cycle.

These differences are sometimes difficult for married persons to understand. For example, often a husband does not realize that his wife approaches the act not in the physical way that he does, but emotionally. Her desire may have its beginnings hours or days before; it depends upon his tenderness and kindness not in the marriage bed alone, but in his everyday regard, care and treatment of her. This fact explains why the husband who is discourteous or inconsiderate at other times may fail to evoke interest when he tries to initiate the marital act.

A wife who recognizes these basic differences will not conclude that her husband is lascivious because his desire is aroused by the mere sight of her at night. Nor will the husband conclude that his wife does not care for him because she does not show enthusiasm for intimate love when she has housework to do or is concerned about a sick child.

Other differences become apparent once the preliminaries of the marital act have begun. Very few things will divert the typical husband from his objective. He is usually oblivious of distractions. A child cries, the telephone rings—these will quite possibly not disturb him. His wife's reaction is generally the opposite. Even when love-making is well advanced, she can be distracted by outside noises, calls by children, even the dripping of a faucet. And once the spell is broken, she finds it difficult to recapture her mood.

A husband's climax to the marital act varies markedly from his wife's. He usually can reach an orgasm—the climax of his sexual urge—with little difficulty. If he does not try to forestall it to permit his wife to achieve satisfaction, he may easily achieve an orgasm within a minute or two. A wife generally requires a much longer period of time—often five or six times longer. Almost invariably, the act is concluded for him with the discharge of his semen into his wife's vagina. Her climax is seldom, if ever, so definite. Depending upon her mood, she may feel virtually no relief of physical tension or she may experience a tremendously moving orgasm. Few wives experience a climax of the latter type every time. Their very natures enable them to gain emotional and physical satisfaction from the union with their husbands, and they do not need to experience a climax each time to be well-adjusted sexually. The notion that a wife must always achieve an orgasm is mistaken. The wide variety of responses of which she is capable precludes the probability that she will achieve the maximum response every time. Actually, if the act relieves tension and helps promote relaxation and a sense of oneness with her husband, it can be said to provide satisfaction.

A final area of difference is the way in which wives and husbands react after coitus is completed. The husband has actually engaged in physiological exercise and may desire to sleep immediately. A sensitive wife may regard this normal reaction as an indication of her husband's lack of interest in her once he has achieved his own physical satisfaction. She often feels a need for continued expressions of affection after the union, and she cannot understand why the ending should be so abrupt. An understanding by the husband of his wife's needs, and her recognition of his normal physiological reactions, will help to bring the act to an affectionate and mutually satisfying end.

It should be borne in mind that the above discussion of differences between male and female must of necessity consist of generalizations. While most men and women react in the manner described, individuals may differ substantially in their pattern of response and reaction. For example, a young bridegroom will react more vigorously to stimuli than the husband who has observed a silver wedding anniversary. The mother with inner worries over her children's welfare may react more slowly than the healthy, carefree young bride.

Consideration of wife's needs: Some husbands err by thinking that because they are married they can proceed with intercourse as an automatic process. An approach based upon purely physical considerations is completely ineffective in winning the desired response from the wife. Many authorities maintain that the art of courtship learned in the days before marriage must be cultivated to a high degree for the rest of your life. Acts of loving kindness shown to your wife in your kitchen or living room will have their happy fulfillment in love-making, for the act of union is not something that a woman sets apart. Rather it is the physical sign of her inner feelings for her husband. Only if her husband wins her heart will her body express her love.

However, because of the slowness with which even the loving wife responds to physical stimuli, it is both desirable and proper for her husband to try to arouse her desire. He will do this not only by creating a suitable emotional atmosphere, but also by recognizing and making use of the sensitive zones of his wife's body. These erogenous zones are specific areas which, when stimulated, arouse a growing sense of desire for intercourse. In women, these zones may be located in and around the breasts, the tips of the ears, the palms of the hands, the inside of the thighs, and the clitoris, a small organ located at the upper part of the vulva, or opening to the vagina. When these areas are stimulated by means of gentle caressing, fondling, or other contacts, the wife normally responds with an increased sexual interest.

Consideration of husband's needs: The male also has erogenous zones, located primarily on the insides of his thighs, the groin, the underside of the scrotum and in his penis itself. When a husband's excitation comes more slowly than that of his wife, it may be desirable for her to stimulate his erogenous zones by contact.

The husband also needs emotional encouragement. When he spares no efforts in his attempts to be gentle and considerate of his wife's needs, her failure to respond affectionately may cause him to become discouraged and ultimately to lose interest. Even if she does not feel strong desire, it will reward her to welcome and encourage her husband nonetheless. By dwelling on the pleasures which he seeks to provide, she may soon overcome her inhibitions and discover the joy that is possible in sexual fulfillment in marriage.

Achieving mutual satisfaction: Any physical stimulation

which has as its objective natural intercourse, consisting of the deposit of the male semen into the female vagina, is morally permissible. In the interest of mutual love, however, such stimulation should never offend the sensibilities of either partner. A thoughtful husband, seeking to please his wife, will encourage her to make known her individual tastes and needs to him. In a natural, frank and affectionate relationship, she will feel no sense of impropriety in telling him which of his actions induce her greatest sense of desire. Any physical position which is mutually satisfactory and enables the penis to enter the vagina also is permitted.

This preparatory love-making is invaluable and necessary in order to stimulate the reproductive organs and to make them ready for the actual union. When desire is aroused, the wife's genitals swell and become softly firm. Her glands provide a secretion which lubricates the entrance to the vagina and enables the penis—the male organ—to be inserted almost painlessly. The penis consists of erectile tissues which inflate when stimulated. It also becomes firm so that it will be able to penetrate the opening to the vagina, and exudes a small amount of lubricating fluid.

Once a husband and wife begin to experience sexual tension, their excitement tends to grow until a climax—the ejaculation of semen from the penis—is reached. The wife should experience a release of tension at about the same time that her husband reaches his climax. Since the typical male will reach a climax sooner than his wife unless he controls himself, he should learn to delay the peak of his excitement and to caress and stimulate his wife so that they achieve release in unison.

Young brides especially should realize that the reaching of such an adjustment often requires considerable time. Because the act of sex is such an intimate activity, its enjoyment requires the gradual flowering of mutual understanding and a sense of freedom. The husband must learn to recognize his wife's reactions at the various preliminary stages and to govern his own impulses accordingly. Satisfactory adjustment in the sense of simultaneous release may require many months or even years to achieve, and perhaps may never be achieved on a regular basis. You will help this adjustment if you discuss your relationship with love, frankness and an understanding of your partner's fundamental nature and specific responses.

Some husbands are unable to prevent the discharge of their semen before the actual union of bodies. This condition is called "premature ejaculation." By exerting self-control and consciously attempting to remain calm through the preparatory stages of love-making, the conscientious husband can learn to retain his semen until after his wife receives him. When premature ejaculation occurs involuntarily—that is, when it is not the result of the husband's deliberate intention to avoid the deposit of semen into his wife's body—it is not immoral. When such ejaculations are resorted to as a means of preventing conception, they are sinful. It is this sin for which God punished Onan, the first known practitioner, with immediate death.

When stimulation is proper: Since the purpose of contact with the various erogenous zones is to arouse desire and to prepare for the marital act, couples should be cautious about indulging in such contacts when physical union is not intended.

Of course, you should display affection throughout the day even when intimate relations are not planned. Tender glances and affectionate kisses are both normal and necessary for your growth in marriage. However, you should learn to recognize and shun manifestations and stages of love which are likely to arouse you or your partner unduly when complete sexual satisfaction cannot be achieved.

The reason for this is obvious. After a certain point in love-making is reached, most men and women feel a normal compelling urge to increase the excitation until release is obtained by means of physical union and an orgasm. Only with great difficulty can they control themselves once desire is aroused. Thus acts of married love such as petting and fondling, while legitimate in themselves, may be dangerous when indulged in without the possibility of marital fulfillment. There is a risk that one partner may resort to the sin of masturbation in order to achieve an orgasm and to obtain release from the tension which these acts have created.

Partners' "rights" in marriage: The frequency of the marital act, and the specific times when it is performed, should be decided by mutual agreement as much as possible. Ideally, the best time is when both partners feel a spontaneous desire. With experience, you will come to know when your spouse will be most disposed to the physical act of love; if possible, you should try to gear your own desires to those of your mate. The marital act can be engaged in at any time, provided that no deliberate attempt is made to prevent conception. While intercourse during the menstrual period is morally permissible, most wives object to it then for sanitary reasons, and the considerate husband will respect his wife's wishes in this regard.

Sometimes the question of "rights" arises to plague a marriage. From a technical point of view, theologians tell us, the husband has the right to engage in intercourse with his wife except when she has a serious reason to refuse. St. Paul teaches that "the wife has not authority over her body, but the husband; the husband likewise has not authority over his body, but the wife." (1 Corinthians, vii, 4:1) For a wife to refuse her husband's request without a serious reason could be a mortal sin. When is a reason serious? Theologians say that she may reasonably refuse when her husband is drunk, when either has a venereal disease which may be transmitted to the other, when her own health could be seriously endangered as a result, when there is a clear indication that artificial birth control is to be practiced, or when the other party has committed adultery. A husband may refuse his wife on the same grounds.

For the sake of harmony in the marriage, it should not be necessary for the partner desiring intercourse to insist upon his or her right. Since by his very nature it is more difficult for a man to be continent, his wife should readily consent to his request in a spirit of active love. She should not merely tolerate him but should show by her responses that she welcomes his advances and appreciates the opportunity to demonstrate her affection.

There will be times, of course, when she will be unable to respond enthusiastically. The mother who has lost several nights' sleep caring for a child who is ill or recovering from illness, or who grieves over the death of a relative or friend, may not find it easy to develop the mood necessary for satisfactory relations. The considerate husband will recognize these conditions and will not force himself upon her. If he is motivated by charity and the desire to please her, he can easily subjugate his own desires.

Young couples should realize that the occasional practice of abstinence will help them during those periods when prolonged continence is absolutely necessary. Such times may include several months in the late stages of pregnancy and immediately following childbirth, and other long periods when the husband or wife may be absent from home. When the mature and loving couple accept those periods with understanding and patience, they enrich rather than minimize married love. By making your own desires secondary to the needs of your marriage, you may feel more love for your partner in abstinence than in intercourse.

Causes of frigidity: Popular magazines make much of the problem of the "frigid wife." Some writers assert that a majority of American wives might be called frigid—that is, that they seldom if ever experience a climax. There is no way of knowing how accurate such statements are. However, the emphasis given to this problem suggests that there may be a substantial basis for it in fact.

If a wife fails to experience any physical or emotional release as a result of intercourse, perhaps one or several of the following factors are present:

She may expect too much from sex. A great disservice is done American wives by writers of marriage guidebooks who proclaim that women should experience a climax each time they copulate. As we have seen, the patterns of an individual woman's responses vary greatly and depend upon many physical and emotional conditions. The wife who expects complete satisfaction every time, or even a high percentage of the time, is often setting her expectations too high.

She may be inhibited by early training from letting herself participate fully and enthusiastically in the marriage act. She should, of course, rid her mind of the notion that sex in marriage carries any connotations of sin. There is also the possibility that, consciously or otherwise, she fears having children as a result of intercourse. Some wives do not want to make the sacrifices involved in having or raising children. They express their distaste for the prospect by pretending to be annoyed, disinterested, or disgusted by their husband's advances. Some may have heard old wives' tales about the dangers of childbirth—dangers which modern medicine has largely eliminated. Because of fears deeply implanted in childhood, these women cannot bring themselves to enjoy the relationship from which the imaginary terrors of childbearing will result.

Basic conflicts with her husband may make her emotionally incapable of enjoying intimate relations. A wife who suspects that her husband may be developing an interest in other women may find herself unable to participate fully in the act. A wife may become so concerned over her husband's excessive drinking that she is unable to relax in his presence. Basic conflicts over money, relationships with in-laws, and other matters may produce the same results.

Also to be considered as possible causes of a wife's frigidity are lack of understanding and consideration by her husband, or her failure to express to him her needs and desires. These failures may result from improper early training or from a breakdown in communication between husband and wife after marriage.

Doctors state emphatically that almost all cases of women's failure to respond warmly in the marital act can be successfully treated, given time and patience. First, the wife should discuss the problem calmly and frankly with her husband. She may find it necessary to revise drastically her thinking about the entire matter of physical intercourse. She may need spiritual help in accepting the principle—new to her—that this function was created by God to be hers to enjoy and can be the means of her sanctification. The husband likewise may find it necessary to revise his attitudes. Instead of regarding the act merely as a means of relieving his own tensions and as something to be concluded as quickly as possible, he must learn that his obligations to his wife are far-reaching and meaningful.

Together, they must seek to remove causes of friction in everyday living which create mental and emotional blocks and prevent the wife's healthy and normal participation. Sometimes it may be found that minor distractions exert a disproportionate influence. When the distractions are removed, frigidity may soon vanish. Often the solutions to a wife's inability to achieve satisfaction may lie in trivial conditions.

When both partners make a sincere and intelligent effort, a satisfactory relationship usually can be achieved. But if the marital act continues to produce revulsion in the wife and she fails to respond even occasionally to her husband's love, she probably should seek spiritual and/or medical aid.

Male frigidity is also said to be a growing factor in modern life. This frigidity is more properly termed impotence, because the male's active desire is necessary before his penis can reach the state of firmness required to perform the act. He is unlike his wife, who may participate passively as a receptor of his organ. When the husband's desire is absent, he is not capable of intercourse.

Impotence comes to some men in their forties or fifties, and in occasional cases has been known to occur in bridegrooms in their twenties. Some wives adjust to their husbands' lack of interest in sex without difficulty; others become understandably concerned over a relationship that may resemble that of brother and sister more than that of husband and wife.

Doctors state that male impotence usually has a psychological cause. The impotent husband may believe that sex is not something enjoyed by "nice people." Possibly his wife has permitted herself to become unattractive to him or has rebuffed his advances so often that he has given up trying.. When the cause is psychological, psychiatric treatment may help relieve the condition. When the cause is physical, impotence may be treated with varying results by the administration of male hormones.

Many impotent males refuse to seek appropriate medical or psychiatric treatment because they fear the stigma attached in the public's mind to the man who lacks virility. Men who cannot perform the act should obtain medical aid. For just as a husband rightfully expects his wife's co-operation in satisfying his physical needs, a wife can properly demand that her husband do what he can to fulfill his masculine function.

Some husbands abstain from marital relations in the mistaken notion that they will diminish their virility and even shorten the period of years when they can enjoy sex. While it is true that sex indulged in to excess can weaken the body, there is little danger of adverse effects when normal intercourse is indulged in in moderation.

The basis of a happy sex life: From the foregoing discussion of physical factors in the marriage union, it will be seen that marriages do not fail because of "improper sex adjustments" as such, but because of selfishness, lack of understanding or consideration, or other emotional defects on the part of the two persons involved. In seeking a more satisfactory physical relationship, therefore, a couple should look first to their spiritual and emotional communion. Where there is true love, motivated primarily by the spirit and not by the flesh, the physical relationship almost always will be satisfactory.

4

Birth Control and the Rhythm Method

IT IS one of the signs of our times that a chapter on birth control and the rhythm method appears in a Catholic book on marriage. In former times having no children or having only a few children would be so scandalous and so un-Christian as to merit only a short note of condemnation. The small family would be looked upon as something unusual and its parents deserving of sympathy. Fruitfulness in marriage was always considered one of the signs of God's blessing—until the twentieth century. Nowadays it almost seems as if the couple having a fourth or fifth child must defend its right to that child and to more children besides. Tremendous social pressures have been organized in favor of controlled family size—small family housing for one, neighborhood gossip for another, the constant parade of pictures depicting the "ideal" American family, always with two children, the erroneous identification of feminine beauty with infrequent motherhood, the presumption, too often accepted uncritically, that a few children reared in prosperity will necessarily be happier and better than many children brought up in modest circumstances, and the equally common feeling that after a few children pregnancy is more of a pathology than a state of health.

The reasons usually advanced by married couples for restricting the size of their family are usually not real reasons at all. The birth-control state of mind is nowhere more clearly manifested than by many engaged couples who, without any grave problems at all, enter marriage with family limitation uppermost in their young minds. For a couple after ten years of marriage and five children to think in terms of family limitation is one thing. For a couple with two or three children to exaggerate their money, health, or space problems is much more common and much more deserving of criticism. And the fact that the average American woman has her last child several years before she is thirty is certain evidence of a lack of the will to parenthood. "Where there is a will, there is a way," says the maxim. People who will not to be parents will find the way of birth control very easy, even though very wrong.

There is little question, too, that the growth of the birth-control mentality coincides with the desire of many Americans for soft living. Yet, if we are a strong people we may well enjoy modern opportunities for happiness and still do whatever our job requires us to do, even though some sacrifice of comfort or convenience is demanded. The propaganda in favor of the limited family puts a premium on comfort while disparaging duty. It sells American woman the idea that motherhood is a kind of bondage and American man the conviction that the hard work necessary to support a large family is an unreasonable requirement for modern marriage.

The modern Catholic couple must be reminded that parenthood is the business of marriage. This is their vocation. The Catholic husband and wife should do this work with wisdom and prudence, and, where there is good cause, may consider family limitation. But family limitation does not *have* to be considered. Most of you will find that the best evidence of a lifetime of worthwhile work will be your children. You should want children; and parenthood, God willing, should be more than an incidental experience in your married lives. If you have a truly Catholic conscience and a love of children you will find that alleged obstacles can be overcome. Far from losing happiness, you will gain great long-range satisfaction.

Those of you who are blessed by God with the faith and courage to live a heroic married life and accept parenthood cheerfully, far from feeling cheated, ought to delight in your extraordinary achievement. Other couples may not be so well endowed by nature or circumstance, and a small family or even a childless marriage may be your lot. But even here, as long as you are doing the best you can to serve God's purpose, you deserve high praise and should not permit conscienceless neighbors to deprive you of your sense of accomplishment.

The control of births, therefore, should always be the exceptional situation in marriage, never the normal. Even when family limitation is permissible, the methods you use may well make the whole process evil. This is what some people find hard to understand. Having a good reason does not make everything you do right, else many more drunken husbands or nagging wives might be in their graves. The end does not necessarily justify the means. A soldier might get soft living in Korea by selling out his country, or might win a battle for his country by wantonly slaughtering hundreds of women and children to get at a machine-gun nest. Neither course of conduct would receive the approval of American public opinion.

Why, then, should people who have good reason to limit their families feel that it does not make any difference how this is done, as long as it is done? Why do they not see that controlling births under certain circumstances may be good and preventing births under any circumstances is always bad? It is birth prevention that has come under the most dire condemnation of the Church, not birth control by moral means. The control of births by voluntary restraint in the use of the marriage act is to be distinguished sharply from the preventing of births through artificial instruments or chemicals. Contraceptives of any kind, whether they be used by the man or by the woman, have as their only object preventing the union of the male sperm with the female ovum. There is no control required of any couple engaging in this unnatural act, so the title "birth control" is a misnomer. The same is true where the so-called "birth-control pills" are used. Taken by mouth, their purpose is the prevention of ovulation and thus of conception. Such pills are artificial means of preventing births and, as such, are immoral.

People who defend contraception as something good and desirable rarely defend contraception itself. They spend most of their time arguing in favor of not having more children and then assume that because they present good reasons (most frequently the reasons are not valid) the case for contraceptive intercourse is decided. By the same tortuous logic, the soldier overseas might mistakenly make a case for adultery, the hard-pressed father might make a case for theft, or the government official might make a case for bribery. Most of the people who prevent births recognize the practice as unnatural and unsatisfying. The more they keep saying, "There is nothing wrong with birth control," the more they remind one of the little boy suspected of stealing cookies—"I didn't do nothing."

The reason why the artificial prevention of births is immoral is written into the very nature of the sexual organs and the marital act itself. The sex organs were made by God to reproduce the human race. Only when husband and wife unite naturally is the union of sperm and ovum possible. Therefore, the primary purpose of the marital act is the conception of human life. The same act affords an opportunity for the spouses to manifest love toward each other and to satisfy their legitimate sexual needs. Incidentally, too, the physical tensions of the couple are relieved. But these secondary effects accompany the act; they are not its primary purpose. The man who enjoys a good meal experiences a sense of well-being and the toothsome viands give pleasure to his palate. But the primary purpose of eating is to give vitality to the body. The pleasure associated with both these appetites is intended by God as incentives—to coitus and to eating. To make God's purpose impossible of achievement by deliberate interference and at the same time to seek the pleasure He intended as a reward for the willingness to assume the work of parenthood is a complete violation of the Divine Plan. A husband and wife—for many reasons and for greater or shorter lengths of time—may not engage in married love, but when they do they must love as God intended them to love. To do otherwise is to assert a power over their sexual faculties which is not theirs by right. They deliberately alter the purpose of a human faculty. Only God can do that.

A couple using artificial contraceptive devices at any time is guilty of serious sin because this interferes with nature in a serious way. This position was stated by St. Augustine centuries ago. He said: "Intercourse, even with one legitimate wife, is unlawful and wicked where the conception of the offspring is prevented. Onan, the son of Juda, did this and the Lord killed him for it." So serious is this sin that St. Thomas Aquinas considered that the deliberate prevention of conception is, next to the killing of an unborn child, one of the greatest vices.

Now this point of view was, until recent times, the common agreement of all Christians, even Protestants, and if today the Catholic Church stands almost alone in asserting the eternal truth of a long Hebrew-Christian tradition, it is not because this truth is any less valid. Many Protestants, even though emphasizing their devotion to Sacred Scripture, have a difficult time reconciling the scriptural story of Onan with their modern compromise with age-old doctrine. The declaration that contraception is immoral is not merely Church doctrine. It is a matter of God's natural law and binds Jews and Protestants as well as Catholics. If the Church speaks out on the subject with consistent firmness it is not merely preaching Church law. The Church has laws—Mass attendance, Easter duty, fast and abstinence—which will vary from age to age and which can be altered. Many people like to believe that the Catholic teaching on birth prevention can be changed, too. This error rests on the confusion between the moral and ecclesiastical law. A thousand years from now we may be eating meat on Friday, but at that time murder, adultery, and contraception will still be sins. These latter involve God's law and not even the Pope nor a large number of sinning couples can turn wrong into right.

In his encyclical on Christian marriage in 1930, Pope Pius XI stated: "Any use whatsoever of matrimony exercised in such a way that the act is deliberately frustrated in its natural power to generate life is an offense against the law of God and of nature, and those who indulge in such are branded with the guilt of grave sin."

His Holiness also wrote: "No reason, however grave, can be put forward by which anything intrinsically against nature may become conformable to nature and morally good. Since, therefore, the conjugal act is destined primarily by nature for the begetting of children, those who in exercising this deliberately frustrate its natural power and purposely sin against nature, commit a deed which is shameful and intrinsically vicious."

There are many lesser reasons why artificial birth control should not be practiced. No method is fully reliable. The appalling abortion rate in this country—it is estimated that for every four births, one abortion is performed—strongly suggests the failure of artificial methods to prevent birth. Since most criminal abortions are performed on married women, it may fairly be assumed that they tried—and failed—to prevent conception at the time of intercourse.

Moreover, such devices can be and often are definite hazards to health, and in some cases the hazards are significant.

The use of artificial contraceptives also produces undesirable psychological effects. Even many persons who do not accept the Church's teachings regarding the moral evil of birth control object to the practice on psychological grounds. The harmony of the conjugal act is disturbed before, during, or after it by the introduction of devices intended to negate the purpose of the act. By its nature married love is intended to be natural and spontaneous. One wonders how many husband-wife conflicts have their roots in contraceptive love.

Sterilization: The Church's opposition to sterilization is based upon the same moral grounds as its opposition to birth control. By sterilization is meant any operation performed with the intention of preventing any organ necessary for conception from fulfilling its normal function. For example, surgeons can remove female organs so that the ovum will be unable to travel its appointed path to unite with the male sperm. Or surgeons may cut and tie off male glands to prevent the sperm from being discharged. One who submits to an operation of this type in order to copulate without the possibility of conception is guilty of self-mutilation and sins against the Fifth Commandment. This Commandment, "Thou shalt not kill," requires us to care for our bodies—not only to avoid committing murder, but also to avoid injuring or destroying any bodily faculty.

In certain operations, sterility results as a secondary effect. Such operations include a hysterectomy—a cutting out of the uterus—which is necessary to prevent disease. A woman without a uterus cannot give birth, and thus this operation sterilizes her permanently. But the operation's purpose is to save the woman's life—not to make her sterile. Thus it can be performed morally.

Occasionally a woman is advised by her doctor that she should not have additional children. She may have had one or two babies by Caesarean section, an operation by which the infant is delivered through an incision made in the abdomen rather than in the usual way through the vagina. Even though many women can and do have multiple Caesarean sections safely, a particular doctor may tell her that it is inadvisable to deliver additional children in this way. Inasmuch as the abdomen will be open in the course of delivery, he may offer at the same time to cut the Fallopian tubes. This procedure will permanently prevent the sperm from reaching the ovum. Catholics may not permit this. The health of the woman can be safeguarded in other ways.

Like those who practice artificial birth control or interfere with the natural law in other ways, persons who are sterilized to avoid parenthood often suffer deep and lasting remorse. Sterilization is permanent; once performed, it can never be reversed. The sterilized man or woman can never become a father or mother. When they reach later life and their capacities for other pleasures have diminished, they will look about them and see homes made happy by the presence of children while their own remains empty. The realization that they can never rectify their error will haunt them until they die.

Ill-advised persons who are sterilized may later discover that the conditions that caused them to undergo the operation have changed radically. Those who do not want children because "they can't afford them" may win economic success. The mother who "has enough children" may lose them through death. The woman who for health reasons "cannot bear children" may later improve so that carrying a child would not be even remotely dangerous. In fact, medical progress in recent years and the prospects of more dramatic progress to come encourage the belief that many diseases now regarded as incurable may soon be brought under control.

THE RHYTHM METHOD

The rhythm method is often described as Catholic birth control. This description is erroneous. This method is neither sponsored nor endorsed by the Church. The Church merely permits its use under specific circumstances outlined below.

What is the rhythm method? It is a scientific fact that a woman is fertile only during certain days in her menstrual cycle, which usually lasts about a month. On other days in this cycle, she is not capable of conceiving a child. By means of the rhythm method she can isolate the particular days in her own cycle during which intercourse is likely to result in conception. By avoiding intercourse on those days, therefore, she will not become pregnant.

The fundamental difference between the rhythm method and artificial methods of birth control is that rhythm erects no physical barrier to the normal process of conception. The fact that a child is not conceived results from the simple fact that intercourse has not occurred.

To understand this basic difference fully, it is necessary to understand the marvelous way in which a woman's body is constantly prepared for the reception of a new life. A woman is born with thousands of immature ova, or eggs. By the time she reaches the age when she is physically capable of carrying a child—in Western civilization, this is about the age of fourteen or fifteen—she has also developed an immature egg to maturity. Approximately every month from the time that she begins to menstruate until menstruation finally ceases at the menopause, an immature egg is brought to maturity in one or the other of her two ovaries. Thus nature constantly prepares a woman for motherhood, whether or not she avails herself of the privilege.

At a specific time in the monthly cycle, a structure called the Graffian follicle discharges the egg from the ovary. This procedure is called ovulation. A hormone—progesterone—also is discharged, apparently to help the womb nourish the egg if it becomes fertilized. This progesterone plays a vital role in the success of the rhythm method, for reasons to be described later.

The egg leaves the ovary, enters the abdominal cavity and then slowly moves through one of the two Fallopian tubes to the uterus, or womb. This entire trip from ovary to womb takes almost a day.

Conception can occur only if the male sperm unites with the ovum while the latter travels to the womb, or for a short time after it reaches it—little more than twenty-four hours in all. An ovum not fertilized during that time will die. In dying, it will make unnecessary the special lining of the uterus which has developed to nourish it in the event it arrives fertilized by the sperm. The death of the egg, therefore, is a signal for the lining to be disposed of through menstruation. The lining remains only if the egg is alive. Thus a woman's failure to menstruate is usually the first indication that a child has been conceived.

Male fertilizing cells also have a short life span. Medical men now believe that sperm loses its ability to penetrate the egg within twenty-four hours after being deposited in the female. During a wife's entire monthly cycle—from the time she begins one menstruation until she begins another—she therefore is fertile only two days: one day before ovulation, and one day after it. Sperm injected on the day before ovulation will live to fuse with the egg when it is released by the ovary. The egg will live another day after ovulation and will die unless it is fertilized.

The rhythm method depends upon successfully forecasting the ovulation period—the only time in the cycle when intercourse can result in conception. Coitus can then be avoided at this time. Three basic ways of predicting this fertile period have been developed.

The Ogino-Knaus method: The first and earlier method was developed by two scientists working independently—Dr. Kyusaku Ogino of Japan and Dr. Hermann Knaus, now of Vienna. It is based upon an assumption which has proved true in most cases—the assumption that ovulation takes place fifteen days before menstruation.

The next step is to determine when menstruation will start. Some women menstruate with clocklike precision every twenty-eight days; therefore they ovulate on the thirteenth day in each cycle. However, most women have somewhat irregular cycles. One may be twenty-eight days and another thirty days. A cycle may be lengthened by illness, such as a cold, and also by emotional upsets. It may also be shortened or lengthened by sudden changes of climate or altitude, excessive physical or mental exertion, excessive fatigue, and the like. In order that a woman's definite pattern can be learned, she may be required to keep records of her periods for from six months to a year.

The Ogino-Knaus method is put to practical use as follows: A particular chart shows that the previous twelve menstrual cycles varied in length from twenty-five to thirty days. It must be assumed that either of these cycles—the short or the long—may recur.

Suppose that the twenty-five-day cycle is repeated. Ovulation time would be fifteen days before the beginning of menstruation—the tenth day of the cycle. Inasmuch as sperm can live outside the ovum only for a day, conception would not occur if the sperm entered the vagina before the ninth day. And since the ovum loses its ability to be fertilized about twenty-four hours after ovulation, conception could not occur after the twelfth day. In this twenty-five-day cycle, therefore, the wife is fertile only between the ninth and twelfth days.

A similar computation for the thirty-day cycle will show the fourteenth day as the earliest in which conception would occur, and the sixteenth day the latest. A formula to cover a twenty-five to thirty-day range therefore would consider conception possible from the tenth day of the cycle through the sixteenth. Thus, according to this theory, coitus during the first nine days after menstruation begins or after the sixteenth day and until the next menstruation would not result in pregnancy. As these calculations indicate, when a menstrual period follows a consistent pattern—every twenty-eight days, for example—the possible fertile period is of shorter duration.

The body temperature method: The second method of predicting ovulation is based upon body temperature. Many scientists consider it to be a more accurate method than the other.

As was noted earlier, when the egg leaves the ovary, the level of the hormone progesterone rises in the body and the body temperature rises by almost a full degree. A wife who kept careful temperature readings a few days before and during the expected period of ovulation thus could say with good accuracy whether ovulation had occurred. In his pamphlet, *Family Limitation,* Dr. John Ryan describes how ovulation can be predicted by means of a thermal chart.

This chart records temperature variations at different stages of the cycle. A typical chart shows a low temperature during the early stage of the cycle, just after menstruation, and a higher level before menstruation. Between these two levels there is a sharp rise, sometimes preceded by a dip. When the chart shows this rise and the higher level is maintained, it is an indication that ovulation is about to occur or has just occurred.

Dr. Ryan states that the first infertile period ends about twenty-four hours before the low temperature rises. The second period begins when the thermometer registers the higher figure for two or three days. A doctor can examine a woman's past record and determine her expectable rise in temperature and the number of days that the higher temperature must be maintained.

A doctor can also interpret possible variations in the record. For example, the line showing the temperature rise may not be smooth, but may ascend in steps. This often occurs in delayed ovulation. Or the chart may show several up-and-down lines. These variations sometimes accompany mild inflammations in the pelvis. A doctor can treat this condition with antibiotics so that the readings will return to normal.

Dr. Ryan states that when women are given proper directions they can determine for themselves when ovulation has occurred. They take their basal temperatures for three or four days in any given cycle. The basal temperature is the body's temperature upon waking, when it is completely at rest and before food is taken. Since a fraction of a degree makes an important difference, a special basal thermometer is recommended. It has a different temperature range from that of ordinary household thermometers and is marked so that temperatures can be read in tenths of degrees instead of fifths.

Daily temperatures are recorded over periods ranging from three to six months. The doctor then studies these, together with such information as the starting dates of six consecutive periods and their duration, and illness or emotional upsets which might influence the reading. Once her pattern is established, the doctor can explain how the patient can interpret temperature readings to determine her precise ovulation time.

It is claimed that ninety per cent of wives have menstrual patterns sufficiently reliable to enable them to determine their ovulation period by this means. It is also claimed that this method pinpoints fertile periods with greater accuracy than the Ogino-Knaus method and makes it unnecessary to abstain from intercourse for as long as when the O.-K. theory is used.

The Test Tape Method: Within the past year a new test, based on cervical mucus, has been devised to determine the time of monthly ovulation in the woman. A piece of test tape applied to the cervical area will change in color from yellow to green during ovulation. Research indicates that this method of determining the period of fertility shows considerable promise. Childless couples may use it with profit to facilitate a fertilization. In situations where pregnancy may be undesirable, periodic continence need be practiced by couples using this method for a shorter duration than presently recommended. Provided that the normal moral conditions for the use of rhythm are met, it is a proper means of limiting family size.

Holy Father's statement on rhythm: Who may practice the rhythm method? A clear answer was given by Pope Pius XII in 1951 in an address to the Italian Catholic Union of Midwives. His Holiness pointed out that married couples are obliged to procreate and to help conserve the human race. In the Pontiff's words: "Matrimony obliges to a state of life which, while carrying with it certain rights, also imposes a fulfillment of positive work connected with that state of life."

This means that rhythm is not to be used indiscriminately. The small-family or no-family state of mind is not necessarily good simply because contraceptives are not used.

The Pope recognized, however, that under certain conditions a couple might be excused from fulfilling its obligation. He said, "From the obligation of making this positive contribution, it is possible to be exempt, for a long time and even for the whole duration of married life, if there are serious reasons, such as those often provided in the so-called 'indications' of the medical, eugenical, economic and social order. It therefore follows that the observance of the infertile period may be licit from the moral point of view; and under the conditions mentioned, it is so in fact."

The four "indications" cited by the Holy Father when the practice of rhythm might be justified may be further explained as follows:

1. *Medical:* A doctor may advise a couple against having children. For example, a woman recovering from a serious operation might lack the strength to carry a child. A woman suffering from an incurable disease might face the likelihood of death soon after her baby is born. A husband's health might be so poor that he might not live to support a child.

It is important for you, however, not to accept the judgment of a single doctor as infallibly decreeing death with the next pregnancy. Too many of us know of women so instructed who bore many children safely. A doctor can be wrong. The better the doctor, the less is he inclined to lay claim to infallibility in making these observations, particularly as he realizes the medical improvements possible with a few years' time. Unfortunately, some women are scarred psychologically for life by the ill-considered statement of a doctor. It should be remembered, too, that doctors, though men of science, are not always scientific in their practical determinations. Like anyone else, they may have the small-family mentality and are quick to convert their patients to this way of life. If a woman should ever receive such an edict from a doctor, her first move should be to consult an obstetrician in a Catholic hospital. In the face of confirmation, she may then feel justified in considering rhythm.

2. *Eugenical:* When there is a great probability that a couple will produce defective children or pass on serious physical diseases, use of the rhythm method might be justified. Some diseases considered at least partly hereditary include epilepsy, a certain type of cataract, and a rare type of diabetes.

3. *Economic:* The obligation of parenthood does not require a couple to have as many children as is humanly possible, as some critics allege. However, they should have as many children as they can support reasonably. This does not mean that they must be deeply in debt to the loan companies before practicing periodic continence. Nor does it mean that rhythm is justified until they have sufficient savings to insure a college education for the child.

4. *Social order:* As one example, poor housing conditions may force a couple to live in such crowded quarters that an additional child would create a great burden. In another case, a man might expect to be sent to work in a distant place for a number of years. He might be required to leave his family behind and therefore could not fulfill his responsibilities as a father.

As can be inferred from the examples cited above, one can merely suggest possible instances where couples might justifiably practice rhythm. Each case is an individual one and can only be decided with a full knowledge of specific circumstances.

Additional conditions required: Assuming that in one particular case, circumstances of a medical, eugenic, social or economic nature justify confining intercourse to the sterile period, two additional conditions must be met. These are outlined by Father John A. Goodwine of St. Joseph's Seminary, Dunwoodie, N. Y., as follows:

"First, both partners must be willing to abstain during the fertile period. Neither partner may insist on abstinence against the reasonable protest of the other. The reason for this is the marriage contract. By that contract each partner agrees to satisfy the reasonable and serious request of the other for marital relations; for one partner to default on this contract would be a serious violation of justice. Accordingly, the practice of periodic continence would be lawful when, and just as long as, it is mutually agreeable to the spouses.

"The second requisite is that both husband and wife must be able to practice continence during the so-called fertile days. The use of periodic continence demands no little self-control. When a couple attempts to restrict the use of marriage to the sterile period, there may arise occasions of serious sin. The attempt may lead to sins of self-abuse, to mutual fondling to the point of culpable pollution, and even to infidelity. These dangers are especially great in the case of men; but women are by no means exempt from them."

If the necessary conditions are not met in a particular case, would a couple commit sin in practicing periodic continence? And if it is sinful, how serious is the sin? Writing in *The American Ecclesiastical Review,* Father Goodwine has answered:

"If any one of the required conditions (that the parties be willing to abstain, that they be able to abstain without proximate danger of serious sin, and that they have a justifying reason) is not met, recourse to periodic continence will be sinful. In certain cases it may even be seriously sinful.

"For instance, if the first condition is not verified and the practice of periodic continence is insisted on by one partner against the reasonable objections of the other, a sin of injustice would be committed. In such circumstances one partner would be unjustly depriving the other of his right to the marriage act during the fertile periods. So also, if the second condition is not met and the practice of periodic continence becomes a proximate occasion of sins against chastity, there would be serious sin. The otherwise permissible practice of periodic continence becomes seriously wrong when it leads to grave danger of other mortal sins. Similarly there would be serious sin if the practice involves a proximate danger of divorce or breakup of the marriage, or of other sins against the obligations of married life."

Large families the Christian ideal: Pope Pius XII has described large families as "those blessed by God, beloved by the Church and considered by it as one of its most precious treasures."

In an address to the Association of Large Families of Rome and Italy, His Holiness restated a truth that is sometimes forgotten—that "faith in God supplies parents with the strength necessary to face the sacrifices and renunciations required for the rearing of children; Christian principles guide and lighten the difficult task of education; the Christian spirit of love watches over the family's order and tranquillity while it dispenses, almost drawing upon nature itself, the intimate family joys common to parents, children and brothers. . . .

"But God also visits large families with His providence, to which the parents, especially poor ones, give an open testimony by placing in it their entire trust when human efforts are not sufficient. It is a trust well founded, and not in vain . . . God does not deny the means to live to those He calls to life."

In this connection, the following comments by Father Goodwine should be carefully considered.

"There is a tendency to limit the discussion of periodic continence to questions of strict morality, to concentrate almost exclusively on right and wrong, to attempt to draw the line between what may and what may not be done without committing sin," Father Goodwine states. "All too often such discussions lose sight of the Christian ideal of family life. Hardly ever do we hear any mention of the ideal of parenthood or of family life as the ideal type of married life.

"God instituted marriage as the means for the propagation of the race. The fruitful marriage, therefore, and not the sterile marriage, is the marriage that falls in best with God's plan. Having children is the primary goal of marriage. The family, therefore, consisting of father, mother and children is the ideal for the Christian.

"There is something amiss when a couple wishes to marry, yet does not want to have any children; or determines to postpone having children for one, two or more years; or intends to have only three or four or six children but no more. A priest friend of mine likens such people to a young man seeking ordination to the priesthood who makes the stipulation that he will never have to say Mass, administer the sacraments, preach, or take duty. Such a young man would be seeking to avoid the very purposes for which men are ordained to the priesthood. So, too, the married couple who, without sufficient reason, seek to avoid children, fail to fulfill their purpose in life. Even the couple who has sufficient reason for practicing rhythm can be counseled to do more than is required by duty; to strive deliberately and consciously after the ideal.

"The present Holy Father has said: 'It is one of the fundamental demands of right moral order that a sincere inner acceptance of the office and duties (of parenthood) correspond to the use of conjugal rights.' There must then be a willingness on the part of married persons and on the part of couples entering marriage to 'serve' motherhood and fatherhood—a willingness to become parents. Perhaps more attention should be paid to what Dr. John Kane, of Notre Dame, calls the 'almost unanimous conclusion' of sociological studies on marital happiness: 'Happiness in marriage is not associated with the presence or absence of children in the family, but with a strong desire to have children.'"

Disadvantages of rhythm: Even when the conditions outlined above justify using the rhythm method, its practice has definite disadvantages. For example, neither the Ogino-Knaus method nor the basal temperature method, like contraception itself, is completely reliable. If a wife fails to keep careful records or miscalculates by a few days in the first method or misreads the thermometer in the second, she may become pregnant unwittingly. Because of this lack of complete certainty, a couple unwilling to accept the possible consequences of childbirth often find themselves in a state of tension, fearing that pregnancy may have occurred. Tension of this kind leads to irritability and resentments. It does not help to make a happy marriage.

Constant use of the rhythm method also may cause a husband and wife to repress their natural feelings of affection toward each other. The marital act is the most important way by which a husband and wife express their mutual love. The normal relationship of living together produces many occasions when a couple may wish to express this love. It is not natural that they should consult the calendar before deciding whether to carry their spontaneous relations to the natural conclusion. Because use of the rhythm method sometimes requires husbands and wives to restrain their normal feelings for long periods, some may respond by curtailing expressions of affection at all times.

The rhythm method, therefore, may tend to overemphasize physical aspects of intercourse and to repress its spiritual and emotional aspects. Another danger is that continued periods of abstinence may cause open or unconscious resentments in one or both partners. Husbands and wives often decide to practice rhythm without realizing all that voluntary abstinence involves. One partner may wish to kiss affectionately but the other, realizing that desire for intercourse may be stimulated in that way, refuses. Result: tempers grow short and bitterness creeps into the relationship. One fight does not wreck a marriage, but sometimes a pattern of resentment is set up which lasts for years.

Practicing rhythm is particularly inadvisable for young couples. During the early years of marriage, the emotional and physical needs for intercourse probably are at their greatest. Moreover, a young husband and wife who abstain during the "fertile" period have no way of knowing whether their marriage really will be fertile. If they do not take advantage of their fertility when it is at its peak, they may discover later that they have lost their opportunity to have children. And if they are not fertile, the best time to discover this condition is when they are young—and when cures for sterility have the best chance to succeed.

In conclusion, we should state that periodic continence is not the Church's method of birth control. The Church neither approves nor disapproves *per se* restricting marital intercourse to the safe period. If a man and wife wish to restrict intercourse to stated intervals and meet the proper conditions, the Church finds no objection, since the marital act is performed as God designed it. The couple so deciding, presuming the honesty of their motives, do not need the permission of the priest before they begin its practice. While they may wish to consult a priest about the morality involved, the basic decision to have four rather than six children belongs to the couple themselves. It is important, also, to consult a competent doctor on the best way of determining the safe period. The average couple is usually unqualified to determine the time of ovulation. Care, however, must be exercised in the choice of a doctor. Some doctors do not themselves know a great deal about the latest research done in this field of fertility. Some do not want to take the time or share the responsibility of deciding the mechanics of rhythm with the couple. Others are devotees of contraceptive devices and will consider nothing else. At all events, if you are justified in using rhythm, you are entitled to practice it as efficiently as possible.

The abortion horror: The Church teaches that at the instant the male sperm fertilizes the female ovum, life is created. Obviously, anyone who intentionally and deliberately takes that life then or at any time thereafter violates the Fifth Commandment.

Probably few Americans realize the extent of the abortion problem in the United States. Exact figures are impossible to obtain, but informed experts have estimated that of every five pregnancies, one is terminated by deliberate abortion. As a direct result of their attempts to avoid giving birth, hundreds of women die every year and thousands suffer permanent injury and sterility.

The most appalling fact about abortion is that the women involved are not unmarried. In nine cases out of ten, they are said to be wives between the ages of twenty-five and thirty-five—the very ages when they are best equipped physically to carry healthy babies.

An abortion performed solely to prevent childbirth is illegal throughout the United States. As a result, women seeking to have their pregnancies terminated in this way usually are referred to unscrupulous doctors, midwives or others who charge exorbitant fees and often perform the delicate operation under the most unsanitary conditions. The danger of death from an illegal operation, even when performed in a sanitary setting, is twice as great as that from delivering a child. Other women fall prey to the peddlers of quack nostrums and preparations which are sold for overinflated prices and often permanently damage the sensitive tissues of the female organs.

The Catholic Church never permits deliberate abortion at any time or under any circumstances. In fact, this offense is so grave that the woman who deliberately aborts her child is automatically excommunicated. Only the Bishop can give her absolution. The penalty of excommunication also is automatically incurred by any persons who have encouraged the abortion in any way, as well as doctors, nurses and others who have helped to perform it.

Persons outside the Faith sometimes misinterpret the laws covering abortion. These persons cite the example of a woman whose physician tells her that her health and perhaps even her life may be endangered by pregnancy. Cases like this are rare in actual practice. In fact, many doctors with decades of experience say that they have never encountered a situation where such a choice had to be made. In most cases like this, something can be done to save both mother and child, and the Caesarean section usually saves both.

Referring to rare instances of this type, however, Pope Pius XI declared in 1930: "However much we may pity the mother whose health and even life is gravely imperiled in the performance of the duty allotted to her by nature, nevertheless, what could ever be a sufficient reason for excusing in any way the direct murder of the innocent? This is precisely what we are dealing with here. Whether inflicted upon the mother or upon the child, it is against the precept of God and the law of nature: 'Thou shalt not kill.' The life of each is equally sacred, and no one has the power, not even the public authority, to destroy it."

It more frequently happens that the infant's life is endangered in the course of medical or surgical treatment of the mother. For example, an emergency appendectomy must be performed upon a woman to save her life. But the fetus—the unborn child—might die as a result. May the mother be treated to save her own life? The Church answers yes, for the infant's death is not intended. Such cases were discussed by Pope Pius XII, in an address, "Morality in Marriage," delivered in 1951. His Holiness said:

"If the saving of the life of the future mother, independently of her pregnant state, should urgently require a surgical act or other therapeutic treatment which would have as an accessory consequence, in no way desired nor intended but inevitable, the death of the fetus, such act could no longer be called a direct attempt on an innocent life. Under these conditions the operation can be licit, like other similar medical interventions, granted always that a good of high worth is concerned, such as life, and that it is not possible to postpone the operation until after the birth of the child nor to have recourse to other efficacious remedies."

Studies by Raymond S. Pearl established that abortions were from three to four times more numerous among those who used contraceptives than among those who did not. When the contraceptives failed, abortion was the next step. Another report by the Milbank Research Study stated that there are ten times more abortions among users of contraceptives than among those who did not resort to such devices. Thus the starting point for abortions is the use of contraceptives, and the starting point for the use of contraceptives is the contraceptive mentality. It is this mentality that denies the fundamental truth that the primary purpose of marriage is the procreation of children.

5

The Miracle of Birth

THE marvelous way in which your child is conceived, developed and born is truly an example of the magnificent beauty of God's plan. We tend to take it for granted. Yet when we consider the almost unbelievably complex result—a human being—we can only marvel at the miracle in which parents are permitted to share.

When coitus takes place, from two hundred to five hundred million sperm pass from the man to the woman. That is enough sperm to populate all of North and South America, for any one of these millions of sperm could theoretically play its part in creating a new life. A single sperm is about 1/500th of an inch long—infinitely smaller than a drop of water. Yet it transmits dozens of distinct characteristics of the father—perhaps his red hair, his bent toward music, his aptitude for science.

To some extent, the personality of your child is determined in those first hours after coitus by the characteristics of the sperm which wins the race against its millions of competitors—that sperm which first enters and fertilizes the ovum which is traveling through one of the two Fallopian tubes extending from the ovaries to the womb. This egg is smaller than the dot you would make with a pencil. In fact, a teaspoon would hold a million of them. The egg is almost completely transparent and colorless.

Perhaps a few hundred sperm manage the long, five-inch journey from the vaginal canal into the opening of the tube—a journey equal to a man's five-mile swim in a churning ocean. Fewer sperm enter the tube, which is little larger than the thickness of a hair. And fewer still will reach the egg. But when the first sperm meets the ovum, the race is over.

The ovum is protected by a hard shell cover. Such is the marvelous plan of life that the sperm contains a chemical which softens the covering and enables it to penetrate the egg. And—another marvel—the fertilized egg resists the entry of any other sperm which reaches it.

In that dramatic moment when the ovum and sperm unite, a new life begins. Although the fused ovum can barely be seen, it contains all the infant's hereditary traits—traits that determine his blood type, the color of his eyes and skin, the shape of his nose and his jaw, and his intelligence or ability. The infant's sex is determined by the sperm. One type will produce a girl; another, a boy.

Now growth begins—a growth that will change that single cell into a creature that will emerge after nine months with trillions of cells, all magnificently combined into a human life. The single cell divides; then the newer cells divide; then the newest cells divide.

After three days in the Fallopian tubes, the still-tiny fertilized egg moves into the uterus, where it faces a critical fight for life. For several days it floats about the uterus with only its own fat to provide its nourishment. It must soon find another source of food or perish.

It establishes a position on the wall of the uterus. Next it sends out tiny feelers which penetrate the blood vessels of the uterus wall. Now it can draw its needed nourishment from the mother's blood. Meanwhile, the ovary has begun to secrete a hormone called progesterone. This hormone's job is to quiet the uterus so that the new life will not be cast off. As the embryo increases in size after the second month, the womb requires increasingly large amounts of progesterone. At this stage, production of the vital hormone is taken over by the placenta—the tissue attached to the uterus wall through which the baby derives nourishment and discharges waste.

Reliable tests can determine, within ten days after coitus, whether a woman is pregnant. Unless some such early test has been performed, the first indication that conception has occurred is usually failure to menstruate.

You should visit your doctor as soon as you believe that you may be pregnant. Probably most modern women consult an obstetrician—a doctor who has been specially trained to care for them during pregnancy, in childbirth, and immediately thereafter. Inasmuch as many questions of morality and religion are involved in the bearing of children, you should consult a doctor sympathetic with Catholic teaching. Your doctor will probably use the facilities of a specific hospital; you should make certain that it is one where your religious beliefs will be respected, and which has a good record for the care of mothers and infants. The best medical care is particularly important during the first pregnancy, when lifelong attitudes toward motherhood are formed.

After the doctor has determined that you are pregnant, he will list precautions which you must observe. He will want you to watch your weight, to exercise regularly, and to supplement your diet with vitamins, minerals and perhaps hormones. Your consumption of alcoholic beverages and use of tobacco may be curtailed.

If you can recall when your last menstrual period began, you can easily determine when your child will probably be born. Take the first day of that period and add nine months plus seven days. Thus, if your last period began on January 1, your child will probably be born on or around October 8.

At this time you may also wish to decide whether to deliver your child by "natural childbirth." This method is increasing in popularity throughout the world and is approved by the present Holy Father. You learn early in your pregnancy to develop appropriate breathing techniques and, through exercise, to develop the muscles that will be used in labor. As a result of the natural way of giving birth, the use of anesthetics is reduced to the necessary minimum. You are aware of each stage of labor and are conscious when your child is born. Your husband may also be taught how to assist you in labor, and may even be allowed to remain by your side when the child is born.

Most of the pain that American women associate with childbirth is psychological in origin. The modern American girl is physically in excellent condition to have a baby, but if she has been taught to fear childbirth, her tension may actually cause pain. "Natural childbirth" attempts to allay such fears and to relax the mother. To be conscious and fully aware of a child's birth is a deep emotional experience the mother will never forget. However, there is no obligation to consider "natural childbirth" as the only way of having a baby. Catholic doctors use the same drugs administered in any approved hospital. You need not fear that the pains of childbirth will not be alleviated should you need assistance during delivery. Your doctor will be the best judge of that.

Your baby achieves a truly amazing growth in the nine months that you carry him in your womb. In his first month, his tiny heart begins to beat and he develops his own circulatory system. Before his third month, his body takes shape. By his seventh month, he can move his muscles and change position in the womb. If born now, he has a good chance to live. But in the remaining two months he adds weight and improves his muscular development. When he is born, he will weigh about seven pounds and will be about twenty inches long.

You will be warned that the time to give birth is approaching by the onset of labor pains. These usually begin in the small of the back, around the kidneys. Gradually they move downward and often are concentrated in the lower abdomen.

As the labor pains begin, they may be spaced as much as thirty minutes apart and have a duration of less than thirty seconds. Between pains, there is no discomfort at all. Gradually the pains come at shorter and shorter intervals, until they are coming every three minutes or oftener.

When it is obvious that you are entering labor, you should inform your doctor and arrange to go to the hospital. Your husband should accompany you if he can. Some hospitals encourage husbands to remain in the delivery room while the child is born, thus giving him the feeling that he too participates in his child's birth. Other hospitals are not so inclined to give this permission.

In a modern hospital you can be assured of sympathetic care. The nurse or doctor will examine you regularly to determine how near you are to giving birth. As the time draws near, a discharge is usually emitted. This is part of the sac which surrounded the infant in the uterus and is a mucus with slight traces of blood. Now you may be taken to the delivery room and given straps to pull against. They enable you to bear down with each pain and to help the baby's movement down from the uterus through the birth canal.

Pain intensifies in the final minutes before birth. Perhaps you will recall the beautiful words from the New Testament:

"A woman about to give birth has sorrow, because her hour has come. But when she has brought forth the child, she no longer remembers the anguish for her joy that a man is born into the world." (John, 16:21)

When the baby's head appears, the doctor gently helps it out of the birth passage. Then he eases out the shoulders, then the torso. The infant takes its first breath or is helped to do so by a spank from the doctor. Now the doctor cuts the umbilical cord by which the baby has been attached to the placenta. Soon after, the placenta also moves down through the birth canal. The delivery is complete and you are that most privileged of humans—a mother.

In rare cases, the size of the baby or conditions inside your body may require delivery by means of a Caesarean section. This operation consists of delivering the baby through an incision made in the abdomen instead of through the natural birth passage. The Caesarean section has been performed for thousands of years. In fact, its name is said to be derived from Julius Caesar who, according to legend, was born in this manner. Another explanation for the term is that in ancient Rome the Caesar decreed that if the mother died while giving birth, the midwife must remove the baby through the abdomen. Modern surgical techniques insure that Caesarean sections are usually performed successfully without harm to either mother or child.

Young mothers are often concerned about the possibility of having "RH" babies. Several years ago, the danger of giving birth to such babies was widely publicized, but this danger is greatly exaggerated. The story of the RH factor is very complicated. Before difficulties can ensue as a result of it, a woman with RH-negative blood—blood without a certain chemical in its red cells—must be married to a man with RH-positive blood. Usually two children can be born to such a couple without difficulty. When future children are conceived, the woman's doctor can examine her blood periodically to determine whether a toxic illness is resulting from a mixture of the two kinds of blood. If the infant is endangered, he can be given a blood transfusion immediately upon birth, which will enable him to survive and live normally.

The new mother usually takes her baby home from the hospital after about a week. She should not do any strenuous housework for several weeks after her return. The obstetrician will ask her to appear for an examination about six weeks after the birth. He will examine her thoroughly and discharge her if her condition is satisfactory. Obstetricians usually ask their patients to abstain from coitus until after this final examination.

Breast-feeding recommended: Catholic teachers have always urged mothers to breast-feed their babies. Until this century, breast-feeding was virtually the only way the average mother could supply nourishment to her newborn child. With the development of artificial formulas, however, it became fashionable to substitute bottle-feeding. Mothers were told that it was the "more scientific" way and that it enabled hospitals and doctors to operate more efficiently.

Perhaps it did, but German researchers made an interesting study which proved that the *child* thrives better under breast-feeding. In one section of a hospital they bottle-fed a group of babies under the most sanitary conditions. In another section, babies were picked up by their mothers and fed from the breast whenever they needed food. Unlike the "scientific" babies, these infants were caressed and fondled throughout the day. After only a few weeks of this treatment, the difference between the two groups was remarkable. The breast-fed babies had quieter nerves and obviously were more relaxed and better adjusted. If a nurse closed the nursery door, however gently, many bottle-fed babies would stir uneasily in their cribs or cry out. If a nurse made a similar noise where the breast-fed infants slept, they displayed no reaction.

We now know that bottle-feeding overlooks a basic fact of life. For nine months the child has led a warm, sheltered existence in his mother's womb. All his needs have been satisfied. He has had complete security. Then his birth time arrives and he begins his eventful passage into the world. It is an entirely different world, and an entirely different life from the one he knew—and he has lost the support and security he was accustomed to in the womb. To soften that awful shock of birth, and to make his adjustment as easy as possible, you should give your child support and security similar to the kind he knows. The nearest approximation is the warmth and comfort of your arms holding your baby and giving him sustenance from your own body.

In addition to the psychological value that comes to the child from feeding in his mother's arms and at her breast, there are physical advantages. Doctors find that breast-fed babies often gain weight faster, suffer fewer digestive upsets, and often have fewer allergies than those given synthetic formulas. A mother benefits from feeding her baby, too. During the latter stages of pregnancy, many of her organs—in particular, her breasts—have been developing to be able to provide milk to the infant. Nature has intended that mothers nurse their children, and a mother's bodily functions may be thrown out of gear when this function is bypassed.

Mothers who do not nurse their babies usually resume menstruation within about two months. Mothers who breast-feed their infants often delay the resumption until considerably later. This delayed menstruation has long been regarded as an indication that breast-feeding makes conception of a new life impossible. Although medical men have reported numerous cases of mothers who have become pregnant while breast-feeding an infant, there appears to be some truth to this old belief. In families of a generation or two ago, when breast-feeding was almost universal, the spacing of births was entirely too consistent to have been coincidental: babies came only two or more years apart. When mothers breast-fed their infants and made no attempt to avoid pregnancy, the family with more than six or eight children was an exception.

Two false notions have grown up about breast-feeding. The first is that mothers who breast-feed their babies will lose their glamorous figures. This consideration is hardly serious enough to justify denying an infant what it needs for healthy adjustment. Moreover, it is not true.

The second myth is that breast-feeding ties a mother down. This may be true if you work or lead an active social life away from home. But it is not true of the mother who takes care of her own children. In fact, you are *less* tied down in that you don't need sterilizing equipment, assorted bottles, refrigeration facilities, ingredients of the formula and all the rest. You can leave home for many hours without carrying a large package of formula equipment with you.

One of life's greatest joys is to be found in unselfishly giving of one's self. Such a joy is yours when you breast-feed your infant. You give him nourishment and security—two essentials for his full physical and emotional growth. Few things you will do for him throughout his lifetime will mean more to him—or to you.

The sacrament of baptism: Soon after your child returns from the hospital, you should prepare for his baptism. Of course, if he is in danger of death while in the hospital, he should be baptized immediately. (If he is given emergency baptism and lives, the baptismal ceremonies must be supplied later in the parish church.) Do not delay! Baptizing your child to insure his salvation if he should die is a serious obligation. Before the baptismal ceremony, you must choose a suitable name for him, and you must also select his godparents who will serve as his sponsors at the baptismal font.

The matter of choosing a name should not constitute a serious problem. However, the child must be given a Christian name. There are thousands of such names to choose from, each with a special meaning. We all recall how Jesus named His Apostle Peter because the word Peter meant rock—and it was upon this rock that Jesus intended to build His Church. Some Christian names come from the ancient Hebrew. For example, the name Elizabeth means "consecrated to God." The name John means "God is gracious." From the ancient Romans comes the name Dominic—"belonging to the Lord." Of Greek origin is the word Alice, meaning "truth." The name Agnes means "the lamb," Angela, "the messenger of God," Christopher, "the Christ-bearer." Thus it can be seen that the name you give your child can have a deep significance for him all his life. His name should symbolize the characteristics you hope to instill, and should inspire him to live up to the virtuous qualities it implies. The child also should be taught as he grows up to look upon the saint he has been named after as a special friend in heaven. Your infant's patron saint may therefore be his mediator before God.

Many saints have been neglected by men on earth. Father Daniel A. Lord, S. J., suggests that many of these saints' names be restored to current use. He has compiled a list of male names including Alvin, "pure white"; Anselm, "divine hamlet"; Brockwell, "the strong champion"; Myles, "the Saviour"; and Pascal, "the child of Easter." Among almost-forgotten female names he includes Anthea, "the lady of flowers"; Aurelia, "the golden maid"; Moira, "the soft and gentle maiden."

In choosing the man and woman who will be your child's sponsors in baptism, remember that they assume serious obligations. They promise before God that they will undertake to bring up your child as a Catholic if you are unable to do so. When they agree to be godparents, therefore, they accept a responsibility which may last until the child becomes an adult. Because of these solemn obligations, they must make a profession of faith during the baptismal ceremony and, of course, they must be practicing Catholics themselves.

During the first centuries of Christianity, the person to be baptized was immersed completely in water, as Jesus was baptized by John the Baptist. When the new Christian stepped from the water, he donned a white robe that symbolized the purity of his new faith and the beginning of his new life. When the priest administers the sacrament today, he uses a linen square as the symbol of that new life. He places it on the head of the infant and says, "Receive this white garment and wear it unstained to the judgment seat of our Lord, Jesus Christ, that you may have everlasting life." Many Catholic parents bring their own "baptismal robe"—either a dress for the infant or the linen headpiece—and keep it after the ceremony as a remembrance. Some parents also provide a candle made of beeswax. This candle is used in the ceremony as a symbol of the light that Christians should show in their lives so that they will see the Lord when He calls them.

After the baptismal ceremonies, many Catholic mothers receive the blessing after childbirth. It should be your way of expressing thanksgiving for a safe delivery. This blessing is published in the Appendix.

Miscarriage: When the developing infant—the fetus—dies in the mother's womb before the third month of pregnancy, doctors say that "spontaneous abortion" has occurred. Of course, when such abortion is involuntary on the mother's part, no moral guilt is involved. Because of evil connotations rightly associated in the public mind with the word *abortion,* however, most laymen use the term *miscarriage* to describe the death of the fetus at any stage of pregnancy.

Some women—young wives, mostly—have an exaggerated fear of miscarriage. According to the best available estimates, the danger of miscarriage after one or more menstrual periods have been missed is about one in ten. The other nine pregnancies carry to birth. On the basis of this estimate, most women never have a miscarriage or, if they have a large number of children, they have no more than one in their lifetime. Moreover, these estimates do not reflect recent spectacular medical advances in treating mothers to minimize the danger of miscarriage and to prevent it when its first signs appear.

Wives who fear miscarriage often do not understand the factors which cause the carrying of a baby to be interrupted. Despite what many people believe, few miscarriages result from falls, bumpy automobile rides, or from excessive smoking or drinking. One revealing study, made in Key West, Florida, effectively indicated that bumps and jars are not major causes of miscarriages. Women of Key West can reach the mainland only by a rocky 170-mile automobile trip. Doctors compared the records of 289 pregnant women who made this trip at least once, and of 457 women who remained at home. Surprisingly, the women who traveled had proportionately fewer miscarriages than those who did not. What is the significance of this study? It simply proves that nature provides the developing infant with a protective coating in the womb that enables it to survive all but the most severe damage to the mother's body.

Modern physicians believe that miscarriage usually results from defects in the mother's bodily functions. Many of these defects can now be detected and treated early enough to save the fetus. For example, researchers have noted that miscarriage is more likely if your thyroid fails to function actively. Such thyroid deficiency usually can be remedied fairly easily. Some expectant mothers have been found to lack necessary amounts of the hormone progesterone—the hormone which, as we have seen, is necessary for the fetus to develop and grow properly. Additional progesterone can be given by mouth. Strong evidence also exists that vitamin E—the so-called "anti-sterility vitamin"—can help prevent miscarriage. This vitamin also can be taken in pill form.

When miscarriages occur, they most often take place during the first three months of pregnancy, when the growing fetus is trying to establish its hold upon the womb. This is the period during which you should be most careful of your physical condition. Miscarriage is often threatened when there is bleeding from the uterus or pain of the kind that sometimes accompanies menstruation. These symptoms may occur in normal pregnancies, but if you have them you should advise your doctor immediately. He may advise bed-rest and give you prompt treatment to help you avert the loss of your child.

If miscarriage occurs later in pregnancy, the fetus may be born alive and may remain alive for a short time. The mother should arrange for the infant's conditional baptism. In an emergency, anyone may baptize. Water must be poured over the head of the child while these words are pronounced: "If you are alive, I baptize thee in the name of the Father, and of the Son, and of the Holy Ghost."

The mother who loses a child through miscarriage naturally suffers a grievous sorrow. It should console her, however, to realize that the baptized child goes instantly to heaven and that God has given her a great honor in allowing her to share in creating a saint who never knew sin. Even if the fetus is not baptized, she can also rely fully on the providence of an all-loving Father. The Church teaches that the infant who dies without receiving baptism goes to limbo, where it spends eternity free from sorrow or pain. Its happiness is not so great as the happiness in heaven within sight of God. Yet its state is more desirable than that of no existence at all. The mother who grieves over the loss of her unborn child may therefore be comforted by knowing that thanks to God's goodness, she has created a new life, and that while her child existed only a brief time on earth, it now lives in a state of eternal happiness.

6

Help for the Childless Couple

MOST Catholic husbands and wives realize that a home without children, no matter how luxurious, is not a home in the true sense. The wife who does not want children because they would ruin her figure, interfere with her career or prevent her from enjoying an unrestricted social life is in a tiny minority. Likewise, few Catholic men would reject fatherhood because it might curtail their pleasures or burden them with responsibilities they are too immature to accept. When we see a childless Catholic couple, therefore, we may assume that they are childless against their will and that they deserve our sympathy.

One of the great modern tragedies is the existence of vast numbers of persons who desperately want children but are unable to have them because of physical or psychological reasons. Accurate statistics are not available, but experts estimate that from ten to fifteen per cent of all marriages in this country are barren—that the partners are unable to have children. It is also estimated that an additional six or seven per cent have succeeded in procreating one child but cannot give birth to more.

Until recent years, couples who found themselves infertile could do little to remedy the situation. Medical science was powerless. Now, however, as a result of research findings that have helped in developing the rhythm method and of discoveries along other lines, medical experts estimate that more than one-third of all hitherto childless couples can achieve parenthood. Not long ago, it was also generally believed that responsibility for a couple's infertility rested solely upon the wife. It is now thought that in two cases out of five the cause of sterility lies in the male.

Causes of a wife's infertility: Any one of a dozen reasons could explain a woman's inability to conceive. For example, she may not be producing the ovum—the egg which is the starting point of a new life. By taking the same kind of daily temperature reading as is used in the practice of the rhythm method, a physician can determine whether her ovary delivers the egg in the usual way at the usual time in her menstrual cycle. Perhaps the egg is deposited normally but is defective and will not survive even when fertilized by the male sperm. A thyroid deficiency may be preventing fertilization or may cause immediate miscarriage. There may be a lack of the hormones necessary to develop the newly fertilized embryo.

One of the reproductive organs may be defective. These include the ovary, the Fallopian tubes through which the eggs travel on their way to the uterus, the uterus itself, and the organs through which the male sperm must pass to unite with the egg. Blocking of the Fallopian tubes is a common cause of infertility. They may be blocked as a result of an earlier operation, disease, or other causes. Any well-trained physician can perform a simple test to determine whether the tubes are open. A small quantity of carbon dioxide gas is gently pumped into them; if the gas penetrates, the patient feels a sharp pain. If the gas does not penetrate, obviously neither the egg nor sperm could pass through, either. X-rays may next be taken to determine where the obstruction lies. A minor operation can clear the passage, and in some cases even the simple pressure of the gas will open the tubes enough to permit the egg and sperm to pass through.

Sometimes the uterus does not properly prepare the "nest" in which the fertilized egg may develop. This condition may be caused by a woman's rundown physical condition, by a lack of essential vitamins or hormones, or by other unknown factors.

A woman's mental or emotional condition may also be at the root of her failure to conceive. Without being aware of it, she may fear what she believes to be the dangers of childbearing. Mental tension may cause the Fallopian tubes to constrict during intercourse, making passage of the sperm impossible. The doctor who recognizes that a woman's fears affect her fertility will reassure her that modern medical techniques make the mother's safety during pregnancy and delivery virtually certain.

Conception may also be hindered by an infection in the female organs. For example, all women normally discharge secretions from their vagina. Ordinarily this discharge does not harm the sperm, but in certain cases it may render it impotent. Under proper treatment, the causes of these excessive or harmful discharges can be cleared up fairly quickly.

Causes of male infertility: The hairy-chested, muscular male is not necessarily the most fertile. Fertility has no known correlation with a man's physical build: the short, thin man who weighs but a hundred pounds may be considerably more fertile than one twice his size or weight. The measure of fertility is the amount of sperm which the male ejects, as well as his general health. The average ejaculation includes from two hundred to five hundred million sperm, any one of which can fertilize the egg. It is also believed that unless an ejaculation contains fifty million sperm, the chances of any one reaching the egg are very slight. Some doctors maintain that a far lesser number is enough to make conception probable. At any rate, all doctors agree that the greater the number of sperm entering the vagina, the greater the likelihood that one will swim the channel to fuse with the egg.

The quantity of a man's sperm is determined by such factors as his general physical condition and the length of time that has elapsed since the last marital act. (He requires at least five days of abstinence for the quantity of sperm to reach its maximum potential.) The quality of the germ cells (the ovum or sperm) may be affected by chronic illness, by fatigue, worry or emotional upsets; by overindulgence in alcohol, by an inadequate sub-marginal diet and, in some cases, tobacco.

Modern physicians have many methods of determining to what extent, if any, the husband's or wife's state of health or condition may be responsible for the infertility or barrenness of the couple. Thus, the physician will usually arrange for a simultaneous examination of both partners, if there is a seeming inability to conceive.

Other causes of infertility: Sometimes conception can be achieved by removing unfavorable conditions relating to the marital act itself. For example, Doctor Bernard Pisani comments that "intercourse should take place on the potentially fertile days, which are best determined by consulting a physician who has studied and reviewed the basal temperature or graphs kept by the patient (referred to in the preceding chapter). Some workers in the field of sterility feel that a short period of abstaining from intercourse (three to four days) before the expected target date of ovulation may be of assistance. This should enable the husband to accumulate a maximum amount of sperm, although too prolonged pre-coital abstinence is not warranted, since 'sperm may die in waiting.' These points are to be remembered in the cases where lowered male fertility is present. In other cases, intercourse may be too frequent or not frequent enough.

"The act itself should be performed naturally and in a cheerful relaxed mood, as free from tension as possible," Doctor Pisani continues. "The wife should try to assume a position that will enable the penis to penetrate most deeply into the vagina toward the cervix. This will enable the sperm to be sprayed on the cervix. After intercourse the wife should lie quietly on her back for several hours, perhaps with a pillow under her buttocks, to keep the semen in the vagina. She should empty her bladder before intercourse, not after.

"For presumed sanitary reasons, some women have adopted the practice of washing out the vagina before intercourse. Such douching is not necessary and even plain water before or after intercourse may make the male sperm inactive. Accordingly, washing before intercouse should be limited to careful cleansing of the outside. Nothing should be used in the vagina except as advised by the doctor. Douching after intercourse is forbidden, not only because it is unnecessary, but especially because it is a contraceptive act."

Moral questions: Childless couples occasionally seek answers to questions like these:

"We have been married three years and have not conceived. Are we obligated to seek treatment to enable us to have a child?" The Church teaches that inasmuch as neither partner has acted deliberately to prevent birth, they are not morally required to seek a remedy for their sterility. It would be more in keeping with the ideals of Catholic marriage, however, if such a couple sought medical aid.

"How long should a couple wait before asking a doctor to help them conceive?" Many experts believe that if factors making for infertility are not present, newlyweds who perform the marital act on an average of twice a week will conceive within a year. A couple, therefore, would be wise to seek help if pregnancy does not occur within eighteen months. The older the partners, the more important it is that treatment be undertaken early, for the ability to reproduce decreases with age. Those who delay too long may lose their opportunity for parenthood.

"We are childless. My husband wants children. I do not. Am I obliged to seek medical treatment to enable me to have them?" Theologians answer that if one partner is seriously disappointed over the failure to have children, the mate, in justice, should try to learn what, if anything, can be done to remedy the situation. If a medical examination reveals that only a serious operation would correct the barrenness, you are not obliged to undergo it. If the sterility could be remedied by a simple procedure, however, justice might dictate that you undergo treatment. The absolute answer, therefore, depends upon how serious the treatment would be and how strongly one mate desires children.

"Where can we obtain medical treatment for infertility?" Any modern doctor is probably sufficiently familiar with up-to-date techniques to perform a basic examination. If complicated treatment appears necessary, he can refer you to appropriate specialists.

You should seek treatment from a doctor sympathetic to

Church teaching on this question. In attempting to test the fertility of the husband, some physicians try to obtain a sample of male sperm either by masturbation or by *coitus interruptus*, a form of birth control whereby the penis is withdrawn from the vagina before ejaculation and the semen is captured in a container. Both of these methods violate moral law. Catholics may not use them. A doctor who respects your religious convictions will not suggest them.

Artificial insemination: A husband and wife may be unable for various reasons to have intercourse in the normal way so that the semen is deposited in the vagina. In other cases, the quality or quantity of the husband's sperm remains so low that conception is virtually impossible. In these cases a few doctors have recommended that the practice of artificial insemination be followed. By this method, semen is usually obtained by means of masturbation from the husband or an anonymous donor, depending upon circumstances. The semen is deposited in a receptacle which is then emptied into the vagina. Infants born as a result of this procedure have been publicized as "test-tube babies."

The position of the Church on this procedure is unequivocal. Speaking to the Fourth International Convention of Catholic Doctors in 1949, Pope Pius XII said, "Artificial insemination is something which must not just be regarded with extreme reserve, but must be utterly rejected."

In a talk to the Catholic Union of Midwives in 1951, His Holiness also stated: "To reduce cohabitation and the conjugal act to a simple organic function for the transmission of seed would be converting the home, the sanctuary of the family, into a mere biological laboratory. . . . In its natural structure, the conjugal act is a personal action, a simultaneous and immediate co-operation on the part of the husband and wife which, by the very nature of the agents and the propriety of the act, is the expression of the mutual gift which according to Holy Scripture brings about union 'in one flesh only.'

"This is something much more than the union of two seeds which may be brought about even artificially, without the natural action of husband and wife. The conjugal act, ordained and willed by nature, is a personal act of co-operation, the right to which husband and wife give each other when they marry."

Apart from the overwhelming moral objections to artificial insemination, there are also strong legal objections. For example, in cases where an anonymous donor of semen is involved, lawyers doubt whether the child would be considered legitimate, inasmuch as the natural father has not married the mother. Serious questions also are raised as to the husband's legal responsibility toward his wife's child by another man. Finally, the future emotional relationship of the husband with the child who is not his son may involve difficulties that are unforeseen when conception occurs.

Adopting children: If there is little likelihood that you will become a natural parent, you may wish to consider adopting a child. It is a natural impulse, for it provides an outlet for every wife's motherly instincts; it changes an often lifeless house into a home happy with the sound of laughter; and it gives a child his greatest gift—parents who love him.

A century ago, orphans were numerous in our society. Today, thanks to better medical care for mothers, safer working conditions in mines and factories, and the general lengthening of the life span, relatively few children are available for adoption. In fact, there are more prospective parents for orphaned children than there are youngsters. For example, one large adoption agency receives 2,000 applications from prospective parents each year, but has only 200 babies to place.

According to recent estimates, about 270,000 children live in foster homes, orphanages and similar institutions throughout the United States. But only about ten per cent—30,000—are available for adoption. Parents of the other 240,000 are living, but for various reasons cannot care for their children properly at this time. However, the possibility remains that they may be able to do so in the future. In any event, they will not sign the necessary papers to enable another couple to adopt their children legally. Inasmuch as about three million couples in the United States want children but are physically unable to have them, it is obvious that the demand for boys and girls to be adopted far exceeds the supply. Nevertheless, if you can meet the qualifications necessary to give a child a good upbringing, have the humility necessary to undergo close scrutiny, and the patience to wait for many months, or even years, you may ultimately be successful.

Adoption agencies are extremely careful about the persons to whom they give a baby. They will want to know a great deal about you. Your health—if an examination reveals that either prospective parent suffers a disabling disease, or might not live until the child reaches maturity, an agency would not entrust a baby to your care. Your income—adoption experts have found that usually neither the very rich nor the very poor make the best parents. If you have an average income and can give a child an average home, your prospects are excellent. Your religious history—a child is placed only with a family of his religion. Records of adoption services prove unmistakably that husbands and wives who faithfully practice their religion provide the kind of home in which children grow most happily.

Your own personalities will be considered. Psychologists can detect a great deal about your character by talking to you and observing your attitude generally. Many such interviews are conducted before a child is awarded. The husband and wife who are considered most desirable as parents are those with an easy, relaxed relationship toward each other. When the husband acts like a dictator, the woman nags, or the couple places too much emphasis upon material possessions, the trained workers in adoption agencies have learned to proceed with great caution.

Your other aptitudes and interests also are a factor. Agencies often conduct many tests to determine the interests and intelligence of the children and their prospective parents. If a boy shows an aptitude for working with his hands, for instance, an effort may be made to give him a father skilled along that line.

Before applying to an adoption agency, both husband and wife should deeply want a child and should be fully prepared to make any sacrifices necessary to provide a loving home. Ideally, you should want to take on the responsibilities of rearing a child because of what you believe you can do for him, rather than what you think he might do for you.

It is unfair to seek a child as a "marriage saver." Frequently a husband and wife, unable to settle marital difficulties in any other way, decide that adopting a child will solve everything. Husbands who drink to excess or cannot hold a job convince themselves that "everything would be different" if they had the responsibility of providing for a child. Usually adoption will not work under these circumstances. The child's coming may bring peace to the couple for a short time, and the husband may make a strong effort to shoulder his responsibilities. But adoption agencies have found that the basic causes of the couple's difficulties must be removed, or they probably will return. And when they do, the causes will be magnified greatly, because a child has now joined the ranks of the sufferers. Fortunately, adoption services are experienced in detecting applicants who have underlying motives of this type, and the number of unsuitable parents to whom children are given is constantly diminishing.

Couples considering adoption often ask how they can be sure that their child will be normal and healthy. Physicians, psychologists and other experts examine each child thoroughly and appraise his mental and physical condition as accurately as possible. They try to match the youngster to the parents. Whenever possible, a child with high intelligence will be placed with parents who are equally gifted and who will help him to develop his capabilities to the fullest extent. A youngster of average intelligence will be placed with a couple in the same category, and so on.

Because most babies available for adoption have been signed over by unwed mothers, some couples also seek assurance that the child they adopt will not grow up to be "tainted morally." Such an attitude is, of course, both un-Christian and unscientific. Whatever the child's parentage, he will reflect the moral influence and training of the husband and wife responsible for his upbringing.

It is normal for every man and wife to seek a child who is healthy, bright and vivacious. The cute, curly-haired, bright-eyed babies are the ones who spend only a few months in an institution while many different prospective parents clamor for them. The less perfect children often go unwanted. These may be youngsters who suffer from minor or major physical defects—harelip, clubfoot, partial blindness or deafness, or who are below average in intelligence. It is children such as these who can profit most from the loving care and attention which you can provide. To take such youngsters into your home and to give them your fullest measure of affection is to be parents in the most glorious sense of that word. Natural parents always face a possibility that their child may have some physical, mental or emotional defects. They usually meet their problems with love and trust in God. So too might the parents of an adopted child who desperately needs the care which only a loving mother and father can give.

To avoid possible legal repercussions later, you should deal only with an established, reputable adoption agency. So-called "baby-brokers" occasionally offer to provide a child to a couple lacking the patience required by an established service. These brokers promise to produce a child for from $500 to $5,000, depending upon what the traffic will bear, but they may neglect to complete the many legal steps involved in adoption. For instance, the child's natural parent or parents must sign a statement relinquishing all rights to him. Adoption services make certain that such papers are in order before placing the child in a new home; baby-brokers are not so meticulous. In some cases, natural parents have returned after many years to demand the child from a couple who mistakenly believed that they were the legal parents.

A thought for the childless: Reaching doggedly for something you can never have will bring frustration and unhappiness. There will be many married couples who in God's Providence will never be parents even by adoption. No one can explain this mystery satisfactorily, so the best thing for such couples to do is to resign themselves to childlessness. They will find this easier if they seek a child from an agency not for any advantage they expect to receive but because of the advantages they can give the child.

The world has not ended for the childless couple. They may well discover that God has a fulfillment of another kind in store for them. For one thing they have full opportunity to cement their love for each other and to create a bond that in itself is very satisfying. For another thing, they can channel their parental instincts in other directions. Their freedom enables them to do more for others in the church and in the community than ordinary parents could ever do. There is a vast field of social and charitable work awaiting this kind of "parent." Their childless lives do not have to be empty and barren of affection. The grass in their garden will be as green as anyone else's if they realize that God apparently has given them a destiny different from other married couples', a destiny capable of satisfying even their parental needs if they merely accept His Will.

7

Danger Signs in Marriage

MOST Catholic marriages are happy marriages. They have their stresses and storms, their trials and errors; but when a Catholic man and woman seek God's sanctifying grace and subdue their own selfish pleasures, the result is mutual salvation and joy. The truly Catholic husband can take his wife's hand after thirty or forty years and say to her, "Ours has been a good life together."

Not all marriages are lived out so happily. Somewhere along the line, selfishness, stubbornness or false pride enter the picture, and a union which might have led to mutual sanctification becomes a source of bitter unhappiness, shame and remorse. The fact that a marriage is performed in the Church and before God's priest is no automatic assurance that it will succeed. No less than members of other faiths, Catholic couples need to develop many virtues to achieve a harmonious life together and to avoid pitfalls that exist everywhere. Even though they cannot end in divorce, Catholic marriages can fail. They can reach a state where the husband deserts his wife and children, where husband and wife no longer live under the same roof, or where husband and wife may remain together but in a state of permanent animosity. Even though hope for reconciliation remains, no one could deny that such marriages are in desperate trouble.

Marriage counselors, divorce court judges, social workers, and other experts unanimously agree that couples do not reach such troubled stages overnight. Long before a husband deserts his wife or lives with her under circumstances in which calm communication with each other is impossible, there have been many early danger signs predicting that this trouble would come. For just as early symptoms forecast the coming of physical disease, so too do simple signs often indicate when marriages may be headed for trouble.

Many serious marriage problems start from simple differences. Unless the couple recognizes these differences early and tries to meet them with understanding and mutual consideration, the symptoms may continue to grow and become a deadly disease. Some of the danger signs will be discussed below.

In reviewing this list, you might profit from the experience of the middle-aged woman who appeared before a marriage counselor with tears streaming down her face. She pleaded with him to tell her what she now could do to win back the husband she had divorced a year before. She had wanted to be a social leader in her town. She permitted her ambitions to grow unchecked even though her husband did not care for a social life but preferred to spend his evenings quietly reading at home. Looking back over her past life, she realized that all her marriage troubles started when she permitted herself to join a bridge club of wealthy women. From that point on, she made life with her husband a living hell, demanding that he take her out almost every evening. "If only I knew in time where this social climbing would lead to," she said, "I never would have nagged my husband the way I did. I would have worked hard to save my marriage." But it was too late. She should have acted when the problem was a small one and probably could have been settled in a friendly way through a calm discussion with her spouse.

In addition to money problems, in-law problems and the tendency to drink to excess, which will be discussed in detail in the following chapters, sources of friction which should be eliminated now, lest they grow to endanger your union, include:

Inability to agree on "little things." One husband and wife prepare for an evening out together. Before they leave, however, there is a sharp interchange over how she should dress. Then they bicker over the restaurant where they will eat. In the car, the wife sharply criticizes her husband's driving and his choice of a parking spot. Throughout their dinner, they argue about which movie to see. What lies behind their inability to reach friendly conclusions about little things? Generally it is a sign that something deeper and more basic is gnawing at one or both. For instance, such continual warfare often occurs when husband and wife are struggling to dominate the marriage. Of course, no couple goes through a lifetime without many minor disagreements, but in the normal marriage the areas of conflict decrease with time instead of increasing. When a husband and wife find themselves quarreling more often than they have in the past, they should stop and think of basic causes which may be involved.

The wife nags more often. Of all the complaints which husbands make, the one that their wives "nag them to death" is probably most common. When a husband makes such a statement, he probably does not realize that he may be revealing a fundamental fact about himself—the fact that he fails to give his wife the understanding and appreciation that she needs. Psychologists say that nagging indicates that a wife is unsure of herself and of her husband's love. She wants to reach out and hold him. The easiest way that occurs to her to do this is to call his attention to her as often as possible.

Judge Paul W. Alexander of the Domestic Relations Court of Toledo, Ohio, tells the story of a businessman who hired a beautiful and talented secretary. One day the wife paid a visit to the office, took a look at the secretary and began to worry. Soon thereafter the businessman had to travel to New York to close a big contract, and he took his secretary to help him. Unable to control herself, the wife began to nag, to try to impress her own presence on her husband. The nagging continued until the secretary eloped with an army captain. The businessman hired a new secretary, a middle-aged woman who offered the wife no competition. When the wife's feeling of emotional security returned, she stopped her badgering.

Few cases of nagging begin so simply or end so abruptly.

Moreover, nagging is a matter of degree. Every wife finds it necessary at times to remind her husband of the screen door that needs mending or the window pane that must be replaced. But nagging does become serious when the tired husband cannot read his newspaper in the evening without constant interruption. Once nagging becomes a problem in marriage, the typical husband may retreat into himself—or into a bar. The basic cause of the nagging—the wife's feeling that she is neglected—may be intensified and the problem grows.

One or both partners neglect their religious duties. Research by social scientists unanimously confirms the fact that religious couples have a greater chance to achieve happiness than those without a true belief in God. As Paul H. Landis of the State College of Washington declares in his book *Making the Most of Marriage,* "It is an established fact that those without religious affiliation are a greater marriage risk than those with acknowledged religion."

Mr. Landis continues: "Not only is religious training significant, but also whether or not a couple remains actively associated with some church organization is specifically important. Even as early as the engagement period, church attendance has been found to be a factor in the success or failure of the relationship. One study found that more than half of the engagements in which the girls attended church more regularly than the boys were finally broken. This was also true of engagements in which neither had religious affiliation. Fewer engagements were broken among those couples who attended church once a month or more.

"This association with a church, which contributes to success in engagement, is even more significant in marriage. Higher marital happiness scores were registered by couples who, after marriage, continued attending church regularly. It has been found, too, that striking differences in marriage adjustments are associated with the circumstances under which a couple marries." He concludes that "all the evidence adds up to the fact that a religious background is an asset in marriage, or to state it negatively, that those without religion are less likely to achieve success in courtship and marriage."

Frequent reception of the sacraments virtually obliges a husband and wife to consider their obligations to make their marriage a success. The person contemplating his own sins in preparation for the sacrament of penance is less inclined to be critical of his mate. When husband, wife, or both, grow lax in the practice of religion, therefore, they lose the advantage of the unifying grace which the sacraments can provide.

Husband and wife quarrel over religious questions. These quarrels naturally are more prevalent in mixed marriages. Sometimes religious differences do not pose a serious problem until children are born and the question of educating them in the Catholic faith arises. The non-Catholic partner may be unwilling to have his child taught principles which he cannot accept. He may try to influence the child away from Catholicism. Conflict results. Sometimes the nonbelieving parent carries on a rear-guard action: wherever and whenever possible, he directs sly digs and sarcastic asides against the Faith. The result is an underlying tension which may be reflected in conflict over other matters.

Serious disagreements over religious matters sometimes occur even in marriages between two ostensible Catholics. Occasionally, a husband will refuse to abstain from meat on Friday or will discourage his child's enrollment in a parochial school. Sometimes differences develop over a mate's desire to practice artificial birth control in violation of divine teachings.

Whether these religious differences are between Catholics and non-Catholics or practicing Catholics and fallen-away Catholics, the fact remains that unless these can be resolved somehow, the very fabric of the marriage is threatened.

Husband and wife find it more difficult to talk to each other. Psychologists term this condition a "breakdown in communications." It is an indication that at least one of the partners no longer has the same interest that formerly existed in the other's problems, feelings and opinions. There is no longer a full sense of oneness in the marriage.

It is probably impossible for one human being to know another completely; all of us have inner fears and hopes which we do not reveal to another soul. We may be naturally reticent about physical problems, sex relationships, or money matters. This reticence is to be expected in any marriage. When it increases rather than declines, however, it indicates that the sense of companionship necessary in a happy partnership is not being achieved.

A breakdown in communications may result when the husband is always too busy to hear his wife tell of the problems she faces with the children all day; when she refuses to listen to his report of his difficulties at the office or, worse, usually takes his employer's side in the argument; when they cannot discuss politics without violent disagreement. Sometimes a sensitive wife tries to discuss hidden fears about her health; her husband ridicules her symptoms and refuses to extend the sympathy she so obviously seeks. Sometimes a shy husband ventures to express his deep feelings of affection and his busy wife laughingly rebuffs him.

The inability to talk freely with each other develops slowly and in two stages. In one case, a husband became passionately attached to the hobby of photography—a wholesome hobby, within reason. However, he could not go near a photo supply shop without buying something. He turned his basement into a fully equipped darkroom, and he constantly traded in his cameras, enlargers and slide projectors for newer, more expensive models.

Since he was a city fireman with a modest salary, his wife thought that he was spending too much money on his hobby—money that could be put to better use around the house. She tried the first step—telling him frankly that she thought he should spend less on himself. He answered angrily that how he spent the money he earned was no concern of hers.

Obviously the difference of opinion remained, so the first stage in the breakdown in communication resulted. The couple began to bicker constantly over his spending. There were bitter quarrels whenever the children needed clothing, the house needed painting, the kitchen linoleum needed replacing. But the husband remained unmoved; there was seldom a pay day when his wife did not see him carrying a new purchase from the yard to his basement darkroom.

When quarreling failed to achieve her objective, the wife retreated into stony silence. Whenever she found it necessary to walk from supermarket to supermarket to save a few pennies on groceries, she despised her husband for his selfishness. Gradually she found it increasingly difficult to discuss any common problem of their marriage with him. A wall of silence was erected—a wall which represented defeat for the mutual happiness they had hoped to achieve.

This breakdown of communications is a particular danger in mixed marriages. After recognizing that their opposing religious beliefs cannot be reconciled, a husband and wife may conclude that no further purpose can be served by discussing them. The question of religious differences subsides, but it does not die. Father John L. Thomas, S.J., of St. Louis University analyzed twelve hundred broken mixed marriages and concluded that while religious differences are factors in marital instability, they often do not lead to direct quarrels over religion. Father Thomas explains:

"As a rule, people do not argue about religious differences, even, or especially, in mixed marriages. Religious beliefs by their very nature involve the emotions to such an extent that it is impossible for most people to argue about them with any degree of calm or objectivity. As a result, after a few attempts, most couples give up trying to talk over their religious differences. Finding this approach rather hopeless, they silently agree to disagree." In this cold-war atmosphere, other serious tensions develop and lead to cruelty, desertion and adultery.

Inasmuch as the inability to communicate usually stems from the inability to discuss problems without rancor, every married couple should learn the art of settling differences in a peaceful way. If there is any sign of breakdown in communications in your marriage, you should read with special care the section in this book on "How to Disagree with Your Mate."

One or both mates become increasingly careless of personal appearance. Every young man and woman naturally tries to make a good impression upon his prospective mate. Consequently engaged couples probably go to extremes of personal adornment to attract each other. After the ceremony, some letdown is inevitable; rare is the marriage that retains all the charm, glamour and romance of the honeymoon. But both husband and wife should maintain high standards of personal hygiene and dress with taste and dignity.

The wife becomes a careless and indifferent housekeeper. Most wives want to maintain a home that is reasonably presentable. Of course, housekeeping standards vary considerably. One woman may be a perfectionist who cannot bear to see a speck of dust on her living-room rug. Another may leave breakfast dishes unwashed until dinnertime. Both women may have happy marriages. But when there is an appreciable lowering of their established housekeeping standards, a danger signal may be flying.

The wife who formerly was reasonably conscientious about her housekeeping chores and who suddenly becomes careless, may be reflecting a "what's the use" attitude about her obligation. A deep problem may be disturbing her—perhaps the feeling that she is being neglected, that her husband does not appreciate her.

If she has been a good cook and suddenly stops preparing meals she knows her husband will like, she also usually betrays an inner dissatisfaction with her marriage. An interesting study reported to the American Association for the Advancement of Science found that wives often use meals as a means of expressing their true feelings toward their husbands. The wife who resents her mate will serve him overdone vegetables, meat that is too rare or too burned, and desserts that take no effort to prepare. (Even the most loving wives sometimes are unable to prepare a meal that is up to their usual standards. The study does not refer to such occasional lapses, but rather to a wife's persistent indifference toward the meals she serves.) Another survey found that the amount of time and thought a wife spends on preparing dinner usually is in direct proportion to the contentment and sense of security and love she feels toward her mate.

Like other symptoms of troubled marriages, the sloppy home and inferior meals often accentuate the very condition that caused them. Every husband likes a well-kept home to return to after his day's work; if it ceases to be attractive or even repels him, he may be tempted to spend his leisure hours elsewhere.

Sex relations grow less satisfactory to one or both partners. The marital act is primarily an expression of mutual love and consideration. In a normal marriage, the satisfaction of both partners from physical communion should increase with growing understanding, adjustment, and responsiveness to each other's needs. Unless there is an underlying physical reason, such as illness, fatigue or worry, a diminishing enjoyment from the conjugal relationship therefore indicates that serious strains and tensions may exist elsewhere in the marriage.

As we have seen, emotional harmony is of basic importance in this act. The woman who resents her husband may hide her feelings at other times, but her true emotions will make mutually satisfying marital relations difficult. What is wrongly called "sex maladjustment" is therefore actually a sign that tension and frustrations exist in other areas of domestic life, and not until these emotional conflicts are settled will the sexual relationship adjust itself.

Conflicts over money matters increase. Financial problems exist in every marriage. But more important than the presence or absence of money is the attitude of the husband and wife toward material wealth. The lives of many millions of exemplary Catholics prove that a couple with emotional maturity, secure in the knowledge of their love for each other, can sail through any financial storm. Money problems therefore are usually not the root of domestic strife. When conflicts over money appear, they are almost always the outward expression of deeper tension or friction that can be traced to the selfishness of one or both spouses.

They do fewer things together. The question, "Is it right for my husband to spend one night a week out with his male friends?" is frequently asked by young wives. Most priests experienced in marriage counseling would answer that a night out for the husband with his male friends, or a night out for the wife with her woman friends would not generally be considered a source of trouble in marriage. Signs of danger exist, however, when husband and wife want to stay away from home frequently, and they want to do it—whether they are consciously aware of this motive or not—to escape from each other. This intense desire to seek the bulk of one's recreation away from one's partner has been termed "psychological desertion."

One sees frequent examples of husbands who appear to be deeply devoted to hobbies. The reactions of their wives vary—possibly because the wives can sense the true motives. One man is a golfer who spends most of his weekends on the golf course. His wife shrugs her shoulders and good-naturedly accepts his hobby. Another man disappears into his basement workshop every night and does not rejoin his wife until bedtime. She fiercely resents his hobby. In the first case, the wife recognizes that her husband's enthusiasm for golf is a genuine interest in the sport. The second wife suspects that her husband's woodworking activities merely cover his desire to be away from her.

When a husband begins to spend a great deal of time on recreation away from home, the normal wife feels let down. She has a right to expect that her husband should spend more of his leisure time with her than anywhere else. She wants to know that if he had to make a choice, he would choose her ahead of any other interest.

If his wife complains about the time he spends on his hobby, a husband should recognize that her complaints may really be legitimate. He should ask himself: Just why do I pursue this hobby or sport or recreational activity so diligently? Is it something I turn to because I really enjoy it, or do I use it primarily as an excuse to get away from my wife?

Do I purposely seek recreational outlets that do not include her? For example, hunting offers many thrills for a sportsman, but it is primarily a male sport and some men find that its chief advantage is that it takes them away from home.

Did I know in advance that taking up this sport or activity would irritate her? A husband married for any length of time can usually predict his wife's reaction. If he seeks nights out with friends for whom he knows she has little regard, perhaps he is subconsciously using this method to get away from her.

The husband who answers yes to any of these three basic questions should consider where his actions may be leading, for if he continues a selfish course of activities that disturbs his wife he will probably bear the major responsibility if the marriage deteriorates further.

Husband or wife becomes unduly attentive to a member of the opposite sex. A married man or woman can be pleasant to members of the opposite sex, but so-called "harmless flirtations" should be viewed with reserve. A man or woman who demonstrates overly active interest in the other sex obviously is searching for some satisfaction which is not being obtained. Perhaps there is a lack of excitement, a need for glamour, or a desire to feel attractive which one's mate has not satisfied. Or the man or woman may be emotionally immature and incapable of living up to the obligations of marriage. In any event, so-called "innocent flirtations," if unchecked, may produce a deadly result. They may lead straight to adultery.

One mate resents the other's attention to the children. When some immature men marry, they seek not a wife, but a mother —someone to baby them and give them undivided attention. When children come, this type of husband discovers that he has a competitor for love. He often reacts jealously, like the first child who feels pushed aside when the second baby arrives. Some wives also resent their husband's love for a child, feeling that it has been diverted from themselves.

Parents who resent their children are often young in years as well as in emotional control. In one case, two twenty-year-olds were married and had a baby a year later. The father had never been truly separated from his mother's apron strings, and felt in need of his wife's complete love. When the baby arrived, the mother responded naturally. She gave the child the attention and love he required. Her husband could not stand much of this. Before long he was spending his evenings at bars with his old school cronies and often never came home at all. In this case, a parish priest was able to help the husband grow up in time before serious harm was done to the marriage. Many other parents who are jealous of their children also require help from experienced counselors because no marriage can thrive amid such immaturity. It is true that in some cases a parent will smother a child with affection, completely leaving the spouse out in the cold and with a justifiable resentment. But such cases are rare.

One of the partners becomes noticeably indifferent to displays of affection. When you were first married, you probably spent hours with your bride or bridegroom, holding hands and showing your affection in other ways. Of course, honeymoons do not last forever, and requirements of the workaday world make such demonstrations impractical. However, there will always be affection manifested in the healthy marriage. The husband who fails to kiss his wife as he leaves for work or when he returns may merely have important business matters on his mind. Such occasional lapses probably happen in every marriage. But if they recur often, a dangerous habit pattern is being established. Affection thrives on demonstration of affection and dies from the lack of it. Moreover, the failure to kiss in the morning and evening, failure to use the courteous words, "please" and "thank you," in everyday relationships, the husband's failure to open the door for his wife when they enter a building—all these lapses suggest that mates may be losing interest in each other. Gallantry and chivalry as manifested by kind words and tender acts are most desirable traits to cultivate; seldom does a marriage experience serious difficulties when these displays of mutual affection are made.

Husband or wife gambles to excess. Most gambling is harmless, and probably every husband and wife have gambled at some time in their lives. Such innocent gambling may involve a few pennies on a raffle or a few dollars on a horse race. When indulged in as a sport, and when the sums involved are not required for the family's basic needs, gambling is not sinful. It becomes a sin and a source of danger to a marriage when it is indulged in with money needed for life's everyday essentials.

Like other vices, gambling does not become a vicious, all-consuming habit overnight. It gives many warning signs: increasing preoccupation with the horses or whatever; diminishing awareness of responsibility toward one's family; and, ultimately, inability to resist the temptation to stake all on the hope of amassing quick riches. A person conscious of his family obligations would do well to rout all gambling out of his system, once he observes that his interest in it exceeds the casual, indifferent attitude of most normal persons.

Husband (or wife) fears that the other holds him back. Some executives of business corporations now interview wives of their employees before making important promotions. The executives reason that a wife's influence may be the factor which determines whether or not her husband is capable of filling a higher job. A wife is often expected to be a good hostess, a clever conversationalist, one who is adept at cocktail parties and who looks as though she had just stepped from a beauty salon. Whether she is a truly good and inspiring wife and mother on the spiritual and emotional levels is seldom, if ever, considered; the primary question is whether she will help her husband serve the corporation. This concept of the wife as her husband's helpmeet in business is also growing among independent businessmen and professional men. By these standards the ideal wife makes a good social impression on men and other women and encourages them to patronize the husband's shop or hire his services.

In view of this emphasis on the wife's business talents, it is no wonder that as many husbands climb to material success, they find fault with mates who do not progress with them. The biographies of American business leaders abound in stories of the man whose wife served him well in the early years of marriage but was unable to transform herself into the party-loving, cocktail-pouring hostess that he required her to be to further his business ambitions. Of course, to expect a wife to be an assistant businessman is a perversion of the Catholic ideals of marriage.

Many wives also develop ambitions—mainly social—and find fault with their husbands for failing to keep up with them. For fifteen years of his married life, one happy-go-lucky carpenter attended wrestling matches every Friday night, and his wife usually went with him. She enjoyed watching the matches and talking about them with him during the week. He was a home-builder and after the war he became wealthy. He and his family moved to a more prosperous neighborhood, drove a more expensive car and wore custom-made clothing. Immediately the wife began aspiring to a higher social level. She joined a woman's club, attended art classes and symphony concerts, and began criticizing him for his interest in a "lowbrow" sport. After several years of growing tension, the wife realized that her one-sided social aspirations could in time lead to nothing but grief, and she wisely decided to accept her good husband and his interests as they were.

Where one partner feels that the other is not making sufficient progress, a reasonable compromise should be attempted. No husband should reasonably expect to place the burden of his business success upon his wife. On the other hand, loyalty for her husband should inspire the wife to treat his business associates courteously, to dress becomingly, and to reflect the gracious, happy nature of her relationship with him. She should also be willing to inform herself about current events in order to carry on an intelligent conversation.

A husband should also tolerate, if not encourage, his wife's efforts at self-improvement. For example, if he makes an effort to overcome his prejudices against such cultural interests as music, literature and painting, he may even discover that he likes them, or at least that he can endure them occasionally.

One partner feels bored or ill-at-ease in the other's presence. Some unions seem to wither from pure boredom when a husband or wife fails to make life interesting for the other. This frequently occurs when the main basis for the marriage is sexual. After the first months of physical exploration, there is little mutual interest to sustain the relationship. The coming of children, which gives the husband and wife a continuing experience to share together, is an especial blessing in such cases.

When a husband or wife feels uncomfortable, it may indicate that the other partner is a perfectionist—one who seems to be waiting to pounce on some fault. The person who is ill-at-ease may also be doing something of which he is ashamed and of which the other partner is not aware. When two persons realize that their personalities are at odds, they should try to appraise the causes objectively. For the bored partner and the ill-at-ease partner are traditionally the ones who cultivate the dangerous vices of drinking, gambling, or engaging in extra-marital affairs.

How to handle the danger symptoms. It should be emphasized again that inasmuch as no marriage is perfect, you may detect indications of some of the above danger symptoms in your own union. Where these symptoms are not a major cause of tension, they should not be a source of worry. But you should try to remove any defects which a survey of your own marriage might reveal.

Once you recognize the trouble areas, try to learn what conditions cause them. Ask God to help you see the real factors clearly. In analyzing them, try to understand your partner's feelings, motivation and needs. You may discover that you are primarily at fault. Maybe your partner's attitude toward you stems from your behavior; or maybe you have at least contributed to the situation in question. Few problems in marriage are the fault of one partner entirely.

Once you believe that you clearly understand the problem, talk it over with your mate. Resolve not to become angry, regardless of the turns the discussion takes. Select an occasion when you have enough time to discuss the problem leisurely. Try to view the problem constructively—in terms of what you can do in the future to make conditions better, rather than rehashing old incidents which may have led up to the problem. You will gain nothing—and may lose much—if you attribute to your mate an unwillingness to solve the problem or accuse him of obstinacy because he fails to see things your way. Try to reach an understanding—even if only a partial one on a small point. If you can conclude your discussion feeling that something has been gained from it, the door will be open for future talks and more progress later.

What if these approaches fail and the danger symptoms grow to constitute a real threat to your married happiness? You probably should then obtain outside guidance. By consulting your pastor or an experienced Catholic marriage counselor, you can usually obtain a helpful perspective. Often a husband or wife is blind to basic factors in marriage which an observant, experienced outsider can detect easily. If possible, both husband and wife should visit the counselor together. By talking to both, he can often gain a quick understanding of the true nature of the difficulty, and if both parties truly want to eliminate the sore points, he usually can suggest a workable compromise. In extreme cases, psychiatric help may be needed.

Some Catholic dioceses have established marriage reconciliation courts where persons with serious grievances are encouraged to work out their problems under the guidance of trained counselors. Thanks to these courts, couples are saved future misery on earth and perhaps damnation in eternity; and children who might otherwise grow up without proper spiritual and physical care are given a chance to lead normal lives of sanctity and happiness. The benefits, not only to the family involved, but also to society in general, can hardly be estimated. All that is necessary is the willingness of both spouses to discuss their problems calmly and, when the fault is established by an impartial observer, to amend their lives in the necessary way.

When seemingly insoluble marriage crises occur, try to use your sufferings to improve your trust in God and your acceptance of His Will. As Christians, we must remember that Jesus did not promise that we would not be obliged to bear a cross but rather that we would have one. The promise you made on your wedding day to love your mate "for better or worse" clearly foresaw that you would experience days in which your faith and fortitude would be severely tested. You do have Christ's guarantee, however, that any cross can be made bearable with His Help.

8

How to Disagree with Your Mate

COMING from different backgrounds, a husband and wife do not view all of life's problems in the same way. They have different ideas on how money should be spent, how the household should be run, on health habits, recreation, eating, sleeping and many other activities of daily life. No couple can reasonably hope to live together in a continuously serene atmosphere, unbroken by disagreements. We all prefer to do things in certain ways, and these preferences—plus our weaknesses of character—make it certain that any two persons will have some differences. However, there are no differences, no matter what their seriousness, which cannot be handled on a peaceful basis. Even if the problem is one that is vitally important to both of you, you can resolve it in a calm, affectionate way and thus strengthen the bonds of your marriage. On the other hand, if your approach involves bitterness and stubbornness, you may not only fail to solve your problems, but even add deep and long-remembered wounds.

Mature husbands and wives disagree; they do not fight.

There is a difference—the difference between a happy marriage and one with an underlying fabric of tension and bitterness. Discussions of disagreements are the friendly way to reconcile different backgrounds and experiences so that you can work together to achieve your common goal. Fights tear apart the unity of marriage; they are the means each mate uses to gain his own way without considering the other partner. They lead to name-calling, raking up of the past, a spirit of hatred. Therefore one of the most important ways to insure married happiness is to learn the art of disagreeing in a friendly way. You can acquire this skill by mastering nine principles.

1. *Don't blow up trivial differences.* Dozens of minor irritations occur in everyone's life every day. Overlook them! Don't make an issue of them. Your wife does not have the breakfast toast ready with the eggs; your husband drops his pajamas on the bedroom floor and neglects to hang them up before he leaves for work; your wife invited friends to dinner last Saturday and forgot to tell you until Saturday afternoon—all these occurrences are trivial. Yet these incidents were sparks in actual marriages and set off fires that were not extinguished until there had been agonizing hours of charge and countercharge, accusation and counteraccusation, name-calling and recrimination.

It seems obvious, yet all of us must constantly remind ourselves that we are not perfect. Your mate's habits may irritate you, but you doubtless have habits which are also minor irritants. Do you expect your mate to correct annoying mannerisms? Then prepare, in justice, to correct your own. Would you rather keep your habits because they give you pleasure? Then extend the same privilege to your spouse.

If any incident upsets you, ask yourself if any harm results because things are not done your way. If so, mention the incident to your partner in an affectionate way. Two wives add too much starch to shirt collars when laundering them. One husband shouts, "When are you going to learn how to starch a shirt?" The second husband puts his arm around his wife and says, "Honey, my neck is growing more sensitive to stiff collars." Which wife will correct her error more willingly?

2. *If you have a grievance, get it out of your system.* Psychologists say that the person who continually suppresses deep anger

creates a reservoir of resentment which may ultimately break out in a violent form. In a typical case, a bookkeeper employed by a large corporation was continually urged by his father-in-law to seek a position as a department head. The young man did not feel qualified for the position. At first, he simply smiled when his father-in-law mentioned the matter. But whenever they met, the older man asked, "Did you get that job yet?" The bookkeeper began to see this prodding as a reflection on his own judgment. He seethed inwardly. One day, his wife mentioned that they had been invited to her parents' home for Sunday dinner. He exploded with a barrage of invective against her father. She responded by dredging up complaints against his relatives. The battle did not end until dozens of old wounds in their relationship were reopened. It is now fifteen years later, but both partners feel resentment toward the other when they recall the hateful things said that day.

This situation would have been avoided if the husband had told his wife promptly that he felt annoyed at her father's suggestion because he, the husband, was in a better position to decide when he should bid for a promotion. If he had pleasantly explained his feelings, she could have supported him whenever the question arose or could have urged her father to drop the subject. But by keeping his feelings to himself, the husband built up anger that was certain to explode eventually.

A habit that weakens many marriages—the habit of pouting—also can be averted by bringing grievances into the open. Instead of telling his wife what irritates him, the pouter retreats into martyred, sulky silence. He realizes that the annoyance is not important enough to justify his actions and that he will appear silly if he mentions it. But he enjoys the self-pity in which he clothes himself.

If you are a pouter, you especially need to apply principles one and two: If the matter is trivial, pass over it. But if it continues to irritate you, bring it out into the open.

3. *Always guard your tongue.* For more than forty years, Father John A. O'Brien has advocated a way to enable couples to settle disputes without rancor. He states that this technique can reduce the number of estrangements by fifty per cent or more. He has seen it carry thousands of couples through difficulties

which otherwise would have overwhelmed them. In addition, it has prevented heartaches and deepened happiness in countless marriages.

After every wedding at which he officiates, Father O'Brien explains in his book, *Happy Marriage,* he takes the couple aside and tells them:

"In an impressive ceremony you have just pronounced your vow of conjugal fidelity and I know you will keep it. There is another vow which is scarcely less important in safeguarding the happiness of your wedded life. I almost hesitate to suggest it to a couple who have just plighted their deathless love. It is implicit in that vow, of course, but it is well to make it explicit: to promise each other that no matter what difficulties arise you will not speak an angry word to each other.

"Right now you can scarcely conceive of differences arising between you; but they will arise, for you are only human. There is no difficulty, no divergence, no matter how serious, however, which can't be settled if you will bring to it mutual understanding, good will, and, holding hands, talk it over in a calm, friendly manner. Similarly, there is no difference, no matter how trivial, which can be settled *unless* you bring to it sympathetic understanding and a willingness to talk it over in a friendly spirit.

"Are you willing, then, to promise that, no matter what provocation may arise, you will never stab each other with sharp angry words but will discuss any differences in a calm, friendly manner?"

Father O'Brien adds, "Never have I had a couple refuse.

"Then I have them pronounce a second vow of matrimony: 'I solemnly promise always to speak in a kind, friendly, and affectionate manner to my beloved wife (husband) and never to utter an angry, mean, bitter, or spiteful word that would hurt and wound her (him). So help me God.'

"My whole ministry has been spent among young people on the campuses of three universities—Illinois, Oxford, and Notre Dame. For forty years I have mingled intimately with tens of thousands of young people at three large universities, listened to their problems, heard the cry of their hearts reaching out wistfully for friendship and love, introduced thousands of young couples, married great numbers, and followed them in their enlarging family life. Never have I heard of one such marriage hitting the rocks or even being clouded by serious domestic strife."

When you discover your emotional temperature rising, also remember that the subject is not worth angry words. If you have been married for several years or longer, try to recall subjects over which you had bitter words in your first year together. Probably only in rare cases can you do so. How many of the specific subjects that you recall remain a major issue in your marriage? If you are like the typical couple, you will recall few specific disagreements worthy of the intense language you may have used in discussing them. But this is the key test: You probably remember the harsh, cutting words spoken by your mate in anger although you have forgotten what caused the argument in the first place.

Guarding your tongue requires diligent practice. The ancient Greek philosopher Epictetus advised, "Reckon the days in which you have not been angry. I used to be angry every day; then every other day; then every third and fourth day; and if you miss it so long as thirty days, offer a sacrifice of thanksgiving to God."

4. *Keep discussions within bounds.* When arguments get acrimonious, it is usually because this rule is not observed. When the monthly statements arrive, John sees a bill for a woman's hat at fifteen dollars and asks Joan if she bought it. Perhaps feeling guilty over buying something she did not need and no longer even likes, she admits that she did. But to justify herself, she recalls the time John met some friends at a restaurant and insisted upon paying the large bill for the entire party. John recalls Joan's expensive winter coat which she can no longer bear to wear. She mentions the vacation two years ago when John lost eighty dollars at the race track. Unchecked, the discussion moves to the spending habits of the in-laws and of every neighbor on the block. What began as a simple question—not even a difference of opinion—suddenly got out of hand because Joan and John failed to keep the discussion within the limits first set for it.

Judging from comments of husbands, this inability to stick to the subject is a common failing of wives. But men are guilty too. We all have a powerful sense of self-defense, and we recognize that in war the best defense is a good offense. When facing a situation in which we are wrong, we tend to cover our defects quickly by pointing to the other's shortcomings. This may be good military strategy but it is poor marital strategy.

If you must defend your actions, only two conclusions are generally possible—you are either wrong or right. If you are wrong, why not admit it and let the matter rest there? If you are right, why not defend yourself solely in terms of the subject under discussion, explaining your actions as calmly and pleasantly as you can? After your explanation, if your mate disagrees with your reason, at least you both will realize that there was a logical basis for what you did. And you will have kept the area of difference as small as it was in the beginning.

5. *If you must criticize, criticize the act—not your mate for performing it.* One wise couple had developed this principle to a fine art. When the bathroom faucet continued to leak for months, the wife complained about the high water bills—never her husband's laziness in failing to repair it. If his socks remained unmended, the husband commented upon his discomfort when wearing them—never upon his wife's fault as a housekeeper. Of course, their criticisms of actions diminished over the years, because both were willing to correct conditions called to their attention in that inoffensive way. Their egos were not involved, so they did not feel it necessary to defend themselves.

What if your husband or wife has shortcomings which require direct correction? Take a tip from corporation executives who have mastered the science of getting the most out of people: Always precede serious criticism with a statement of genuine appreciation for some good quality. You *feel* both; *express* both. Don't speak out only when you have something negative to say.

6. *Keep disagreements between yourselves.* Never carry them outside to in-laws, friends, or neighbors. In every good marriage, the husband and wife always feel free to communicate their innermost thoughts to each other. Often they make statements which, if repeated out of context, would make them appear foolish, vicious, or worse. If you repeat your mate's confi-

dential statements and hold him up to ridicule to outsiders, he will not speak freely to you again. The precious art of communication will be lost.

Sometimes young wives report quarrels to the husband's mother or father. They could hardly conceive of a more effective way to feed the flames. The typical husband will be angrier than before when he learns that his wife is trying to align his family against him—and angrier still if they agree with her.

7. *Give in on little things.* Because of your particular background, you have stronger convictions about certain aspects of life than upon others. So, too, has your mate. Considerate partners give in on matters on which their mates feel much more strongly than they.

One man was taught as a boy that it would hurt his health to sleep during the winter with the window open. His wife had slept with the windows open as a child, but she did not feel strongly on the subject. After marriage, when the question of open or shut windows arose, there could have been a prolonged argument. Disputes over this issue, in fact, have reached the courts in the form of divorce suits. However, the wife wisely recognized that her husband had powerful convictions and she did not care strongly enough to make an issue of it.

A typical husband "blows his top" over trifles. He explodes if his wife misplaces his cuff links or delays dinner a few minutes, or if the teen-agers turn up the radio volume while he pores over his newspaper. The wise wife knows that his anger will disappear rapidly if she remains quiet. But if she chooses to dispute him, a full-scale battle may be under way. Even if his anger is completely unjustified, she gets more constructive results by waiting until he can discuss the problem calmly. After their anger subsides, most husbands will admit that they were wrong in losing their tempers.

A humorous story illustrates the point that husbands and wives should remain silent amid the other's outbursts. An eighty-year-old man appeared at a doctor's office for a checkup. After examining the man from head to toe, the doctor remarked that he was in excellent physical condition.

"One thing is responsible for my good health," the man explained. "Sixty years ago, when Ellen and I were married, we made a promise to each other. Whenever I got angry, she was to leave the room immediately and do her housework elsewhere. When she got angry, I was to leave the house and take a long walk until she cooled off.

"And, Doc," the man added, "for sixty years I've had the greatest outdoor life you ever did see."

To apply this principle of giving in on little things, you must reject the false notion that marriage is a "fifty-fifty proposition." At times you will demand ninety per cent, whether you are aware of it or not. At other times, you will be asked to give the ninety per cent. But marriage is not a ball game with a score keeper. It does not matter whether you get forty per cent today and sixty per cent tomorrow, or even whether you continually provide more than an exact fifty per cent. The important thing is that your contribution and your mate's contribution add up to one hundred per cent.

However, there is a way for you to determine whether you demand too much from your mate. If you frequently disagree with other people too, perhaps you habitually expect too much and give too little. Occasionally a strong-willed man cannot make or hold friends because he constantly demands his own way. At home, all is tranquillity. This peace is almost always due to the wife's spirit of self-sacrifice which enables her to bow to him as a matter of course.

8. *Develop an outlet.* As certain as death and taxes is the fact that sometimes you will be frustrated in your marriage. Despite your best intentions, and even when you discuss disagreements in a temperate way, you and your mate sometimes will fail to see eye to eye. Perhaps you suppress a deep sense of futility over your mate's inability to see a problem from your logical point of view. You feel that you must vent your feelings on something.

For your mental and physical health, work off anger or frustration by engaging in physical activity—sweeping the sidewalk, walking to the post office, transplanting your shrubs, washing the car. One man has a woodworking shop in his basement. In moments of frustration, he retires to his shop and pounds boards for hours. Often after such exercise, he can appreciate that his wife's opinion rests on a logical basis. Whenever problems with her husband reach a stalemate, a certain wife mops the kitchen and bathroom floors; her hard work helps her feel less tense and more willing to view matters from his position.

Whenever you seem unable to settle your problem after a reasonable period of discussion, postpone further talk about it for a while. Attend evening devotions, take a walk together, or look at television. You will often be surprised at the new outlook you acquire after giving the subject a rest.

9. *Never let bitterness carry over the night.* Even if you cannot agree, give each other the benefit of good intentions. Kiss each other good night. This simple, tender act at the end of each day insures starting the next one on a loving basis. You will be less inclined to spend a restless night brooding, and often you will awaken with a new understanding of your problem. Moreover, if discussion is renewed it will be on a friendly basis.

It is not always easy to prevent rancor from entering into your disagreements. Habits of name-calling, raking over old coals, using sarcasm and ridicule to gain one's way perhaps must be unlearned. Making progress may be a slow process. But it will be worthwhile. For if you truly follow the principles outlined above and learn to resolve your differences in an atmosphere of affection and mutual respect, you will develop a deeper love for each other than you ever had before.

When serious conflict persists over a long period of time and threatens the stability of the home itself, then a trained marriage counselor ought to be consulted. Sometimes one of the parties, usually the husband, even when he may be more sinned against than sinning, strongly resists taking his problems elsewhere. But the wise man is never so stiff-necked as to prefer a broken home or an unhappy home to an honest airing of differences before a neutral and skilled listener.

9

Money Values in Marriage

MODERN society places such an appalling overemphasis on material things that some friction over money problems is probably inevitable in every marriage. Wherever we turn, we are besieged by appeals to spend and overspend. On radio and television, in newspapers and magazines, in the bus on our way to work and on the highway where we take a Sunday drive, we face a ceaseless urging. We may not have enough money to buy a postage stamp; we are assured on all sides that we can pay later. Would you like a new two-tone, 300-horsepower automobile, wall-to-wall carpeting for your bedroom, or a trip around the world? You need only write your name on a contract. Payments can be gloriously deferred until some remote time.

As a result of the great pressures exerted upon us and the ease with which we can accumulate possessions, we Americans are literally engulfed in luxury. We have more cars, more radios, more household appliances, more gadgets of every conceivable kind, than any other people on earth. We have twice as many television sets as the rest of the world combined. The typical American smoker spends more on cigarettes each day than millions of human beings earn by their labor. We spend more on alcohol than on education, millions of dollars more on beautifiers than on books.

Very few families in this fantastically prosperous America live in actual want. Even the poorest of us usually has adequate food, shelter and clothing. One glance at almost any current magazine will convince you of that: the unending volume of articles telling us how to reduce by means of new "wonder diets" is vivid evidence that our major problem is not how to get enough to eat, but rather how to avoid the consequences of eating too much.

When we speak of families as being poor, therefore, we probably do not refer to their lack of necessities—for they usually have these, but rather to their lack of the luxuries which we have come to believe are essential to the enjoyment of life. Thus, an underprivileged family in the prevailing American view may be the one with a car five years old or even, in some circles, the family with only one automobile. Sympathy is extended to the youngsters whose parents cannot send them to summer camp; to the housewife who lacks an automatic dishwashing machine; to the father who postpones parenthood because he does not have the wherewithal to give children a college education.

In the face of these prevailing standards, Catholics find it difficult to develop and maintain a true perspective about why we have been placed on earth. We must remind ourselves constantly that God made us, not to be consumers of industry's products, but to save our souls by prayer, mortification and sacrifice. We must remember the words of Christ: "For what does it profit a man, if he gain the whole world, but suffer the loss of his own soul?" (Matthew, 16:26) We must reflect upon the truth that the search for luxury can never lead to true and lasting happiness but usually results in misery.

Once embarked upon a course that puts material things first, a family will probably never reach a stage at which it is satisfied. The husband and wife who set as their goal the owning of a car with all the available push-button gadgets or of an appliance-filled "dream house" in the most socially acceptable neighborhood will find that their desire for possessions feeds upon itself. When first obtained, the two-tone car with buttons that manipulate hundreds of horsepower will seem the fulfillment of a dream. Soon, however, a new model in the showrooms will make their car seem woefully obsolete. The couple who allow themselves to be unduly influenced by the siren calls of the materialists, therefore, are insuring for themselves a life of frustration and dissatisfaction. They become pliable consumers to be manipulated—consumers who *must be made unhappy* with their present possessions in order that advertisers can sell them something new.

An added danger of a materialistic philosophy is that it makes couples "contraception-minded." The husband and wife who come to believe that they should have a new car every other year, that dinner must always be preceded by cocktails, that frequent visits to theaters and beauty establishments are essential, will find it difficult to welcome the new being which may take those luxuries from them. Many couples say that they cannot afford another baby because "a child would cause them to forego actual necessities." Actually the sacrifices would be made exclusively in the area of luxuries. The cost of supporting an additional child may often turn out to be less than the family's liquor bill.

If you wish to avoid pitfalls in your marriage, you must develop a spiritual philosophy of life that firmly turns away from the materialism of the day. You can take your inspiration from the words of the Saviour: "Do not lay up for yourselves treasures on earth, where rust and moth consume, and where thieves break in and steal; but lay up for yourselves treasures in heaven, where neither rust nor moth consumes, nor thieves break in and steal. For where thy treasure is, there also will thy heart be." (Matthew, 6:19–21)

God expects man to use his intelligence and his energy productively and to enjoy their fruits. Among farmers that might result in a larger yield of wheat and increased income. For industrial workers productive labor usually means better pay and more leisure. Whatever advantage or enjoyment is gained by the sweat of one's brow or the wrinkle of a thinking forehead may be properly enjoyed. The Church is not puritanical. She does not eschew pleasure, even luxury. Whether you have much or little money, the important thing is that you be its master, that you be not overly depressed at being poor or live riotously because you have more than you need. The importance of money in a family should never get out of proportion, because going without can be just as much fun as having. The key word is "detachment." Work for what you need and a little more, but live as if you needed very little.

Danger of the "meal-ticket" husband. When you learn to resist the pressures of the day and to live within your income, two dangers—the danger of the "meal-ticket" husband and the working wife—can be averted. Of course, it is the husband's duty to support his family. He should provide not only the basic necessities but also common comforts, if possible. Nevertheless, it sometimes happens that incessant demands for luxuries—extensive wardrobes, new furniture, expensive entertainment—drive a husband onto a treadmill where he tries to earn enough to pay for these things. He may come to place financial progress above every other value. One often sees executives and professional men who spend little or no time at home with their families. They work day and night and travel for long periods, beset by the ambition to provide material comforts.

But no amount of luxury can compensate for the absence of a husband and father. Often the marriage itself suffers seriously because there is no companionship between husband and wife; the upbringing of the children is neglected because the father's guidance is lacking; and even his health is destroyed because of the way he drives himself to gain material success. The satisfaction that a man once had in making ends meet has been taken away by his struggle to live better this year than he did last year.

Danger of the working wife. The increasing number of working wives also creates serious problems. The working wife is a relatively new figure on the American scene. Sociologists state that the increase in employed married women results from the growing desire of families for luxuries not obtainable on the husband's salary alone. In 1890, only four per cent of married women in the United States were gainfully employed. By 1940, that number had increased to fifteen per cent, and by 1956 thirty per cent of all married women held jobs outside the home. Once the working woman was almost certainly unmarried; today, wives outnumber "bachelor girls" two to one. Nor are these wives childless. There are 2,500,000 mothers of small children at work —18.2 per cent of all the mothers with children under five years of age in the United States.

The wife should work outside the home only in cases of great necessity. Experience teaches that the path of the working wife is strewn with difficulties, both for herself and her family. All too often, the wife who takes a job with a temporary objective (to buy new living-room furniture, for example) soon discovers that living standards have risen to meet the new income and that the family needs her wages to live on the scale to which it quickly has become accustomed. Once their wives help support the home, some husbands tend to become lazy and to neglect their own duties as providers. In other cases, if the wife's income approximates or exceeds that of her hsuband, his pride may be deeply wounded, and friction may easily develop over the question of who is head of the household.

Work outside the home may also foster traits undesirable in a wife. She may become economically independent, and be less willing to make sacrifices and emotional adjustments to keep relations with her husband on a happy basis. She is often flattered by other men, with the possibility of flirtations and serious romantic entanglements. She faces the danger that she will overemphasize the importance of dress and adornment, and that there will be a lessening of her womanly qualities and refinement. The greatest danger of all, of course, is that in her pursuit of material benefits, the upbringing of her children will be seriously neglected. Social workers uniformly attest to the fact that delinquency rates are greatest among those children without mothers at home to supervise their activities.

When a working wife carefully analyzes her expenses, she sometimes discovers that her net financial gain from working is not worth the effort. First, she must pay an income tax, and inasmuch as her income is added to her husband's, the rate she must pay on each dollar earned is considerably higher than the rate applicable to her husband's salary alone. Secondly, her net income may drop still further when deductions are made for the wages of others she may hire to care for her children or to do housework which she no longer has time to do. Thirdly, she will have considerable expenses in traveling to work, dressing appropriately, and buying lunches. Finally, since she no longer has time to spend in shopping for the best values, she usually must buy food, clothing, and other necessities at the most convenient stores and at higher cost. (It has been estimated that as much as 20 per cent of total living expenses can be saved by prudent spending on the part of the wife.) When these hidden expenses are deducted from her salary, the amount remaining may not be large enough to compensate for all the other losses involved.

Budgets help prevent money conflicts; the wheels of marriage will turn more smoothly if a husband and wife learn the art of intelligent money management. By educating yourself to avoid traps set up for unwary consumers, following a plan of family spending, disciplining your tastes, and learning to make things last longer and to do without, you can make your income buy more for you.

Many families find that a budget helps them to develop habits of thrift and limits spending for unnecessary items. A budget can help you find leaks through which your money flows. It can also lessen your financial worries, because you always know exactly where you stand. A budget helps you keep accurate records showing the cost of various elements in your standard of living. You are then able to choose intelligently the expenditures which may be increased or cut down.

Before a good budget can be determined, two things must be considered—who will draw it up and the principles according to which it should be composed. As to the first, it seems agreed by most experts on family finances that the entire family, including the older children, should sit in on budget conferences. Particularly is it important that husband and wife work the program out together. Too frequently conflict arises because the husband does not appreciate what happens to food money or because the wife does not realize how heavy the fixed family expenditures are. The principles underlying a good budget are simple. Spend money first on *absolute necessities,* food, clothing, shelter; then on *conveniences,* which are a normal part of living for your walk of life, the television set, the radio; and finally on *luxuries,* the high-priced car, the expensive vacation.

The actual budget ought to consider four items: *fixed expenses,* an *emergency fund, day-to-day expenditures,* and *savings.* Before anything else is considered the couple should set down all the fixed obligations they have for the year—rent, insurance, gas and electric, union dues—and divide the total by fifty-two so that they know how much remains of the weekly wage for other living costs. Some money, even though a small amount, ought to be reserved weekly for emergencies such as the inevitable winter sickness, tooth extraction, parish building campaign, etc. If a person makes $100 a week of which $65 automatically must be deducted for fixed expenditures and the emergency fund, he knows that he has only $35 for his day-to-day expenditures to be divided among the various needs of husband, wife, and children. Every family ought to save at least one dollar a week, not only for the discipline it encourages, but to provide the extra decencies that make for warm family living around Christmas, birthday time, etc.

You will be more inclined to maintain a permanent budget if you keep records simple. An allowance of $25 per week for food is easier to live with than a detailed record specifying so much for milk, so much for meat and so much for vegetables. If you spend more for meat one week, you can make up for it by cutting down on desserts or elsewhere within the same broad category. It is also wise to recognize your own limitations when making a budget. If you allow too little for essentials, you may become discouraged at your repeated failure to remain within the established limit. You may then be tempted to drop your budget entirely.

In working to make ends meet, the intelligent couple will learn to avoid three wasteful types of buying: credit buying, installment buying, and impulse buying.

Credit buying, through the use of charge accounts, is a great convenience, of course. But it often makes it too easy for you to buy things you do not really need. Stores encourage you to be a charge customer because they know from experience that customers who buy on credit invaribly buy more merchandise than those who pay cash. For instance, surveys have established that if you have a charge account in a store, there is a 57 per-cent chance that you will buy something when you shop there. Moreover, those with charge accounts tend to shop less critically. It is easier to say "Charge it" than to go to another store where the same merchandise may be sold for cash at a few dollars less.

Installment buying also makes it easy to obtain things you do not need. The habit of buying "on time" is particularly serious for young couples. Many newlyweds do not even bother to ask the full price of merchandise; their sole concern is the cost per month. When you buy "on time," you pay about 12 or 15 per cent more in carrying charges than if you pay cash. When you pay cash to the store, but borrow the money to do so from a commercial bank, you also generally pay about 10 per cent extra. On loans made at finance companies, you may pay interest amounting to 36 per cent per year. Obviously, the couple that learns to pay cash can make their income work much more effectively for them.

Impulse buying is the kind you do when you purchase items you never intended to get when you left home. University researchers who investigated factors that cause budgets to go haywire found that impulse buying heads the list. Usually you do not think about impulse purchases very carefully. The attractive hat on the bargain counter, the expensive toy which Junior will play with for a few days, then discard, the brightly packaged delicacies which stand invitingly by the supermarket's checkout counter—you probably would never miss these items if you did without them. If purchased, however, they may leave little money at the end of the budget period for more important things.

Excellent books have been written by home economists on the subject of money management. Several are listed at the end of the book. By reading them, you can discover many other ways of avoiding stress on your family budget. You can learn efficient shopping practices. For example, by buying your necessities at sales whenever possible, paying cash, dealing at self-service stores and carrying purchases home instead of having them delivered, you often can obtain everyday necessities at prices 20 or 30 per cent below those generally paid. You can learn to do home maintenance jobs yourself. Experienced persons in this field claim that painting a house inside and out, doing minor plumbing, heating and carpentry repairs, mending furniture, etc., can be learned by almost anyone. You can cut automobile maintenance bills substantially by being careful about oil, grease and tires; tests have proved that the average motorist who learns to drive ten miles an hour slower than his present speed can save fifty dollars a year on gasoline consumption alone.

In addition to adopting ways of keeping expenses down, you can avoid friction over money matters by cultivating saving habits. Probably the best way to build up a reserve for rainy days is to set aside a certain amount in a savings account each pay day. Insurance savings policies, government bond purchasing programs and company pension plans in which employees participate all have the merit of deducting a certain amount for savings before you receive your salary; what you do not have in your hand, you are not tempted to spend. Other devices can be used to make savings automatic. For instance, you might decide to save every nickel or dime which comes into your hands and to deposit these in a piggy-bank. You might yourself perform some service for which you usually pay (ironing shirts, for example) and put away what the service would have cost. You might also eliminate one luxury (the weekly bowling game or the weekly "night out," perhaps) and add the amount to your savings.

Who should manage the money? Difficulties about money in the home usually stem from two sources: the problem of who should manage the money and the question of how much a husband and wife each should spend for personal purposes. Each couple will have to answer these questions in their own way. Before husbands and wives adopt an inflexible attitude on this subject, they should recognize that their opinions about money management are probably based primarily on their experiences in their childhood homes. The husband who as a child has seen his father keep a tight rein on family finances will conclude that this is the proper way to handle money matters. As a child, the wife may have seen her father turn over all his wages on pay day and then beg for spending money every day. This childhood experience will naturally color her outlook. If husband and wife were brought up in an immigrant environment, they have to learn principles of partnership which were not practiced when they were young.

The question of who should manage the money can be an explosive one. It should be discussed calmly by both husband and wife. The answer, it probably will be concluded, depends on which partner does the best job at it. Some men have no head for figures and hate to balance a checkbook; others feel that since they have full responsibility for the home's financial welfare, they can fulfill their obligation only by controlling family expenditures. The husband, however, should never abdicate his authority to make decisions when necessary.

An arrangement that works well in many marriages is one in which the husband handles the major expenses (rent or mortgage payments, medical bills, utilities, etc.) while the wife has a regular allowance to cover food, household expenses, etc. No major purchases (of a car, television set, or living-room sofa, for example) are made without the prior agreement of both partners. The husband has an allowance for his personal expenses (lunches, cigarettes, etc.) and the wife has an allowance for her personal expenses (hairdressers, accessories, etc.). Neither husband nor wife need explain how this allowance is spent. This type of arrangement makes both partners responsible for spending the family income efficiently, yet gives each a certain amount of freedom.

To make this or any other financial arrangement work in marriage, both partners must develop an unselfish attitude. Whenever disputes over money matters reach a point where outside aid is needed, marriage counselors almost always find that the problem has its roots in a lack of understanding and in the selfishness of one or both of the partners.

10

The In-Law Problem

THE in-law problem is one of the most talked-about aspects of marriage. It provides an endless number of jokes for cartoonists, after-dinner speakers and television comedians. But unfortunately, in-laws are more than a mere source of amusement. Marriage experts agree that the success or failure with which young couples adjust to their in-laws is often the major factor in determining the success or failure of their marriage.

Whenever you come across a married couple rich in love and strong in character, you usually find that they have a close bond of kinship with other members of their families. How many of us born of large families still enjoy the holiday or anniversary celebrations with our twenty or thirty sisters, brothers, their husbands, wives and children! As such gatherings become less frequent with advancing age, they still evoke nostalgic reminiscences. So the frequent visits and many telephone calls of married sons and daughters, far from injuring the conjugal relationship, for the most part add to its strength. The same virtues a son displays toward a parent very frequently are directed also toward a spouse.

People who complain about in-laws forget that they are in-laws too. They certainly do not seem to remember that the extended family with its three generations and countless uncles and aunts is really a wonderful group to behold. Even though Americans have lost many of their family traditions and no longer take pride in the family name or its achievements, they are still close enough to the past to value the help, support, and insurance to be found in close ties with so called in-laws.

Grandparents make wonderful baby-sitters and the small children dote on their attention and understanding. But vastly more important is the contribution that they can make, together with other blood relatives, to a married couple, socially, economically, emotionally, and religiously, particularly in times of trouble. How many ordinary sons and daughters with a minimum of talent for the marital relationship, or parenthood, have not been prodded on to great accomplishments in both fields by the example or advice of a parent or brother?

It ought to be remembered, also, that animosity toward in-laws is sometimes a smokescreen used to cover up the true causes of marital conflict as well as the personal weaknesses of a husband and wife. And while wives are more inclined to look upon mother-in-law as the "other woman," immature husbands too often are inconsiderate of the attachment between a good mother and the good daughter who happens to be his wife. Charity begins at home but it need not be restricted to the couple's home. It ought to embrace the blood relatives and in-laws.

The foregoing does not mean, however, that the so-called "in-law problem" cannot be serious. A study by Father John L. Thomas, S.J., of 7,000 cases of troubled marriages which were brought to Chancery Courts for adjustment revealed that in-laws were cited as a disruptive factor in fifteen per cent of the cases. Another study of 544 couples in their early years of marriage revealed that the newlyweds considered their partners' relatives to be their major concern. The in-law problem is greatest at the beginning of marriage, when the new husband and wife must end their dependence on their parents and begin an entirely independent life of their own, and again in much later stages when a parent is unable to support himself and needs help from the married children. The problem can also arise at any time when in-laws show a tendency to interfere in any way with the marriage.

The in-law situation can get out of hand so readily that certain rules should be rigorously observed. The most important is that when you marry, your mate's interest must always come ahead of those of your mother and father. Speaking of marriage, Christ taught that "For this cause a man shall leave his father and mother, and cleave to his wife, and the two shall become one flesh." (Matthew, 19:5) For this reason, every couple should make an independent life for themselves. They should live in their own home, away from parents, so that they can make the many adjustments necessary to achieve a harmonious union together.

Sometimes couples are anxious to marry before they can maintain their own home. They decide that they will live with one set of parents until they save enough money to furnish their own place. Experience teaches that this is extremely hazardous. The couple's chances for happiness would be greater if they moved into a furnished room. They should postpone marriage until they can begin their life together under their own roof.

Living the early years of married life away from the influence of parents is desirable for three major reasons. First, every young couple needs a period of time so that they can learn to know each other, adjust to each other's personalities, and decide such matters as spending their income, sharing responsibilities and using leisure time. They are usually unable to do this in the presence of in-laws, for only the rare parent relinquishes complete control over a son or daughter who marries. The parents' temptation to tell them how to do things is almost overwhelming—and the newlyweds' temptation to resent such suggestions is equally difficult to resist.

Secondly, married partners must be able to put into practice the joint decisions they have reached. For instance, they should be free to come and go as they please, to eat food of their own choice when they want it, to entertain their own friends, to listen to their favorite television programs, to play their own music. If they live in the home of in-laws, they cannot do so. They probably will be forced to bow to the elders' wishes on such matters. They may even find themselves unable to speak to each other intimately unless they go to their bedroom and whisper. Thus they are constantly frustrated.

Thirdly, living with in-laws makes it much too easy for one or both of the partners to run to Mother or Dad whenever there is a disagreement. Almost inevitably, the in-laws find themselves taking sides. Even if they line up against their own flesh and blood to support the son-in-law or daughter-in-law, their participation will be resented. Moreover, the tendency to run to a parent at the slightest sign of trouble soon becomes a habit. Instead of cutting ties to the parents, the couple finds that a life of independence—one in which they are free to discuss and reconcile their differences—is denied to them.

Most newlyweds will elect to live by themselves in the critical first years of marriage, or can be persuaded that setting up their own household is the best thing to do. Occasionally, however, a man or woman will refuse to marry unless the couple will then live with his or her parents. When the parents are fully capable of caring for themselves, this determination often conceals a dangerous immaturity—an unwillingness to accept responsibility on one's own. The man or woman who insists upon living with parents after marriage may be looking for someone to handle obligations which he or she is unwilling to assume. Psychologist Alexander A. Schneiders, Ph.D., tells of a young couple, married three years and with two children, who were referred to him by a Catholic agency. They had been living apart for eight months, and every time they tried to discuss a reunion, the discussion ended in a free-for-all fight.

After a few interviews, it became apparent that the woman had decided to get married partly because she feared that if she missed this opportunity, she might become an old maid. After the wedding, she had told her husband that they would live with her parents for a year to save money. Three years later, they were still living with her parents and the husband had grown to despise every member of her family. At this point he moved into separate quarters.

The psychologist concluded that the root of this troubled marriage lay in the wife's fear of leaving home. She did not want a husband to protect and cherish her; she wanted a sex partner. When sex lost its alluring qualities through satiation, the responsibilities of marriage became overwhelming. The young lady wanted to stay with her mother, who would maintain a home for her, and her husband was expected to satisfy her wishes and desires like a servant. After several months of treatment, the couple were persuaded to live together again—but in their own home. There they learned to adjust to each other in a way they had neglected to do during the first three years of their union.

Parents in our society tend to be overprotective toward their married children. This results in two undesirable conditions—excessive interference by the old folks in the lives of the youngsters, and excessive dependence by the newlyweds on the parents.

Dangers which parents and close relatives should avoid in dealing with newlyweds include:

Checking up. Some parents refuse to let go of their children, and make frequent phone calls or visits to make certain that the new marriage is proceeding smoothly. This conduct implies the parents' lack of confidence in their children's ability to solve problems of marriage without outside help. The parents want a step-by-step report of what the newlyweds are doing and usually the oldsters' next move is to criticize openly or to make unsolicited suggestions which the children resent. Such parents must realize that married people want to be left alone. While it is normal for parents to be interested in their children's activities, they should not give the slightest indication that they are prying into the newlyweds' affairs.

Making things easy. Some marriages degenerate into a competition between the bride's parents and the bridegroom's parents to determine who can do most for the youngsters. Her mother and father lavish gifts upon the couple; then his parents cannot be outdone, so they make even more expensive presents. A race is on. Soon the newlyweds are living in a state of luxury which they come to consider as normal. They are not forced to make the sacrifices and to work out financial problems which other married couples face. When the race ends, as it inevitably must, they suddenly find that they must live on the man's income alone. Sometimes the pampered pair are unable to make the necessary sacrifices and the marriage itself suffers.

What attitude should parents adopt? They should realize that young couples do not need luxuries for happiness and that a marriage built on the sacrifice of material things often has the best chance of success. Parents therefore should not overextend themselves. Let the children drive a car that is five years old but which they have paid for themselves. Let them curtail their movie-going in order to buy a new sofa. Let them spend their vacations at a low-priced resort which they can afford on their own income. By doing things for themselves, the youngsters will develop a necessary sense of self-reliance. Of course, if the newlyweds are in actual want—if they need help to pay medical bills, for example—a parent who can afford to aid them would be heartless not to do so.

Teaching them how. The typical parents-in-law required twenty-five years or more to acquire their present experience. They are tempted to teach their married children all they know about childbearing and child rearing. Some parents succumb to the temptation and try to correct every mistake that they imagine is being made in the upbringing of their grandchildren. Other parents decide that nothing is too good for their grandchildren, who can do no wrong and never require correction. They not only spoil the grandchildren but often try to prevent their own children from disciplining the little ones properly.

A particularly unwholesome type of mother-in-law is the one who conducts a constant propaganda campaign against parenthood. She feels it her duty to express dismay when her daughter or daughter-in-law becomes pregnant for the third time; she is all too ready with unsolicited recommendations for artificial birth control. Other parents may not advocate birth control directly; however, they instill such a materialistic point of view in their children that if their advice were taken, contraceptive practices would be followed of necessity.

To avoid the dangers described above, parents must accept the fact that they now occupy second place in the affection of their married children and that they are outsiders insofar as the new marriage is concerned. They might well recall their own early years of marriage when they too sought to establish a new life without interference. They should willingly give the same opportunity to their children. Parents also should now treat their married children like grownups who are capable of reaching their own conclusions about their problems and of deciding what is in their best interests. Difficult as it may be to do at times, parents should not take sides in arguments. If a son or daughter reports personal disagreements, the parents might suggest gently that disagreements be confined to the marriage. Sometimes their children virtually force parents to listen to tales of marital conflicts. When this happens, parents should try to play the role of peace-maker. In the long run, the in-laws' refusal to take sides will win respect for themselves and will encourage the young couple to solve their own problems.

When serious troubles over in-laws arise in a marriage, it is often found that the newlyweds share at least some of the blame. For example, they often impose upon their parents shamelessly. Sometimes doting grandparents find that they have become perpetual baby-sitters who are called upon to care for their grandchildren not only for an occasional evening but for long periods when the parents themselves are off on vacations. Grandparents are often treated like finance companies, except that they are not expected to want the loan repaid. When the grandparents decide that they will not be played for easy marks, their children often resent the withdrawal of what they have come to consider as their rights. Thus tension over in-laws frequently develops because the younger people lack the maturity to shoulder their own obligations and resent their parents' unwillingness to accept their responsibilities for them. While in-laws should help a young couple over genuine rough spots in marriage, they should not be expected to extricate the youngsters from every financial hole. Here, as in other aspects of the in-law relationship, moderation must prevail.

Whether you live with your in-laws or not, you should observe three basic principles:

1. In-laws are a part of your life and you must expect to see them, at least occasionally. Try to make your relationship a cordial one. Bending over backward to avoid resentment over anything they may say or do will help you enormously to avoid more serious friction in your marriage. Remember that your mate

has spent a lifetime to date with your in-laws; they represent more to your mate than you will ever appreciate. Try to avoid incidents in which a choice must be made between you and your in-laws.

2. Try to ease your entry into your mate's family by calling the mother by the same term of endearment that he or she uses. Try to stay on a friendly basis with the sisters and brothers—never on a competitive one. To keep the relationship noncompetitive, a husband should not tell his wife what wonderful homemakers and cooks his mother and sisters are; and the wife should not parade the perfections of her father or brothers before her husband. The husband should not permit his family to criticize his wife under any circumstances, nor should the wife permit her family to criticize her husband. This rule implies, of course, that neither husbands nor wives will carry tales about their partner back to their families.

3. Any discussion of in-laws' shortcomings should be strictly out-of-bounds whenever a disagreement arises between husband and wife. In one case, the husband's father was unable to hold a job; whenever husband and wife disagreed over any matter, she could not resist the urge to tell him that he was like his "shiftless" father. Although she always treated the older man courteously, her husband could not believe that her show of affection was not mere sham. He always felt uncomfortable when his wife was with his family; he found himself wondering what incident would occur which she would use against him later. Her angry outbursts became etched in his memory and beclouded the in-law relationship for years.

Problems in caring for parents. As a result of the average increase in the life span of Americans, many parents now reach an age when they can no longer support themselves and need help from their children. The question is often raised as to how much support a married couple should give their parents. Obviously the first responsibility of husband and wife is to each other and to their children. They are not morally obliged to deprive their children. However, they are obliged to help parents in desperate need even if they must suffer some privation themselves.

Children have an unfortunate habit of overlooking the tremendous sacrifices their parents made on their behalf. If your parent is penniless today, it probably results directly from his inability to save while spending thousands of dollars on your upbringing. Therefore justice requires that you repay your parents when the latter lack adequate food or shelter. However, you are not obliged to support them in a state beyond that in which you yourself live. Sometimes an older man could pocket his pride and do work to pay at least part of his living expenses. Sometimes the older woman could obtain baby-sitting jobs in the neighborhood to defray some costs. They should earn what they can to ease the burden upon their children.

Even parents who are supported by their children should have separate living quarters, if possible. An elderly husband and wife in a simple one-room flat will be happier than if they shared a luxurious home with their children. When conditions make it necessary to allow an in-law to share the home, the guest should be made to understand in a kind but firm way that he or she will not be permitted to interfere in the couple's right to run it in their own way.

Overprotecting the elderly. Some couples go to the harmful extreme of refusing to allow their elderly parents to do anything for themselves. Whenever a parent tries to move, the younger people jump up to help him. If an elderly woman wants to cook a meal, she is told to sit down while her daughter-in-law cooks it. The elderly man who could repair the squeaking door is told not to do it, but to let it squeak until his son-in-law finds time to repair it.

This overprotection of the aged is on a par with the overindulgence of children. It gives old people the feeling that they are unable to perform even basic chores for themselves and it destroys their self-confidence—their most precious possession. To help your elderly parents feel that they are still useful, encourage them to do things for themselves.

Often retired men who have financial security will nevertheless take part-time jobs in occupations lower in prestige than those they formerly held. Children should disregard what "people might think" and should encourage the elderly man to do what makes him happy. One retired corporation executive took a job as a clerk in a stationery store. His children were shocked that he would "lower" himself in this way. They overlooked the fact that he wanted above all to feel that he could contribute a service to society. Moreover, working in the shop enabled him to meet and talk to many friends; it was a pleasant way to pass the day. Nevertheless, the children exerted pressure upon him to quit the job, and it is probably no coincidence that he died soon thereafter. For the sake of your parent's mental and physical health, therefore, permit him to work as long as he wants to, and as long as he can.

Sometimes old persons have deteriorated mentally or physically to such an extent that the married children cannot care for them properly at home. It may become necessary to place them in an institution for the aged. Before making the decision to do so, a couple should search their souls to determine whether they have exhausted all other means of providing proper care. For example, the younger persons should be certain that proper medical attention has been provided. Many medicines and treatments have been developed recently to enable doctors to extend the usefulness of older persons by many years.

If a home is chosen, it should be one which will enable the parent to enjoy the solace of the Faith in his declining days—either a Catholic institution or one which a priest regularly visits. Every effort also should be made to assure him that he is being placed in the home for his own welfare. He should be made to understand that you are motivated by love—not by a desire to be free of him.

Regardless of whether the old person possesses all his faculties or is senile, can provide for himself or depends upon charity, young children should be taught always to treat him with the utmost respect. Sometimes a husband and wife laugh at a parent's eccentricities. Their children ape the parents and do likewise. The grandparent soon occupies a position of ridicule in which all his opinions are ignored. He becomes a pet who is humored but not taken seriously. Adults who permit this condition to develop do not give their parents the respect which is justly deserved. Moreover, they establish a pattern which may haunt them. For their children, taught to ridicule parents who are at the end of their days, will teach their own youngsters to act in a similar way. In this instance, the sins of the parents will return to be visited upon themselves.

11

The Problem of Alcoholism

OF ALL the threats to the stability of marriage, excessive drinking is without doubt the greatest. In his study of marriage failures, Father Thomas found that this problem accounted for the failure in approximately one third of the cases among those marriages enduring from six to fifteen years, and in over forty per cent of the marriages of more than fifteen years' duration. In another study of 1,434 divorce cases in Philadelphia, the charge of excessive drinking was listed more than cruelty, adultery, bigamy, fraud and sexual complaints combined. A veteran divorce court judge, John A. Sharbaro of Chicago, was asked by a newspaper reporter what, in his experience, was the most frequent cause of broken marriages. Without hesitation, Judge Sharbaro answered, "Drink."

Few Americans apparently are aware of the terrible human suffering which alcoholism causes. According to estimates by the Alcohol Section of the World Health Organization and by the Yale School of Alcohol Studies, alcoholic beverages are consumed by 70,000,000 Americans. Of these, approximately one in fifteen—or 4,500,000—are alcoholics. It is also estimated that every such alcoholic directly affects the lives of four other persons—his wife, parents, children, brothers or sisters. Therefore, approximately 17,000,000 Americans suffer in one way or another because of excessive drinking.

Alcoholism is the greatest single reason why families are forced to seek relief from government agencies. Welfare Commissioner Henry L. McCarthy of New York City says that one of every four families asking the city for financial help does so because the father is an alcoholic. In Mr. McCarthy's experience, the dependent children become "second-class citizens." According to Judge Luther W. Youngdahl of the United States District Court in Washington, "Alcohol addiction is one of the most devastating factors contributing to juvenile delinquency and the breakdown of the home."

Our appalling accident record—more than a million persons are injured in automobile accidents every year—results to a large extent from the mixture of alcohol and gasoline. In one survey made in New Hampshire and reported by Andrew J. White, director of motor vehicle research for that state, liquor is involved in "nine out of ten" serious highway accident cases.

Another startling fact is that the number of women victims is increasing at a terrifying rate. Twenty years ago—a few years after the repeal of Prohibition—only one out of ten victims of alcoholism was a woman. Today, the number is three or four in ten. For the first time in our history, the woman "repeating alcoholic"—the woman with a police record for repeatedly disturbing the peace—is becoming a common sight in city jails. About twenty per cent of all women inmates in U. S. prisons are there because of drunkenness.

We still do not know much about the causes and cure for alcoholism. We do know, however, that many old-time attitudes are unfounded and have been disproved scientifically. Here are the basic facts.

There is no "alcoholic type." Many persons believe that alcoholics are found only in "Skid Row" or in other low environments. Actually, alcoholics are representative of the population at large. They include persons who have never gone to school

—and those with several postgraduate degrees from leading universities. They are from poor and humble environments—and from the wealthiest sections of the country. They are laborers and college professors, truck drivers and doctors, beggars and bankers.

The underlying causes of alcoholism are not clearly understood. Through the centuries it has proved frustrating to priests, doctors, psychiatrists, social workers and other professional people, because no one has ever isolated the factors that make the alcoholic different from the normal drinker. For example, it is commonly believed that he has certain personality characteristics which set him apart from other people. However, Professor Raymond E. McCarthy of the Yale Center of Alcohol Studies says flatly that "there is no such thing as an alcoholic personality." Edwin H. Sutherland of Indiana University studied thirty-seven surveys which sought to determine the precise characteristics in the personality of the alcoholic. He found a singular lack of agreement. According to the researchers, alcoholics could be shy or friendly, happy or sad, brooders who always want to be alone, or back-slapping extroverts who always want to associate with others.

Alcoholism also has been described as a condition resulting from the drinker's loss of sense of spiritual values. The evidence seems undeniable that failure to trust in God often contributes to the problem, but there is no basis for believing that alcoholism is primarily a spiritual disease. If it were, prayer and the sacraments would be a complete answer to it. But persons who in apparent sincerity try to stop their compulsive drinking behavior by the use of the sacraments are not always successful.

Some scientists believe that the primary factor is physical. They maintain that as a result of basic defects because of which the body cannot absorb alcohol properly, a powerful inner force drives alcoholics to drink more and more. Some researchers have suggested that this defect results from a vitamin deficiency. Others say that the alcoholic's system lacks hormones of a certain type. Others think that he has a defect in handling blood sugars in his system. Regardless of these theories, no effective treatment has been devised that can change the chronic, compulsive drinker into a normal drinker.

Persons who habitually drink to excess and whose drinking behavior causes concern to themselves, their wives, business associates or friends, have one thing in common. It is that they drink alcohol. Wherever treatment of this condition has been effective, it has been so by pinpointing alcohol as the basic cause of the problem. Regardless of the individual's basic defects—whether they are emotional, spiritual or physical—it is alcohol that accentuates them and makes them unbearable.

Alcoholism and marriage. Alcohol as a cause of marriage breakdowns probably has never been given the attention it deserves because of the mistaken belief that the person who drinks excessively does so because other factors disturb him. It has been thought, for example, that no man who was otherwise happy would overindulge habitually. As a result of this belief, when many marriage counselors have encountered drinking as a problem, they have spent much time seeking causes for the drinking instead of trying directly to eliminate the drinking itself. They overlooked the fact that uncontrolled drinking can stem simply from social drinking, and alone can endanger married life.

In his study of disrupted marriages upon which he reported in his book, *The American Catholic Family,* Father Thomas wrote: "Whatever may be the reason why men drink, serious frustration in marriage does not appear to play a major role. Rather, the habit was acquired gradually and had started disrupting smooth family relationships before its full seriousness was recognized. By that time, the individual found himself enmeshed in a whole web of relationships—on the job, at home, during weekends, after the day's work, having a 'few' with the boys—so that he found it impossible to break with the habit. By the time the case reached the separation court, the whole gamut of family relationships had been undermined and disrupted, so that reconciliation appeared hopeless short of an extended period of rehabilitation for both partners."

Stages of alcoholism. There are four stages in the consumption of alcohol: the normal stage beyond which fourteen out of fifteen adult drinkers do not go, and three stages which mark the emergence of the problem drinker.

The normal drinker enjoys alcohol for its mild, relaxing effects, or for the mild pickup it gives. He may usually have a cocktail or two before dinner, but it is no great sacrifice for him to omit them. When he goes to a party, he anticipates its pleasures in terms of the people he will talk to rather than the drinks to be served. He may drink wine or beer with meals, as he learned to do if his parents were of European origin. In any event, he does not drink to get a "severe jolt" or sense of excitement. His attitude toward drinking as a legitimate means of mild exhilaration or relaxed pleasure conforms to the spirit of the Bible: "Wine was created from the beginning to make men joyful, and not to make them drunk. Wine drunken with moderation is the joy of the soul and the heart." (Ecclesiasticus, 31:35–36)

The first stage on the road to alcoholism is taken when a drinker uses alcohol for other purposes. After working hard, he may find that several drinks before dinner relieve his nervous tension. If he has had trouble getting to sleep he may drink so that he drops off immediately. He may discover that whenever he is troubled or upset, a few cocktails make his world seem right again. If he is afraid to meet people, he may find that highballs change him into a "regular fellow." In each case, he uses alcohol to do a job for him, and he finds it increasingly difficult to do the job without it. Thus he is becoming dependent upon alcohol.

The second stage is one in which storm signals are flying. Now he often finds himself drinking without any occasion to justify it. He may drink by himself, or consume his drinks faster than other persons. He may control himself at social gatherings, then return home to continue drinking. After an evening of imbibing he may be unable to remember all that happened the night before. Perhaps his boss now warns him about his drinking habits. His wife begs him to cut down. He has severe remorse after drinking bouts, and may even promise to do better in the future. He may swear off for a time, then perhaps conclude that he can again drink normally. By now, however, it is quite likely that he has crossed over the line to alcoholism. One drink will start a chain reaction and usually he will not be satisfied until he becomes intoxicated.

In the latter part of this stage, many of the traditional evils of drink appear, and they often shake the foundation of the marriage. He becomes irresponsible. Money needed for food, for the baby's clothing, for long-overdue medical bills or apartment rent, is thrown onto a bar for alcohol. Now he may lose his job because of his many absences, or because his work has become slipshod and unreliable. If he drives a car, he may become involved in accidents. His wife becomes increasingly worried, tense and unresponsive to him. Putting the blame everywhere but on himself, he may find doubtful companions elsewhere.

If the alcoholic is a woman, she may shut herself in her room for long periods, neglecting the care of her children and her household duties. She becomes a lonely, solitary drinker. Knowing the verdict that society renders against the alcoholic woman, she often tries to hide from the world. For long periods, she may refuse to leave her room, will not answer the telephone, and will go to extremes to avoid facing friends. She becomes a voluntary outcast from society.

The third stage of alcoholism is one which no longer can be hidden from the world. By now the male alcoholic has either lost his job or is on the verge of doing so. Friends and neighbors know of his condition. Unless he has had much wealth at the beginning of his alcoholic progression, he probably will be deeply in debt. If he still lives at home, his family has learned to run from the sight of the bill collector. His children dread his coming, for they realize that in his drunken state he may beat them violently or create disturbances that will arouse the neighborhood. Perhaps his wife has been forced to take a job to support the family. She is now father and mother, and he is ignored whenever possible. The fact that he is no longer recognized as head of the house infuriates him still further.

There often are definite manifestations of insanity. The alcoholic may put the blame for his passion for drink on his wife, his employer, his children, even upon God. He is overwhelmed by the problems which have piled up at home, at work, and elsewhere. It may seem to him that his only solution is to flee. He may desert his family. But unless he can somehow regain his senses, he may move from jail to jail, to the depths of Skid Row, to psychiatric wards of hospitals, and ultimately to an institution for the insane, or death.

The pattern of alcoholic behavior is described in detail in the hope that those who suffer from this disease in any of its stages will do something about it before it is too late. For it is practically certain that one with the early symptoms will, if he continues drinking, pass on to the advanced stage.

Once a drinker passes over the line from normal social drinking to compulsive drinking, there is no turning back. Medical and psychiatric authorities all agree that he can never drink normally again. No matter how long he abstains, the first drink he takes will probably set off a chain reaction which will not stop until he is completely intoxicated. The only treatment is total abstinence. But the reason drink takes such a frightful toll is that alcoholics often cannot permanently stop by themselves. In fact, this inability is given as a characteristic of the disease by the Catholic Encyclopedia. It describes alcoholism as "The condition of those whose excessive drinking creates serious problems in the management of their lives and yet who usually are unable to stop drinking, even if they want to, without outside help."

But hope does exist for the alcoholic. He can obtain temporary physical help in a hospital or by means of medications which a doctor may administer. Massive doses of vitamins may help him overcome the intense nervousness, tension, and state of depression which almost inevitably follow a prolonged bout. But while doctors may ease the pain of hangovers, they have no magic pill to prevent the patient from drinking again.

Experience has taught that reformation of the alcoholic can come only through spiritual and emotional help, coupled with whatever physical assistance is available. The inspiring story of Matt Talbot, the Irish alcoholic who conquered his desire to drink by cultivating a new life of the spirit, shows that the resources of our religion alone can change the compulsive drinker into a respected member of society. But Matt Talbot was exceptional. Most drinkers in the advanced state of alcoholism have refused countless opportunities to partake of God's grace during the time of their decline, and their spiritual resources now are unequal to the task they face.

Several hundred thousand alcoholics have been helped to sobriety through the unique organization of Alcoholics Anonymous. Father Edward Dowling, S.J., who has made a thorough study of this organization, thinks that "they have an answer that no one else has been able to supply." Father Dowling states that "they ask only one thing of the prospective member. He must say that he wills to be helped." The drinker then is taught that he is powerless over alcohol and that he needs a Higher Power to help him achieve sobriety. He learns that he must concentrate on avoiding the first drink for, if he does take it, the inevitable compulsion for more will be set into motion. He learns to put into practice a "twenty-four-hour program," in which he concentrates on solving the problems of one day at a time and does not disturb himself with remorse over the past or undue anxieties for the future. He also learns to recognize emotional responses like resentments which may create tensions that lead him to drink. Above all, he learns to place complete reliance upon the will of God. In doing so, he often experiences a spiritual rebirth which has been described as the "Miracle of A.A."

This treatment is not always successful. Sometimes the alcoholic does not truly wish to become sober. Sometimes he insists that he can stop by himself "when he wants to." And sometimes he is so far advanced that no program of recovery can make an impression. Nevertheless, those who continue to attend these meetings and try to conform to its suggested steps of recovery almost invariably achieve a large, if not full, measure of success.

Because of the alcoholic's traditional perversity, it is difficult to recommend any single way to call his need for A.A. to his attention. Sometimes an employer will threaten to fire him unless he stops drinking and joins. Sometimes a doctor, recognizing the limitations of physical methods of treatment, will recommend this step. Often the parish priest will suggest it. The wife herself should proceed delicately, for in most cases the alcoholic's relationship with her has reached such a sad state that almost automatically he rejects any suggestions she makes. Perhaps the most advisable procedure is for her to wait until he shows signs of remorse—usually after a prolonged bout—and obviously is groping for a way to stop. She might then delicately suggest that he interest himself in A.A. Its members will gladly call upon him and help him get started on the road to sobriety.

In extreme cases, the wife may find it necessary to leave him to protect herself and her children. She should not take this drastic step without first consulting her spiritual adviser, because leaving an alcoholic to his own feeble resources often causes him to drink even more, and makes recovery all but impossible.

An alcoholic may also be a psychoneurotic who would benefit from psychiatric treatment. A psychiatrist might be able to help the drinker understand what he is running from, diminish his feelings of guilt or inadequacy, and help him compete with the world on better terms.

The trouble is that most excessive drinkers don't want the help of outsiders, and that is precisely what they need most. Usually they are people who feel adequate only under the influence of liquor, and yet when sober are as proud as peacocks. But they do not know themselves. Before anything can be done they must accept the truth that there is nothing shameful about consulting a psychiatrist or joining A.A. Psychiatry is not just for the insane nor is the A.A. exclusively for "Bowery bums." The fact of the matter is that many people have been helped by both, particularly when they sought the help in the early stages. Unfortunately many people have to hit bottom before they will acknowledge their need for help.

What is needed in the nondrinking spouse is great patience and faith, the capacity to bear the injuries and the shame, and the faith to call for God's grace. One old lady in the midst of her husband's drinking bouts would always march up to the church on a dark morning. Kneeling before the altar rail, she "demanded" the help of Our Blessed Lord for herself and the husband. She always asserted that Christ never let her down whenever she needed sacramental grace. Once when she was asked why she had not separated from her husband long before this, she answered, "If I left Jack, I am sure he would lose his soul." This type of faith and determination kept the husband more sober than he would have otherwise been.

Total abstinence is often advisable. Couples in their early years of marriage should consider carefully the horrors that can result from excessive drink. They should also realize that this wretched affliction could come to them. If there is any indication that drink is or could be a problem in your life, by all means stop drinking immediately. If you could visit the alcoholic wards of hospitals, sit on the benches of the nation's courtrooms, visit social welfare agencies and witness the suffering deprivations of children that result from alcoholism, if you could view the records of chancery court which reveal how once ideal marriages have been ruined by excesses of drink, you would fully agree that complete abstinence is the only course open for anyone susceptible to this disease.

Total abstinence is not the joyless existence that drinkers sometimes make it out to be. Abstinence is a natural way of living; drinking is not. "There is a mistaken notion current among many Catholics in this country that there is something puritanical, or slightly un-Catholic, about the practice of total abstinence," comments the Rev. John C. Ford, S.J. "This is a false idea. Total abstinence has the highest approval of the Church and her theologians, and Catholic total abstinence organizations in this country and elsewhere have been enriched with indulgences by the Holy See.

"It would be false, however, to say, as some of our non-Catholic brethren do, that total abstinence is obligatory on all Christians. And it would be an exaggeration to say that total abstinence is always the more perfect way of practicing the virtue of sobriety. After all, Our Divine Lord drank wine. He was not a total abstainer. Yet he practiced the virtue of sobriety, as He practiced all other virtues, in a perfect degree.

"However, given the tremendous abuses of alcohol which are widespread in the United States, total abstinence is a peculiarly fitting and appropriate method of self-denial and self-discipline. It not only safeguards the total abstainer from the dangers of excess, but when practiced for a supernatural motive —for example, reparation to the heart of Jesus for one's own sins and the sins of others—it can become a means of advancing in perfection."

12

The Menopause and Old Age

MIDDLE AGE—the mid-forties and early fifties—is often the critical period in marriage and in life. It is a time of physical and emotional stress. You are startled to realize that you can no longer do many things you have always taken for granted. You cannot eat rich foods as you used to, you cannot keep late hours, you must sit and recover your breath after running a few yards to catch the bus. As your physical powers wane, you also realize that many dreams you nourished in adolescence and early adulthood will not be realized.

When we were young, we were certain that we would somehow leave our mark upon the world. We would invent some machine that mankind needed. We would gain renown for our skill as a surgeon. We would be the great actor, write the great books, stir the masses with our great oratory. We would produce superior children who would lead their class in scholarship, win medals for athletic skill and excite admiration everywhere for their attractiveness and charm. When we reach middle age, however, we usually realize that we will not realize our early dreams. Even those of us who have attained our goals find that success does not produce all the happiness we had supposed it would.

In middle age, we face reality. We realize that, to a large extent, the pattern of our lives has been set. We must face the fact that death is approaching; we are drawn as by a magnet to the obituary pages to learn who among our acquaintances is the latest to succumb.

Important changes occur in marriage itself. By now the physical attractions which drew man and woman together have become submerged; the marital act depends more than ever upon spiritual and emotional adjustments achieved over the years. If mutual affection and consideration have not been cultivated to make the act a true communion of spirit, one or both partners' interest in sex may die entirely. Also at this time, the children usually leave home to set up their own households. For many years, husband and wife have occupied themselves with the problems of childbearing and child rearing. Now they are again alone together. How they adjust to this new situation will depend almost entirely upon how well they have come to know and to respect each other when they were busy with their responsibilities as parents. If there was affectionate companionship, the middle-aged couple will find unexpected pleasures in each other's company. If the children have been their only interest, they may experience a painful period—almost a second courtship—when they must learn to know each other anew.

Because of the many adjustments, stresses and strains of middle age, it is not surprising that researchers have found that this period coincides with a low point in happiness in the average person's life cycle. Recent evidence indicates that your marital happiness may decline from a peak in your twenties and early thirties—when your family is being formed—to a low in the forties for women and the fifties for men, when physical and emotional facts of life must be faced squarely. Evidence also indicates, however, that the low point is temporary. Once you adjust to the new condition, your happiness rises—and usually continues to climb well into old age.

A spiritual life softens the blows. In middle age, the virtues of an active spiritual life become completely apparent. If you now hold the firm understanding that you received life to prepare for an eternity with God, you can face the prospects of illness and death with serenity. If you have acquired qualities of gentleness and charity through your active life in Christ, you can anticipate your remaining years with your mate with serene confidence. When you see your children leading wholesome lives as adults, you can feel satisfaction that you have been a good parent. You can also draw inner strength from the realization that by helping your mate achieve sanctity you have fulfilled well your vocation in life.

Changes in women in middle age: Husbands and wives pass through this critical period with fewer difficulties if they have an adequate knowledge of physical and emotional changes which take place. In women, the most pronounced change is the menopause, or "change of life." This time has been described as "adolescence in reverse." Instead of the changes in the body's physical make-up which take place in the teens to enable the woman to conceive and bear children, the powers to conceive gradually wane and childbearing becomes no longer possible.

The menopause occurs when a woman stops menstruating. According to records of thousands of women compiled by Dr. Emil Novak of the Johns Hopkins Medical School, Baltimore, the average age at menopause is about forty-seven years. Fifty per cent of all women experience the menopause between the ages of forty-five and fifty. One woman in four stops menstruating before forty-five, and another one in four stops after the age of fifty. There is an apparent relationship between the mother's menopause and that of her daughter: both usually experience this change at about the same age. The earlier a woman first menstruates, the longer her active childbearing life usually lasts. Childless women often reach their menopause earlier than mothers.

Menopause does not cease abruptly. Rather, it comes to a gradual stop. Perhaps a woman menstruated regularly every twenty-eight days. Now her cycle will lengthen—to thirty days, to six weeks, to several months. During her earlier years the flow of blood may have lasted four or five days. As the cycle lengthens, the quantity of discharge decreases—finally it lasts for less than a day, then stops entirely.

As menstruation tapers off, the ovaries, which discharge the egg necessary for human life, become less active. The body produces smaller quantities of hormones needed to bear and carry a child to term. Thus a woman's ability to conceive coincides roughly with her ability to menstruate.

In adolescence, increases in hormone production and other bodily changes often cause physical tensions and emotional upsets. During the change of life, there may also be periods of physical and emotional stress. Not long ago, most women dreaded the coming menopause. They believed old wives' tales that they would suffer intense physical and mental disturbance and might even become insane. Medical knowledge has proved beyond doubt that these old fears are groundless. According to the best available statistics, eighty-five per cent of women pass through the menopause with either minor symptoms or no symptoms at all. The remaining fifteen per cent experience some difficulty but can be helped tremendously by hormone injections and other medical treatments. In short, no woman should fear the menopause as anything worse than a mildly disconcerting and passing stage in life.

Common symptoms, in addition to the ending of menstruation, are a slight increase in nervousness, occasional feelings of depression, and possible inability to sleep as soundly as before. Sometimes hands or feet tingle as though they are "falling asleep." There may be occasional itching of the skin and so-called "hot flashes"—passing sensations of heat around the neck and face caused by an irregular contraction and expansion of the blood vessels.

In the relatively few cases when symptoms of the menopause are more disturbing than those described above, doctors can prescribe sedatives to reduce tension and make passing phases more bearable. In extreme cases, they can supply hormones to relieve physical discomforts which may be felt at this time.

Since most difficulties associated with the menopause are psychological and not physical in origin, the woman who adopts a proper mental attitude usually will pass through this period with a minimum of difficulty. The husband should be gentle, considerate and reassuring. If his wife appears to be having trouble during this period, he should encourage her to visit a competent physician who will prescribe any necessary medicine and relieve her mind.

At this stage, some women tend to review their lives in a critical way. For example, some feel acutely lonely and guilty for not having had more children. Those who have practiced birth control and now face old age without the solace that children can provide, feel this moment in an especially severe way. Some even try desperately to bear a child but find that they have begun too late.

Women also react in different ways to the independence which usually comes as their children now fully care for themselves. Some retreat into an isolated loneliness and develop a passion for self-pity which makes them a nuisance to all. Others, aware of the truth that happiness lies in helping others, become more active in charitable work. Elderly women usually are happiest when sewing for the hospitalized and the needy, helping orphaned children, or performing other good deeds. Husbands should not begrudge a reasonable amount of time spent by their wives on these worthy activities.

The woman who has emphasized physical charms during her earlier years and has failed to develop spiritual and emotional qualities may view her loss of beauty with dismay. One of the saddest human sights is that of the middle-aged woman who is overrouged and overdressed in a frantic effort to look young. At this time, a woman may experience a more intense desire for sexual relations than she has ever felt before. Freed from false fears of pregnancy and childbirth, she may bring a new sense of spontaneity and emotional warmth to the act of physical communion. But now, however, her husband's interest in sex and his ability to perform the act are waning; if her aloofness has discouraged him in earlier years, his interest may now have disappeared almost entirely. She may mistakenly assume that her husband's lack of interest results from her diminishing beauty. In such cases, the husband should strive to compliment her on her enduring qualities and to reassure her that her loss of youth will not cause his affection to lessen.

Problems of the middle-aged man: Important physical changes also occur in the typical man of about fifty. His interest in the act of sex is aroused with increasing difficulty. Stimuli that had always aroused him in his twenties and thirties no longer prove effective. In many other ways he realizes that he is growing old.

Some men do not fully understand that these changes are natural aspects of aging. They fear that they are losing their masculinity and must do something drastic about it. For that reason, this middle-aged period has come to be called the "dangerous age" in men. According to psychologists, at this time some men try to prove that they are as virile as they were twenty years earlier. They make fools of themselves by seeking the companionship of younger girls whom they expect to impress with their charm. Such men are as foolish and foredoomed to failure as women who reach their menopause frantically trying to maintain their youthful beauty.

Although tales of wayward middle-aged men are often headlined in the newspapers, evidence strongly suggests that most men—especially those with a spiritual outlook—move through this period without indulging in such absurd activities. The well-adjusted, mature man accepts symptoms of aging with serenity. For example, his loss of sexual desire usually occurs so gradually that he has ample time to adjust to it. His interest may begin to lessen in his thirties, but he may participate in the marital act after his fifties. Children have been born of fathers who were in their late eighties.

Middle-aged men may feel deflated and depressed for other reasons. The typical male has intense ambition. He wants to be a success in his chosen field, because so much of his prestige with his fellow-men rests upon it. If the man of fifty has failed to accomplish much of what he set out to do in his eager twenties, he may grope for reasons to explain his failure. In his agonizing appraisal, he may conclude that he lacks any worthwhile qualities. This sense of inferiority, coupled with a feeling of defeatism as to future prospects, may plunge him into a depression that leaves his wife bewildered. If she is wise, she will exert her powers of understanding and appreciation to help him realize that he will always be a success in his family's eyes.

The man who has been successful in business often also faces a crisis in his middle years. In his thirties and forties, he had ambition to drive him forward and the energy to reach his goal. His only competitors often were elderly men past the peak of their powers, and often too tired to put up a good fight. Now, however, he is in his fifties and, like the older men he supplanted, he lacks drive and determination. He looks below him on the ladder and discovers many eager, strong young men clamoring to push him aside. He wonders how long he will have the strength to hold them off.

The man who has put all his faith in material success often cannot bear the thought of losing to younger competition because he has nothing to substitute for his all-consuming business interests. A common phenomenon is the middle-aged male who failed to build his marriage on a lasting foundation of mutual love, companionship and understanding. Because he has been too busy promoting his career, he has never really learned to know his wife and children. Faced with the crisis of middle age, he discovers that he can turn to no one who will console him in his inevitable defeats. One often reads of the man who suffers a heart attack and is advised by his doctors to retire from work. The patient rejects the advice because he actually does not know how to live quietly and serenely in his family circle. He knows no other course but to return to work. The inevitable happens: he dies before his time.

In reviewing the problems men face in middle age, you can recognize why you should develop spiritual strength in your early years. The man who learns at the beginning of his career to "render unto Caesar the things that are Caesar's, and unto God the things that are God's," will recognize the futility of unbridled materialistic ambition. He will place a higher value upon the love of his wife and his children. He will realize that satisfactions he can obtain from his role as a good father will surpass any that material success can offer. His family's love will protect him against any adversity he encounters in his business world.

Preparations for retirement: Even if you are now in your thirties or forties, it is not too early for you to consider some problems you and your mate may face after retirement. Four simple principles have helped thousands of couples to enjoy their twilight years to the fullest, and to transform what might otherwise be a time of strain and tension into a golden period when their love for each other reaches its crowning glory.

1. Develop a truly spiritual outlook about life and death. Then the ending of your days will hold no terrors for you. You will accept it as a necessary part of God's plan, and if you have really practiced your faith you can be confident of God's reward. The value on a worldly level of an abiding religious faith has been underscored by Dr. Carl Jung, who has been called one of the world's greatest psychiatrists. He has said that every one of his patients over thirty-five became mentally ill because of a lack of true religious values—and that none ever fully recovered unless they first regained their religious outlook.

2. Learn to know your mate as a person. In later years your spouse will not be your sex partner or even your fellow-parent, for your children will perhaps have left you to establish their own families. You will then need a companion—one in whom you can confide your innermost hopes and fears, one who will comfort you in your days of anxiety and whom you can comfort in turn.

3. Learn to make friends easily. Loneliness has been aptly termed the curse of the aged. Some old persons sink into a kind of stupor and watch hopelessly as their close friends die one by one. Because they have made no effort to cultivate new friendships, they soon are walled in by loneliness. This is unnecessary, for the basic ingredients of friendship—your smiling cheerfulness, your undaunted optimism, your helping hand to all those who need it—are in short supply in our world. To have a friend, you must be one—and if you climb out of yourself to help others, you will develop a true companionship of souls that will add joy to your years.

4. Develop interests that keep you active. Studies of retired men in Cleveland, Ohio, clearly established that those who regarded themselves as happiest after their retirement did things. They visited the children, worked around the house and garden, went for walks together. The unhappiest ones led passive lives—sat or rested much more than they had to.

Not long ago, an eighty-year-old woman died in New York. She was a devout Catholic and was known throughout her parish for the devotion with which she had lived her married life. As the body lay in state, the parish priest came to pay his respects in the late afternoon and to lead in reciting the Rosary. The priest beckoned to the widower and said, "Kneel beside me." The elderly man replied simply, "Father, if you don't mind, I'd like to say the Rosary this evening. Mary and I have said the Rosary together before bedtime for the last forty-seven years, and I would not want tonight to be different." Even in death, the husband wanted to be identified with his wife in the spiritual act they had performed together all their years. That is Christian marriage.

13

"Until Death Do You Part"

WHEN you entered the state of matrimony in the presence of a priest, you made a sacred contract with your spouse. Holding the right hand of your partner-to-be, you took this solemn vow: "I take thee for my lawful wife (husband) to have and to hold from this day forward, for better, for worse, for richer, for poorer, in sickness and in health, until death do us part."

Probably no other sentence you ever speak will have as much meaning as this one. It means that you agree to remain married regardless of disappointments, frustrations or hardships that may later arrive. And it means that the only condition that will terminate your marriage is death.

Everyone married in the Church takes that vow. Every bride and bridegroom has been made aware of its full and awesome significance. No matter how much you may wish at a later date to sever the marriage tie, you can never claim that you did not know the exact conditions of your marriage contract. When you stood before the priest, you knew that this was a sacrament, and that it was for life.

The Church teaches that the bond of matrimony lasts until the death of husband or wife for three basic reasons:

1. In instituting the sacrament, Christ decreed that no human being could revoke it. He said, "What therefore God has joined together, let no man put asunder."

2. You and your mate made a solemn contract when you were married, agreeing that your union was for life. You pledged before God that nothing—neither separation, divorce, nor an attempted marriage with another person—would ever destroy your true marriage bond.

3. It is for the good of husband and wife, for the bodily and spiritual welfare of their children, and for the good of society that the marriage bond cannot be broken, except by death.

You will recall the account in the Bible of the time when some Pharisees came to Jesus, asking: "Is it lawful for a man to put away his wife for any cause?"

The Bible records that Jesus answered:

"Have you not read that the Creator, from the beginning, made them male and female, and said, for this cause shall a man leave his father and mother, and cleave to his wife, and the two shall become one flesh?

"Therefore now they are no longer two, but one flesh. What therefore God has joined together, let no man put asunder."

The Pharisees then asked Jesus: "Why then did Moses command to give a written notice of dismissal, and to put her away?"

"He said to them: 'Because Moses, by reason of the hardness of your heart, permitted you to put away your wives'; but it was not so from the beginning.

"And I say to you, that whoever puts away his wife, except for immorality, and marries another, commits adultery; and he who marries a woman who has been put away commits adultery." (Matthew, 19:3–9)

From these words, some readers have mistakenly concluded that while Christ forbade divorce generally, He made an exception if the wife was guilty of adultery. Such a conclusion is unfounded, however, because Our Lord said without any qualification or limitation: "He who marries a woman who has been put away commits adultery."

That divorce has been prohibited by the Church from its earliest days is proved by the words of St. Paul. In a letter written to the Corinthians almost twenty centuries ago, St. Paul stated:

"To them who are married, not I, but the Lord commands that a wife is not to depart from her husband, and if she departs, that she is to remain unmarried or be reconciled to her husband. And let not a husband put away his wife." (1 Corinthians, 7:10–11)

So that no one could mistake the firmness of his teaching, St. Paul declared, later in his letter:

"A woman is bound as long as her husband is alive, but if her husband dies, she is free. Let her marry whom she pleases, only let it be in the Lord." (1 Corinthians, 7:39)

The Church's teaching has remained unshaken through the centuries. For example, in the fourth century, St. Augustine wrote of the sacrament of marriage: "The substance undoubtedly is that the man and the woman who are joined together in wedlock should remain inseparable as long as they live." As a result of such teaching, the principle that marriage cannot be ended except by death was made a part of the civil laws of every Christian country by the tenth century.

Thousands of quotations could be offered to prove that the Church has always considered sacramental marriage to be indissoluble. For example, in 1880 Pope Leo XIII wrote: "It should further be known that no power can dissolve the bond of Christian marriage whenever it has been ratified and consummated; and that, as a consequence, those husbands and wives are guilty of a manifest crime who plan, for whatsoever reason, to be united in a second marriage before the first one has ended by death." In his address "On Faith and Marriage," in 1946, Pope Pius XII said: "Valid marriage ratified and consummated can be dissolved by no human power and by no other cause but death."

Divorce was practically unknown in Christian countries until the beginnings of Protestantism. Some early Protestants interpreted Christ's teachings to mean that a valid marriage could be ended by a husband or wife if his or her spouse had committed adultery. Others soon broadened the reasons for which divorces should be granted. Today, not even an attempt is made to justify divorce in terms of Our Lord's teachings. Divorces are granted for an almost unbelievably wide and ridiculous variety of reasons, ranging from a husband's refusal to take his wife to a movie because he preferred to watch a baseball game on television, to a wife's "mental cruelty" in refusing to remove the rings around the bathtub after bathing.

Church teachings regarding divorce sometimes may appear unduly harsh to those outside the Faith, and in some instances even to Catholics. In some cases, it may even be true that a wife's life would be happier if she could exchange her adulterous husband for a faithful one. A family might be happier without a shrewish woman who wantonly neglects all her obligations as a wife and mother. However, a few individuals will always be inconvenienced by laws intended to promote the well-being of all men. If you compare the tiny number of cases in which Church teachings may impose a hardship with the almost unbelievable damage that follows when free and easy divorces are permitted, there can be no mistaking the justice and wisdom of the Catholic position.

Consider the situation in the United States, where divorce flourishes. In 1890, one divorce was granted for every eighteen marriages performed. In 1920, the ratio was approximately one divorce for every seven marriages. In 1956, there were 377,000 divorces granted in the United States, and 1,569,000 marriages were performed—a ratio of approximately one divorce for every four marriages. The divorce rate in the United States is approximately five times that of Canada, three and a half times greater than that of England, and twice as great as that of France. With the exception of Egypt and possibly Russia, our divorce rate is now the world's highest. Although divorce is permitted by many non-Catholic sects, probably no responsible religious, political or social leader in the country considers the breakup of marriage as anything but a tragedy. All recognize our divorce rate as an evil which is undermining the very structure of our society. And this evil results mainly from the fact that divorce is allowed.

In its practical application, the Church's teaching that marriage must be permanent has these natural bulwarks:

1. That while there may be disappointments and disagreements in marriage, divorce is no solution; in fact, in many cases, divorce merely takes two persons out of a bad situation and tosses them into a worse one.

2. That many troubled marriages can be salvaged; that a husband and wife can usually find a way either to settle their differences or to live with them in relative harmony.

Almost all experts now recognize that most divorces create more problems than they solve. Magazines tell the stories of women who thought that a divorce court would grant them freedom but who found themselves chained to an appalling loneliness instead. Others discovered that they had stolen something precious from their children by denying them the companionship of a father, regardless of his shortcomings. Others, accustomed to being supported by a husband and untrained to earn salaries in business, found themselves forced to live under conditions of grinding poverty. When some divorced women sought new friends, they discovered that the word "divorcee" attracted only men interested in sexual satisfaction.

Those who had led active social lives as married women thought that things would go on after their divorce as before. But most of their friends were other married couples. Invited to dinner parties or other social events, the divorcees were "extra women" and created problems in entertaining that every hostess dreads. In most cases the number of invitations to social affairs dwindled gradually and finally stopped.

Similar problems affect the divorced male. Not long ago Paul Gallico, writing in the *Reader's Digest,* told from his own experience how divorce can affect a man.

"I have been free now for three years, and I am prepared to report on what this marvelous freedom is like," he wrote. "It's the bunk! You don't know how lucky you are to be married! The disadvantages of living without marital ties, particularly in middle life, far outweigh the delights. You find for the first time how loud silence can be in the chilly glamour of an empty home. The loneliness and silences close in when the rattle of one's key in the front door initiates no answering sound. It is in this moment that the bark of a dog, the meow of a cat, or the chirrup of a bird is no substitute for a human voice. . . .

"No one really cares what happens to you. That is one of the meanings of this wonderful freedom. You are a man or a woman alone. No longer are you the first concern of another person. Nobody bothers about whether you are sick or well, happy or miserable, alive or dead. Friends do not close the awful gap that was once filled by someone called wife or husband. It just isn't the same."

Mr. Gallico quotes a friend who summed up the problem succinctly: "There were irritations in my marriage I thought were intolerable until I found that life without them was even more so."

Almost everywhere, the testimony of those who have been through a divorce and its lonely aftermath is the same. Try anything else first, they say. Learn to accept your marital problems and live with them. Consult a marriage counselor. Visit a psychiatrist. Do anything—but don't get a divorce.

The second assertion—that many marriages can be salvaged—is one which experienced marriage counselors now accept wholeheartedly. They have found, in fact, that many persons who initiate divorce actions do not actually want to end their marriages. Frequently a husband or wife threatens divorce to try to force a spouse to adopt another mode of conduct. When the spouse refuses to conform, the bluff is called. Then the mate who has threatened divorce feels that he or she must save face by filing suit. Sometimes immature husbands or wives become bored with the day-to-day routine of marriage and regard divorce as an adventure. These immature people fail to distinguish between the marriage and a condition of marriage which could usually be remedied easily. If they can be made to realize what divorce really means, they often decide that the annoyances of their marriage are trivial compared to the greater evil they have been considering.

That marriages can be saved has been proved beyond doubt. The experience of Judge Paul W. Alexander of the Domestic Relations Court of Toledo, Ohio, is typical. Judge Alexander has long advocated that every effort should be made to help a husband and wife solve their problems before giving up the marriage as lost. For about twenty years Toledo has had a family court with trained specialists who provide psychiatric or social advice to mates who no longer agree. He has reported that this type of help has been able to salvage between a third and a half of all the marriages that have reached his jurisdiction. In other clinics throughout the country, salvage rates reach as high as ninety per cent—nine out of every ten troubled marriages have been set straight.

Marriage counselors believe that a large percentage of cases which they cannot settle amicably and which finally reach the divorce courts could be solved if one or both of the partners had a truly conciliatory attitude. In such cases, the husband or wife, or both, are too stubborn to admit they have been even slightly at fault. In other cases, pride is involved; for example, a wife's ego may be damaged so badly by the thought that her husband has sinned with another woman that she refuses to forgive him. But this is the important point: almost always the partner who is unwilling to be reconciled is motivated by the thought that he or she can enter another marriage after the divorce action is concluded.

No such prospect is possible in a Catholic marriage. Since both partners know that their contract is for life, they realize that they must make concessions to achieve a harmonious relationship. They must learn to live with each other's faults, to work together, to sacrifice. And in doing so, they achieve a happiness that is denied those who constantly carry with them the thought that they can flee at the first sign of trouble.

Impediments to valid marriage: Occasionally a breakup occurs in a marriage in which one or both of the partners are Catholics. Some time later, a participant in this union is remarried—and in the church. Is this not a sign, non-Catholics ask, that the Church approves of divorce under certain circumstances?

The answer, of course, is that the Church *never* permits the termination of a consummated sacramental marriage except by death. A valid marriage for Catholics is one performed in the presence of a priest and in which other necessary conditions are present. If a Catholic appears before a justice of the peace, he may be married in the eyes of the State, but he is not married in the eyes of God. He is living in sin just as if he had never gone through the ceremony.

Even when a couple go through the marriage ceremony before a priest, certain conditions may exist that make the marriage invalid. In such a case, even if the man and woman are not aware that an impediment exists, they are not truly married in the eyes of God. Some impediments are:

Insufficient age. Church law states that a valid marriage cannot be entered into by a male who has not completed his sixteenth year, nor by a female who has not completed her fourteenth.

Impotence. A person who is impotent is not capable of performing the marital act. Since marriage without the marital act is impossible, it follows that when impotence exists, there can be no marriage. This impotence must have existed when the ceremony was performed and must be permanent. Impotence should not be confused with sterility, which is the inability to have children. If a person is capable of performing the marital act but is sterile, a valid marriage exists.

Consanguinity. Consanguinity is the bond which unites persons of the same blood. For instance, fathers cannot contract valid marriages with daughters, nor can brothers and sisters validly marry.

Spiritual relationship. This impediment arises from baptism. The baptizer and the baptized cannot validly marry, nor can godparents marry their godchildren.

Bigamy. A living husband or wife will always render a second marriage invalid.

There are also other impediments which exist only rarely in modern times.

The obstacle to true consent. Marriage is a contract, and like contracts encountered in daily life, it is not truly binding unless the persons making it know what they are doing and consent to it of their own free wills. The Church therefore recognizes certain "obstacles to true consent" which make a real contract impossible. Such obstacles are want of the use of reason, defective knowledge, mistaken identity, pretense, duress and fear, and intentions contrary to the essence of marriage.

"Want of the use of reason" exists when the man or woman is insane, intoxicated, drugged or hypnotized at the time of the ceremony. Although the use of reason is always strongly presumed, when its absence at the time of marriage is very clearly proved, the marriage will be declared null and void.

"Defective knowledge" exists when the man or woman does not know what marriage is. The bride and bridegroom must know that it is a permanent union between man and woman for the purpose of procreating children. Both must know that children are conceived in a bodily union of husband and wife. They are not required to know the details of the marital act. However, in practice it is almost impossible to prove defectiveness of the necessary knowledge.

"Mistaken identity" exists more frequently in fiction than in fact. For example, Mary goes to the altar to marry John. She believes John is standing by her side when actually the man is Joseph, John's twin brother. Such a marriage would be void at the start. Sometimes a woman may agree to marry a man who says that he is rich and can give her a life of ease. After the ceremony, she discovers that he must count pennies before providing life's bare necessities. Is such a marriage contract valid? Yes, because Church law states that a mistake made concerning a characteristic of the marriage partner does not necessarily make it void. On the other hand, the woman marrying a man previously married and divorced who kept his past secret would not be making a true contract; the law states that "a mistake concerning the person" may void the contract.

"Pretense" exists when one of the parties secretly has no intention of contracting marriage. This, also, is usually unprovable.

"Duress and fear" may void a marriage if it has certain characteristics. A man who marries a woman because her father has held a gun to him and threatened to kill him unless he did so, may be influenced by duress and fear. On the other hand, a woman who marries because she fears what friends might say if she broke her engagement at the last moment, is making a valid marriage, because her fear is caused by herself and is not of grave importance.

"Intention contrary to the essence of the marriage" exists

when the man or woman, or both, intend to obtain a divorce if the marriage does not work out to expectations. Since marriage is, by its nature, for life, an agreement contrary to the essential characteristics—permanency, fidelity, children—makes the contract null and void.

The above discussion has considered some conditions which make a marriage null and void from the beginning. When such cases are brought to the attention of the Church, judges of the Church will decide whether a marriage exists. If they conclude that there has been no marriage, the persons involved must cease to live together or must enter a valid contract if possible. Thus when a marriage is annulled, the parties to it are free to remarry validly in the Church.

The subject of impediments and lack of true consent is highly complicated and the discussion above is intended for general information only. Any person involved in an annulment case should discuss it with a member of the Marriage Court who has been specifically trained for this work and appointed by the Bishop. When conditions warrant, the parish priest will arrange for such a discussion.

It should also be borne in mind that in all cases of this kind, the burden of proof rests upon the person seeking the annulment. A mere statement that an impediment was present will never suffice; the Church requires clear-cut proof.

"It is a rule of law that whatever is done is presumed to have been done correctly," explains Father Stephen J. Kelleher, Judge of the Marriage Court of the Archdiocese of New York. "This means that any time that two people enter a contract, it is presumed that they do everything necessary to make the contract a valid one. There are no exceptions to this rule.

"Where a party alleges that his marriage is not to be considered valid because he is a Catholic and was not married in the presence of a priest, it is necessary that he clearly prove that he is a Catholic, that his marriage did not take place before a priest, and that his marriage was never blessed by a priest. In insanity cases, it must be proved that a party was actually insane at the time of the marriage. Insanity which arises after the marriage never affects its validity. On the several thousand marriages which we consider each year, perhaps only one or two will be declared null because of the invalidating intentions of one of the parties. That is, for example, because one person absolutely excluded children from the marriage. These statistics indicate the reserve with which the Church regards alleged causes for annulment."

Dissolution of the bond. A sacramental marriage legally contracted and consummated can never be dissolved by any human power except through death. A Christian marriage that has not been consummated, a marriage between a person baptized and one not baptized, or a marriage between two unbaptized persons can, however, be dissolved under certain circumstances through a dispensation granted by the Holy See. Such dispensations are rare. The granting of them should never be presumed. Each individual case must be thoroughly investigated by the bishop and his tribunal.

A legitimate, consummated marriage between nonbaptized persons may be dissolved if it is clearly proved that neither party has been baptized and if one partner is converted to the Faith and the other does not wish to live with the convert peacefully without offense to God. The Catholic can then contract a new marriage. This is called the Pauline Privilege because St. Paul taught:

"If any brother has an unbelieving wife and she consents to live with him, let him not put her away. And if any woman has an unbelieving husband and he consents to live with her, let her not put away her husband. For the unbelieving husband is sanctified by the believing wife, and the unbelieving wife is sanctified by the believing husband; otherwise your children would be unclean, but as it is, they are holy. But if the unbeliever departs, let him depart. For a brother or sister is not under bondage in such cases, but God has called us to peace." (1 Corinthians, 7:12–15) This pronouncement was made to protect the faith of Christians. Faith is of first importance to all of us because it is necessary for eternal life.

It is not permissible for a Catholic who is single to keep company with a married person on the theory that the married person may receive an ecclesiastical annulment or dissolution. The Church presumes the validity of all marriages, including marriages between two non-Catholics. Until and unless an annulment or a dissolution is actually granted by the Church Court, it is morally wrong for the married person to keep company with anyone. More often than not, there is no basis for that anticipated annulment or dissolution. Even when such a basis may exist, it may not be provable in accordance with the norms of the Church Court.

Cost of annulments. A libel sometimes made against the Church is that annulments can be obtained more easily by the rich than by the poor. Father Kelleher comments:

"For the year 1956 in the Matrimonial Court of the Archdiocese of New York, the expenses involved in the running of the court amounted to about $60,000. This included the full-time activities of seven secretaries and nine priests. Of this amount the people who were involved in the cases being processed paid approximately $20,000. This means that there was a deficit of $40,000. . . . During the course of the year, more than 2,000 marriages are brought to the attention of the court. When we find there is no basis for nullity, expenses are simply not mentioned, even though we often spend a good deal of time and money in preliminary investigations. In some hundreds of cases we ask for approximately $25 in expenses. In perhaps twenty-five cases we estimate the expenses at between $150 and $250. I use the word "estimate" because if the people cannot afford to pay, their cases are handled anyway. To obtain a civil divorce or annulment anywhere in the United States would probably cost at least $300."

Two kinds of separation possible. The Church recognizes that certain conditions may make it extremely difficult for a man and woman to live together as husband and wife. When a husband and wife cease to live together, however, the danger of adultery is magnified, along with a weakening of the faith and perhaps the ultimate loss of soul. Therefore, the Church always urges married persons to make every effort to reconcile their differences and to try to live in harmony. Separation should be undertaken only after all other attempts to live in peace have failed.

Separation may be of two types—permanent and temporary. Permanent separation is that in which cohabitation is considered out of the question for the rest of the lifetime of the parties involved. So gravely does the Church regard the potential evils of permanent separation that only one greater evil—the evil of adultery—is recognized as sufficient cause for it. When a husband or wife commits adultery, the innocent spouse may refuse to cohabit with the offending party ever again. According to Church law, the victim need not even consult a priest before taking this step. However, the innocent party must be certain that the mate has committed a complete act of adultery with another person; suspicion is not enough. Moreover, the innocent party must not have been responsible, even indirectly, for the commission of the adultery. If a wife habitually refused to engage in the marital act or indicated in any way that her husband should satisfy his physical needs elsewhere, she might have encouraged his adultery indirectly. Nor could she separate if she forgave her husband after discovering the adultery. In view of these conditions, prudence suggests that a priest be consulted before the decision is made to separate.

Temporary separation exists when a husband and wife live apart but with the possibility that they will be reunited if there is a change in the conditions responsible for the separation. Sometimes husbands and wives must separate temporarily for reasons not related to the harmony of their marriage. For example, a husband may be transferred by his employer to a different city in the middle of a school year. His wife remains behind until he obtains living quarters or until the children complete the school term. Or a husband is called into military service and sent to a remote base where facilities for family life do not exist. Such separations are involuntary and do not involve a deliberate decision to live apart; they are not the type which Church law considers.

Before the Church will permit validly married couples to break up their home and go their separate ways, there must be a serious reason for the step. Sufficient reason may exist if one partner has renounced Catholicism to join another religion, or has given up his belief in God entirely; if one insists that the children be educated in non-Catholic schools, when Catholic schooling is available and within the family's capacity to pay; if the husband refuses to provide for his family, or his wife refuses to perform ordinary wifely duties around the home; if a partner is habitually drunk and makes life difficult by disturbances, cruelty, or threats; if the partner leads a life of public sin—for instance, if he is a known and habitual criminal; or if he demands that his mate commit mortal sin with him.

Persons who believe that sufficient reasons exist to justify separation must request permission to do so from their pastor. The pastor will refer the case to the judges of the marriage court established by the diocese.

Even when an innocent victim has a legal right to live apart from an erring spouse, it is often unwise to do so. This may be especially true when a partner has expressed sorrow for his adultery and promises not to repeat it. Although a wife may legally separate, by doing so she may deny her children the advantage of their father's companionship. Her refusal to engage in bodily communion with her husband may lead to future sins of adultery by him and possibly even by herself. By insisting upon the right to live apart, she may show a lack of the Christian virtue of forgiveness.

When faced with the possibility of a separation, the priest will usually advise against it. For trials are the lot of all men. When one of the parties is apparently more bound than the other by the "for worse" clause in the marriage contract, it would be well to remember that there is no strict justice in this world and that first one spouse, and then the other, may bear unequal burdens at different times. Often a little heroism helps a marriage emerge triumphant after a few stormy years. In some cases, a true sense of martyrdom may be necessary; more often, however, the grace obtainable through trust in God, prayer and the sacraments will enable the innocent party to bear the crosses of marriage with serenity.

If separation is finally counseled by the priest and consented to by the bishop, it should never be presumed to be for life. Our Faith teaches that there is always hope even for the greatest of sinners: adulterers repent and drunkards reform, and sometimes they even become more virtuous than they have ever been. The possibility of reconciliation should never be ruled out. If God willingly forgives the repentant sinner, one of His creatures should not refuse to do so.

When civil divorce action is permitted. Church law states that Catholics may not start a civil divorce action with the intention of ending their marriage. As we have seen, a civil divorce or annulment cannot destroy the bonds of any valid marriage. In the eyes of the State, however, two persons remain married until a divorce decree is granted. Therefore it may sometimes be necessary for a Catholic to go through civil divorce proceedings in order to protect his legal rights. When the Church annuls a marriage and states that a true marriage never existed, for example, the parties must obtain a civil divorce in order to be free to remarry in accord with the laws of the State. In cases where the Church permits a couple to separate, a wife may find it necessary to sue for divorce in order to force her husband to support her and the children.

Only a properly authorized representative of the bishop can grant permission to a Catholic to apply for a civil divorce. Church authorities require that the person involved fully understand that civil divorce cannot destroy the marriage bonds. Some dioceses require that the applicant for divorce swear under oath before witnesses that he or she is initiating the action only for civil purposes.

A grave reason must exist before Church authorities will approve a civil divorce application. For instance, the wife may require a court order to force her husband to contribute to her support in the form of alimony. A husband may need this protection against debts incurred by his wife.

Another requirement is that no element of scandal will be attached to the divorce action. The party to the proceedings must always make it plain, in discussing this action with friends, relatives or others, that it is taken solely for civil reasons. Catholics who obtain ecclesiastical permission to begin divorce proceedings must never give the impression to those either in or out of the Faith that their action represents any departure from Church teaching.

14

If Your Mate Is Not a Catholic

AS EVERY reader probably knows, the Church firmly opposes marriages between Catholics and non-Catholics. Her opposition is based upon centuries of experience—centuries in which she has seen a large percentage of such mixed marriages end unhappily, with many Catholic partners and their children lost to the Faith. Despite her constant warnings, however, about three out of every ten Catholics married by a priest in any given year marry non-Catholics. The greater tragedy is that a large proportion of all mixed marriages, approximately forty per cent, are invalidly contracted outside the Church, with little hope that many of these Catholic partners will ever be restored to the sacraments. We can only pray that God will be merciful to them on their deathbed.

Statistics also show why the Catholic in a mixed marriage must work diligently to maintain his faith. An investigation by the Bishop's Committee on Mixed Marriages has revealed that one of every three Catholics in a valid mixed marriage later stops practicing his religion. We have also seen that four out of ten Catholics in mixed marriages automatically leave the Faith by marrying outside the Church. Thus, of every ten Catholics in mixed marriages (valid and invalid combined) six ultimately turn away from the Church in some important respect. Even though Catholic women enter mixed marriages more often, the Church is particularly concerned when the Catholic party is the husband. In such mixed marriages, the apostasy of parents and children is substantially higher.

Catholics and non-Catholics living together in an interfaith union have other differences to encounter besides religion. It is these other differences that breed conflict and make the divorce rates of mixed marriages so high. Different religions breed different cultures and the different cultures form different attitudes in the people growing up under them. How does one amicably decide questions of sex relations, having or not having children, Catholic versus public education, contraception, abortion, whether or not the wife should work, who is the head of the house—in the absence of common attitudes on the principles involved? Perhaps the mixed couple married outside the Church think they have solved the problem by ignoring the Church. However, even bad Catholics and bad Protestants have the uncanny knack of standing up for their family traditions in a real pinch. The apostate Catholic wife who wants the baby named John instead of Stanhope reflects the tradition that Catholic children carry the name of a saint. In the valid mixed marriage, where there was outwardly some agreement on basic principles, where the non-Catholic acquiesced to the proposition that his home would be a Catholic home, human problems are bound to arise. He may have given in grudgingly and will in practice concede the minimum. The children will be Catholic, but there will be no Catholic education for them, no statues in the home, no family prayer, no discussion of religion, birth control in some shape or form. If he is generous and well-meaning, he frequently finds himself a stranger in his own home. He cannot receive Communion with his own daughter. His wife discusses important matters with the children surreptitiously and behind closed doors. As one excellent Protestant wife put it: "The non-Catholic party is expected to make concessions at every turn of the road with rarely a concession in return." This calls for heroism and heroes are few.

If we bypass the greater intensity of the sex problem or the in-law problem heightened by the mixed marriage relationship, it is only to stress that the most obvious obstacle to happiness in a mixed marriage is the children, their bearing and their rearing. Landis, the sociologist, believes that half of the conflict in mixed marriages arises over the training of children. The high rate of childlessness and small families among mixed marriage couples is one of the great evidences of such stirring conflict. The real losers, of course, are the children, but the couple loses, too.

Later we will discuss how the couple should attempt to solve these disagreements. The religious problems in the mixed marriage deserve our first consideration.

If you are a Catholic in a mixed marriage you must intensify your faith by daily prayer, frequent reception of the sacraments, by consulting your confessor regularly for guidance in the special problems of your marriage, and by readings that will deepen your appreciation of Catholicism. You must also have the knowledge to defend your religion. The typical non-Catholic partner—even one tolerantly disposed toward the Church—often has misunderstandings and misgivings about Catholic doctrines. He may be unable to understand why you must confess your sins to a priest. Because of what he was taught in childhood, he may even suspect that there is something sinister about the sacrament of penance. Unless you have proper information that enables you to explain why you believe as you do, you may not only be unable to convince him that Christ instituted the practice of confession; perhaps you will doubt it yourself.

Secondly, you must double your efforts to rear your children as Catholics. This is not an easy task. Although the non-Catholic in a valid marriage has promised to rear the children in the Faith, these promises are not always kept. Studies have established that forty per cent of all children born to mixed marriages are either unbaptized, baptized in a Protestant sect, or baptized in the Catholic faith but given no Catholic training after that time. The Bishop's Study on Mixed Marriages reveals that promises were not kept in about thirty per cent of the *valid* interfaith marriages. The losses from invalid mixed marriages is even more shocking.

Even when the promises are kept, the nonbelieving husband (or wife) may remain indifferent, if not hostile, to your efforts to rear the children as Catholics. Example is always the best teacher, and it is difficult for a child to believe that he must attend Mass every Sunday, frequent the sacraments, abstain from meat on Fridays and say his morning and night prayers, when his father (or mother) does none of those things. In one home, a non-Catholic conscientiously tried to fulfill his promise that his children would be reared as Catholics. Every Sunday morning he helped dress the children so that they could attend Mass with their mother, but he remained at home to read the newspaper. When his son reached the age of fourteen, he too insisted that he should stay home on Sunday. If Dad could do it, why couldn't he?

• • For your own spiritual welfare, as well as the welfare of your children and your spouse, keep before you the prospect of converting him to Catholicism. Priests often find that the Catholic mate adopts an indifferent attitude; as a result, only about three per cent of the non-Catholic partners enter the Church after the marriage ceremony is performed. Everywhere, however, there is evidence that the nonbelieving partner often wants to become a Catholic. He must overcome emotional and intellectual blocks of various kinds, but if you give him understanding and encouragement, he often will be disposed to take instructions in the fundamentals of the Faith.

The non-Catholic spouse sometimes uses various ways to hide his intense longing to believe. He may start discussions about religion in which he takes an anti-Catholic stand. He may ridicule your religious practices and criticize your frequent attendance at Mass and other devotions. If you take him at face value, you may fail to recognize his quest for faith that lies beneath the surface. Never respond in anger or by making religion a subject that cannot be discussed in your home. You can profit from the case of a Catholic wife who asked a priest to advise her how to handle her husband who, she said, had developed an undying hatred of the Church.

"He never misses a chance to ridicule the Church," she said. "When my son goes to confession, my husband questions him sharply. When my son and I leave for Mass, my husband makes sarcastic remarks. On days of abstinence, he always comments on the absence of meat from our plates."

The priest advised the wife to accept her husband's taunts without comment, and to respond pleasantly whenever he raised questions about the Faith. Some time later, the priest met the husband and had a long chat. The man made frequent, friendly comments about Catholicism. Finally the priest commented, "Your remarks surprise me. I had the impression that you were antagonistic toward the Church."

"Oh, my wife and son tell everybody that," the man replied. "I like to kid them about religion, because they're alike—neither has a sense of humor."

The priest next asked, "Why don't you take instructions to see whether you might not want to join the Church?"

"That's a thought," the man replied. "Nobody ever asked me before."

For fifteen years he had been outside the fold, desperately wanting to enter. He was prevented from doing so mainly because his wife failed to realize that his gruff exterior hid a deep desire to participate in his family's religious life. A few months after his talk with the priest, he was baptized.

As a Catholic, you believe that possession of the Holy Faith is the greatest gift that can be bestowed upon humans. Therefore you cannot be indifferent to your mate's lack of it. For if you wish the best for him, you must wish that he receive the gift of faith. But while you cannot be indifferent to his spiritual welfare, you should not be a crusader who is determined to drag him into the Church. He must will to become a Catholic for his own sanctification. You cannot high-pressure him. You can let him know, however, that you will help him in any way possible to learn more about the teachings and practices of Catholicism.

How can you encourage your spouse to take a more active interest in the Church? There are four basic ways:

By prayer and example. St. Paul tells us, "The unbelieving husband is sanctified by the believing wife, and the unbelieving wife is sanctified by the believing husband." (1 Corinthians, 7:14) The Catholic who leads a virtuous life can call blessings down from heaven upon her mate. Her prayers will not only enlist the help of heaven, but will also enable her to regard her husband with greater kindness. Recognizing the virtue of hope, she will continue to pray for him even if he seems to reject any thought of conversion outright.

The power of example can hardly be overestimated. No loving husband can long remain unmoved when he observes the fruits of faith in his wife's life. The typical nonbeliever has a "show me" attitude; he is less impressed by your frequent attendance at Mass and reception of the sacraments than by what your beliefs do for you—by the virtues of patience, humility, self-sacrifice, kindness and forgiveness that your faith gives you. The nonbeliever will accept the truths of religion only as he sees how their application enriches your spiritual life. Here is the area in which the Catholic pays for compromises made over birth control, the Catholic education of children, participation in parish activity, and family religious ritual. The prospective convert is usually married to a convinced and consistent Catholic.

By exposing him to the faith. The adage, "You hate and fear only what you don't know," applies to religion as well as to other aspects of life. Invite him to participate in parish social activities and to take an active part in the P.T.A. if your children attend Catholic schools. Some non-Catholics have been taught from childhood that priests are ogres. Introducing your husband to your pastor or other parish priests should help dispel this notion. Many parishes now conduct annual Cana Conferences in which the problems of Catholic married life are discussed and to which non-Catholics are invited on an equal footing with their Catholic spouses. Parish social affairs are good opportunities for him to learn to be at ease with priests and Catholic laymen. Many informal contacts with priests have helped remove prejudice against the Church and prepared the way for serious discussion of conversion. Invite him to attend, assuring him that his own religious beliefs will be respected. Subscribe to at least one Catholic newspaper or magazine so that he may read about the faith as he chooses.

By identifying him with yourself and the family at periods of religious observance. One of the worst hazards of a mixed marriage is that it separates husband and wife at those intimate moments of family life when they should be fully united: when the baby is born and baptized, when he receives his First Communion and is confirmed, when there is a death of a parent or relative, and on Christmas, Easter and other feast days. Husband and wife should be able to attend church together, to pray together, and to share their moments of great joy and sorrow as a complete family unit. Unfortunately, in many mixed marriages, the Catholic partner tends to isolate her husband from herself and the children at these moments. Even if she does not deliberately close him out, he is aware that he is not a part of the family at the very time when he should be present.

Always encourage your non-Catholic partner to join the family's religious observances. Instead of going separate ways on Christmas and Easter morning, urge him to attend Mass with you and the children. Ask him to listen to his child's catechism answers as the youngster prepares for his First Communion. Almost any husband will feel a closer bond with his children, if he attends the Masses at which their First Communions are received. He might also be encouraged to say their night prayers with them. Ask him to join in singing carols with the family in preparation for the birth of Christ. Other occasions when your non-Catholic mate could join in your religious observances will undoubtedly come to mind. Because he refused a first request is no reason to believe he will refuse a second, or that a more favorable disposition cannot be acquired with the passing of years.

By encouraging him to take instructions. Before permitting a non-Catholic to be married in the Church, many dioceses now require that he be instructed in Catholic doctrines covering marriage. These instructions are necessarily limited. The non-Catholic frequently does not realize that our position is solidly based upon the bedrock of Scripture and tradition. He obtains merely a bare glimpse into the truth and sanctity of the Faith.

He should be encouraged to learn more about Catholicism, if only for the minimum reason that he will then understand why you must confess your sins, attend Mass, obey the rules of the Church regarding fast and abstinence, and perform other religious duties. He should also know the basic teachings of the Church so that he may sometimes help in educating the children.

Many dioceses conduct classes of instructions for non-Catholics. Your husband (or wife) can attend these courses as one of a group of non-Catholics. He can express his doubts freely. He will not be forced to reach any conclusions except those dictated by his own judgment.

Nonbelievers are often surprised at the complete absence of "salesmanship" at these courses. They are told that the Church demands a complete investigation of her teachings and does not wish anyone to be baptized unless he believes them fully, sincerely and without reservation. The Church does not want him unless he first wants the Church. It is one thing to be morally convinced of the truth of the Faith or to admire the Church, and another thing to take steps toward baptism. Most people, even if they have no religious faith of their own (and many of those who marry Catholics are not active in their own religions), are tied to family traditions or molded by strict parental attitudes and youthful experiences which make them wary of Catholicism. Serious consideration of the Church is to them tantamount to rejection of people and ways to which they are sentimentally attached. Hence, formal instruction is the last thing they will consider. Sometimes, however, they are not averse to informal discussion of religious matters in their own home. Such contacts have often helped the non-Catholic to get the feel of things Catholic. Silence on religion in the home or isolation from Catholic neighbors is one certain way to confirm a non-Catholic in his indifference to conversion. Your spouse, therefore, may need your gentle encouragement and patient support to help him overcome emotional barriers that may stand between him and his full acceptance of Catholicism.

By joining with you and your children in your spiritual life, your husband will not only gain the benefits of the Faith for himself but will have the satisfaction of contributing to the spiritual welfare of his wife and children. In this atmosphere of shared religious experience, his sense of oneness with you will thrive.

15

Your Privilege of Parenthood

IF YOU constantly keep in mind the origin of the word "matrimony," you will have a clear understanding of your vocation as married man or woman: your primary job is to perform the function of parenthood.

In the first chapter of Genesis, the first book of the Bible, it is recorded that God created man and woman for parenthood. The Bible states:

"And God created man to His own image: To the image of God He created him: Male and female, He created them. And God blessed them saying: Increase and multiply and fill the earth." (Genesis, 1:27–28)

Man takes too much for granted the magnificent power which God has given him to reproduce human life. Every parent receives a gift far surpassing any other that humans may possess. For example, when the great Michelangelo completed his magnificent statue of Moses, he was so impressed with its lifelike nature that he threw his hammer at it and commanded: "Speak!" Of course, this creation of one of the most gifted of all men remained mute. As a parent, however, you are a creative artist who can produce an actual human being.

Great as is the privilege of bearing children, it is only a small part of your total privilege of parenthood. You are your child's first and most important teacher—the means through which he will learn how to live on earth and to prepare for his lifetime in eternity. As Pope Pius XI taught us, "God wishes men to be born not only that they should live and fill the earth, but much more that they may be worshipers of God, that they may know Him and love Him and finally enjoy Him forever in heaven." It is obvious then that your work really begins only when your baby is born. Your home becomes a miniature church; your function is to teach, rule, and sanctify in Christ's name. Never underestimate your power. You are the most important influence your child will ever know.

The pleasures of parenthood: In our materialistic age, emphasis is often placed upon sacrifices which parents must make to care properly for their children. Persons with a "birth-control mentality" stress that the family with more than a token number of children often must live in an older home in a less exclusive section; must drive an old car that lacks up-to-date conveniences; must patch up and wear clothing that richer people might discard. Obviously, having children involves sacrifices. But the proponents of contraception ignore the truth that the joys of bearing and caring for children far outweigh the disadvantages.

Parenthood is the normal state for a married man and woman. The child is the natural fruit of their love for each other. Moreover, the desire to procreate is inborn. Even in pagan countries, the man who dies without a son and heir is an object of pity; the woman who cannot produce a child is cast away.

In your children, you will find your own happiness. As we have seen, true love can blossom only in a spirit of self-sacrifice and in a willingness to forego selfish objectives for the sake of another human being. In performing your duties of parenthood, you perfect yourself in self-sacrifice and therefore in love. But your sacrifices are like bread cast upon the waters; they return to enrich your life a hundredfold. For children are a pleasure in themselves, a source of comfort and consolation.

Consider the home filled with happy children at Christmas; compare it with one in which the sound of childish laughter is not heard.

Your children give you a worthy goal to work for in marriage. Like the gardener tending rare seedlings in his garden, you watch each stage in your child's development with amazement. You see results today of your efforts of weeks or months ago, and you are encouraged to look ahead to a further blossoming a few months from now. The process of growth continues in a pattern that never ceases to delight and inspire you. The infant who has just learned to gurgle and coo now becomes the toddler taking his first step into a strange new world; soon he asks his first innocent questions about God and life; then he sits by your side, his first reader in his hands. You see him at the altar rail as a first communicant, then with his school diploma. He undertakes his first job; soon he is no longer your dependent son, but a bright-eyed, mature bridegroom. In all of these many stages, you as a parent can feel an unparalleled joy in the part you have played in developing this greatest of all God's creatures—a life more precious than the most exquisite flower ever grown, more beautiful in God's sight than the greatest painting, more inspiring than the most complex machine.

You need only consider divorce statistics to realize that children give stability and happiness to marriage. Almost three-fourths of all divorces are granted to childless couples, most of whom doubtless deliberately rejected the privilege of parenthood because it interfered with their selfish pleasures. Yet in failing to recognize that true happiness comes from self-sacrifice and a worthy goal in marriage, they achieved not pleasure but pain. Forlorn indeed is the man or woman who reaches old age in loneliness, bereft of the consolation that children can give. Childlessness, not childbearing, is the real cross of marriage.

How many children? This question preoccupies couples today probably more than any other question related to their marriage. Actually in too many cases the question is: how few children? Now, while the marriage contract does not specify the number of children you should have and Church teaching merely reiterates for husbands and wives the Scriptural command, "Increase and multiply," many factors enter into the determination of family size. However, the Catholic family which emphasizes God's purposes in creating marriage and which brings God's graces to devoted husbands and wives should by modern standards be relatively large. Something is definitely wrong when the best that the average American couple can do over a fertile period of twenty-five years is to give only two or three children to the Kingdom of God. In some situations, as we have seen, family limitation is permissible and may indeed be desirable. Yet this should be the exception rather than the rule, and for good cause, not just to be fashionable. We know, too, that God's Providence may determine no birth or only a few births. For the most part, however, considering the normal fertility of young people, the average couple ought to be more productive than they presently are.

The large family: Most of us who were born into large families, and poor families at that, are rather proud of our parents for the work they did on our behalf and are quite happy with our many brothers and sisters. All available evidence proves what we know from personal experience that large families—those of five or more children—are generally happier than small families. They are better for parents, better for the children, better for society.

Because the parents always lived by the conviction that their main job was parenthood, they were never distracted by outside interests which often destroy the unity of marriage. The typical parents in a large family are dedicated and selfless people, and most often deeply religious. As the family increases they become tolerant and broad-minded in their treatment of their children. They are not bothered by annoying but transient habits of children which often disconcert parents who have no one else with whom to compare their only child. These fathers and mothers learn to concentrate on important things; they lack the time to worry needlessly over their children. Because they often must forego material possessions, they tend to develop spiritual values instead. As one father commented, "The formula for maintaining a large family on a small income is to learn how to do without things that don't really matter." Thus parents of large families are encouraged to focus sharply on the true, lasting values of life. And as they grow old they are unquestionably gratified by the love, affection, companionship and, when needed, care they receive from their many children. It is a wonderful thing to see how many children keep up the practice of having anniversary and memorial Masses said for their parents, sometimes thirty and forty years after they departed this earth, a prospect which is not equally to be expected by the parents of an only child.

The benefits to a child in a large family are undeniable. He learns how to live amicably with other people—a lesson many youngsters without brothers or sisters never learn until they painfully try to adjust to a partner in marriage. He is trained to work, play and pray with others. He learns to share. He must listen as well as talk. He must respect others' property and rights; if he does not do so, his brothers and sisters have proper ways of dealing with him. He learns quickly that he must give in order to take.

Because his parents are too busy to worry over all his little problems, he soon learns to accept responsibility for his own actions—probably the most important factor in making a mature person. He has more freedom to develop in his own way. But he also learns that rules must be made and observed without favoritism. In teaching him to accept regulations for the common good and to live with both sexes and assorted ages and personalities, the large-family system provides the perfect background to help him take his place as a respectable, law-abiding and well-adjusted member of society.

Parents of large families ought, perhaps, be cautioned to safeguard against certain dangers. They must not place excessive responsibility upon their first-born children and, by exploiting them, deny them the normal pleasures of youth. All the children must learn to share in the responsibilities of the home. Favoritism by one or both parents may create enduring resentment on the part of the overworked ones. Parents should also carefully instill the knowledge that the sacrifices necessary in a large family are made from choice. When children realize that their parents forego material luxuries to support a new life, they regard their poverty as a badge of honor and not of shame.

While death, unemployment, or prolonged illness of the father may provoke an economic crisis and cause serious hardships for the large family, this danger is not so great as it once was. Health and unemployment insurance and other systems of aid to the needy have become so well-established that few families now can be said to live in actual want.

Disadvantages that may exist in large families are by no means as damaging as those in the small family of from one to three children. When parents consciously choose the small family as their way of life, they are often expressing their ambition for material luxury as opposed to the spiritual pleasures which child rearing can give. Mothers of an only child are traditionally those who give him no opportunity to develop under his own power. They follow him about, constantly warning him about getting hurt on the playground, worrying unduly about the influence of his companions, checking every activity of his school and teacher. Every crisis of the child becomes a crisis for the parent. It is no coincidence that the "spoiled little brat"—the selfish monster of popular fiction and newspaper comic strips—is usually an only child.

What do your children need? A child does not ask much from you. First, of course, he depends upon you to satisfy his physical needs—to keep him fed, clothed and sheltered and to obtain medical treatment in his illnesses. He asks only for simple care; he does not require fancy foods, elaborate cribs, lace underclothes.

His basic spiritual and emotional needs are equally simple. Billions of words have been written to advise parents how to rear their children. Much of this advice is helpful. Some, however, is confusing—and parents who conscientiously read the material available on this subject may become overwhelmed by the seeming demands of their job. Relax! For thousands of years, children have been taught to lead good and holy lives without benefit of minutely detailed professional advice. Evidence strongly suggests that parents with a clear understanding of their basic obligations and their children's basic needs can do a thoroughly successful job.

Let us consider what your child requires to lead a happy life of service to God and his fellow-men. You will find that his needs fall into three classifications.

He needs recognition. As we noted earlier, many important elements in your child's personality are determined at the moment of conception. Neither the mother nor father has anything to say about the child's sex; whether your offspring will be a boy or girl is completely beyond human control. Perhaps you wished for a boy but had a girl. Like some parents in similar situations, you could seek to prevent her from developing feminine qualities. You could try to force her to develop athletic skills—to run as fast as a boy, climb trees, dive from the high board. In doing so, you would be refusing to accept her for what she is; you would be denying her her rightful recognition as a female.

A prematurely gray, prematurely bent young man of thirty shuffles along Skid Row in Chicago because of his parents' failure to value him for himself. His father, a lawyer, had built a highly profitable practice which he was determined to pass on to his son. The boy early displayed an ability in art, but had no interest in following his father's steps. The determined father nevertheless forced the boy to attend schools unsuited to his basic interests. The son finally rebelled, left college and enrolled in art school, where he was thoroughly happy. The father disinherited the boy in a rage and refused to have anything further to do with him. Unable to pay for further schooling and untrained to work, the young man became a derelict. His life was literally ruined by his father's refusal to recognize him as an individual entitled to his own honest aspirations.

Of course, this is an extreme case. Few fathers—certainly no father with a Christian concept of charity—would act in such a way. Yet, if you analyze your actions, you may find that you try to impress your own ambitions upon your child in less obvious ways. In one family, the first child is an excellent scholar. He has a high native intelligence. The second child is less bright, simply because he received less intelligence from God. These youngsters' parents are highly intelligent themselves and have high ambitions for their children. They constantly applaud the one child's high scholastic achievements and berate the other for pulling down the family's average. They do not realize that they are refusing their less bright child recognition as an individual, and are imposing unfair standards upon him.

They are trying to make him into something nature has not intended him to be.

To give your child recognition, remember that he has specific inborn traits. You may be justly proud of your scholarship winner, and perhaps you have helped him develop his ability to study. But in most cases, his scholarship results from his native intelligence—an accident of birth. He might also have been born with subnormal intelligence. Many of a child's qualities are more a part of him than his height and weight. One is naturally sociable and enjoys companionship and affection. Another is active, aggressive and dominating. A third is shy, oversensitive and restrained. To a certain extent you can control these characteristics; in fact, you must do so when they show signs of leading to antisocial habits. For example, the child who is dominating by nature must not be permitted to push around youngsters smaller or more submissive than he. But your chances of changing a dominating child into a passive one are nil—unless you destroy the child's personality as well. You must accept your youngster for what he is.

When you give your child this acceptance as an individual, your home can be freed of many tensions. You realize that you cannot stand over him and dictate every action. You permit him to develop in his own ways—to do what comes naturally—and thus to grow as an individual. By developing his God-given talents and qualities of personality, he will achieve greater happiness in life. He will be himself—the person God intended him to be—and not a pallid carbon copy of his mother or father.

He needs affection. He must know that you want him and love him. The child denied love may be more underprivileged than one denied food or clothing—a fact which many parents overlook. An illustration of this is the story of a baby born to wealthy parents not long ago. The father was a successful investment banker; the mother, a figure in New York society. They had a town house in New York, a fashionable summer home in Rhode Island, a winter home in Florida. A few servants accompanied them wherever they went.

The wife gave birth to the baby and two weeks later began a "recuperation cruise" to the Caribbean, while the infant remained behind in a nurse's care. When the mother returned, she found the baby seriously ailing. The nurse reported that many different formulas had been tried without success. Finally the mother called her old family doctor. When he heard the full story, he told her tartly, "You have tried everything but the most important treatment. Your baby is starved for love."

She was instructed to hold the infant at feeding times and to fondle it between feedings. Within a short time, the baby's digestion improved, his restlessness stopped, and he began to thrive.

We human beings need love not only in infancy but throughout our lives. Kind and encouraging words, affectionate smiles —these tell us that we are considered worthy individuals. Such things are important to adults, but even more so to the growing child who is feeling his way. As he meets new situations in his expanding world, he desperately needs assurance that he does the correct things; or, if they are not correct, that you will teach him the right way of doing them. He is unsure of himself; he needs to hold your experienced hand so that you can guide him. When he errs, his very growth as a human being demands that you will be standing by his side to help him and will continue to love him.

Psychiatrists find that many personality disorders which become severe in adulthood often originate in infancy and childhood and result from a lack of love. The psychiatrists explain that their patients often had parents who did not want them, perhaps for reasons the parents did not even recognize. If they were contraception-minded, they may have resented the infant's coming because he forced them to spend money on his care which they might otherwise have used for pleasure. Children who are not truly loved usually have parents who are overrestrictive, overprotective or perfectionist.

Overrestrictive parents handle their child like an army recruit. They set down orders which he must follow blindly. They permit no deviation. The child who does not respond to their orders instantly is severely punished. Such parents lack human compassion and often produce children who are either cowed and fearful all their lives, or who rebel against and reject all authority.

Overprotective parents deny their child his normal right to develop his own powers. Although the child is normally healthy, he cannot run on the street because his mother fears that he may fall. He cannot walk to school by himself; his mother must either drive him or walk with him to make sure that no harm befalls him. He sets his eyes on an expensive toy beyond his parents' means; rather than see the little one disappointed, the father digs into his pocket. Parents who save their children from normal knocks and disappointments prevent them from acquiring the self-confidence they need to become independent men and women.

Perfectionist parents are never satisfied with their child. They often maintain a spotless home where the child would not dare leave a toy in the living room. They sharply criticize him when he returns from play with dirty hands. If he stands third in his class, they want to know why he is not first, and they will not rest until he achieves the top position. True, children need, and respond to, inspiration. But perfectionist parents make no allowances for human frailty and shortcomings. They demand more than the child can humanly be expected to give.

He needs direction. How your child lives—not only in his early years but also as a grownup—will largely depend upon you. From your example and teachings he will acquire his attitudes toward God and religion. He will learn how to get along with other people, how to deal with members of his own and the opposite sex. You will affect his sense of charity and justice, his manners at table, and thousands of other attributes that will make up his whole personality.

That the broad outlines of your child's life are drawn in his preschool years when he is almost wholly under your influence is a commonly accepted truth. An old saying attributed to the Jesuits is that if they could have the first six years to influence a child's life, they would not care who had the rest. Gilbert K. Chesterton commented humorously that a child is not sent to school until it is too late to teach him anything. The poet Alexander Pope remarked that "Just as the twig is bent the tree's inclined." John Milton wrote: "The childhood shows the man, as morning shows the day."

You will direct your child's steps by example, teaching and

discipline. Without doubt, the power of example is the most forceful. "Deeds," said the poet Longfellow, "are better things than words are." You can see striking evidence of this everywhere.

The three children of one family were sent to parochial school, where they were taught to attend Mass each Sunday and receive the sacraments frequently. The parents sent the youngsters to the "Children's Mass" and then climbed back into bed. When the children reached high-school age, all began missing Mass regularly.

A father preached honesty to his thirteen-year-old son. But when they attended movies together, the father paid only half price for the boy by representing that he was under twelve. If a shop clerk erred in the father's favor when computing a bill, the father boasted later about how he had "put one over." He also developed a way to bypass the electric meter so that he could use the utility company's current without charge. But when the son was caught breaking into a candy store, the father insisted that he had taught the boy not to steal.

A mother of three small children chronically complained about the amount of work she was obliged to do. She made it plain to her children that she considered motherhood a necessary evil, not a privilege and pleasure. Her daughter married and immediately practiced contraception. The mother was shocked: hadn't she told her daughter that artificial birth control was wrong?

Many research projects by social scientists have proved the dramatic relationship between what you as a parent practice (not what you preach) and what your child practices. Do you want your boy to aspire to a college education? Research shows that he will probably want to go if he sees you enjoying good books, magazines, music—the fruits of education. Do you want your child to practice moderation in drink? Of college students who do not drink at all, the higher percentage have teetotaler parents. Most persons who drink moderately have seen the example in their own home, and a high percentage of problem drinkers have seen their parents drink to excess. Sanctity runs in families as does delinquency—and it is the power of example which influences both.

You should direct your child to achieve two goals: the salvation of his soul, which, as the catechism tells us, is his basic purpose on earth; and the attainment of earthly happiness. If you analyze how these goals may best be attained, you will appreciate the importance of Catholic schooling for your children.

As Pope Leo XIII wrote: "It is of the highest importance that the offspring of Christian marriages should be thoroughly instructed in the precepts of religion; and that the various studies by which youth is fitted for the world should be joined with that of religion. To divorce these is to wish that youth should be neutral as regards its duties to God; a system of education in itself fallacious, and particularly fatal in tender years; for it opens the door to atheism, and closes it on religion. Christian parents must therefore be careful that their children receive religious instruction as soon as they are capable of understanding it; and that nothing may, in the schools they attend, blemish their faith or their morals. Both the natural and divine law impose this duty on them, nor can parents on any grounds whatever be free from this obligation." When Catholic schooling is available in your community, you are obliged to take advantage of it.

When the moral training you provide at home is reinforced by the school, your child will gain a true and secure outlook on life. He will be helped in his choice of vocation, because he will be made to realize that he can serve God and man in this life and achieve his eternal salvation either as a religious, as a married person or in the single state. You, of course, can help him choose his vocation. Bear in mind that the idealists, those motivated by desire to serve others, and not by hope of great material gains, achieve life's greatest satisfactions.

Parents have a special responsibility to provide that kind of home atmosphere in which religious vocations may flourish. Pope Pius XI said: "The first and most natural place where the flowers of the sanctuary should almost spontaneously grow and bloom, remains always the truly and deeply Christian family." Most of the priests and religious in the Church owe the beginning of their vocation to the example and devotion of their parents and to the family in which the love of God reigned supreme.

Catholic parents should tell their children that a religious vocation in the family is a signal honor and a sign of God's blessing on the home. If they speak always of priests and sisters with respect, the children themselves will quickly learn to revere the religious way of life. If, out of their concern for the work of Mother Church and in appreciation for the work done by priests and nuns in their behalf, they recite in the family gatherings a prayer for the increase of vocations to the religious life, they will certainly be pleasing Almighty God and awakening the minds of their young to the beauty of His service.

Parents must never interfere with the natural right of their children to choose the religious way of life. This will rarely be done crudely or openly. But selfish parents sometimes criticize the religious life unjustly or tie the apron strings tighter or set up other obstacles to deflect the mind of the son or daughter away from the Church. Not every altar boy who says he wants to be a priest will see ordination. In God's own time most of these youngsters will find that their real vocation is to the married state. But no Catholic parent should be responsible for snuffing out the spark of a religious vocation. On the contrary, he should be pleased that his child is noble enough to entertain these aspirations. There is often more resistance manifested to daughters contemplating convent life. The modern world seems to picture the life of a nun in somber colors. Those of us who know nuns realize that they are the happiest women on earth. This worldly reluctance, therefore, to encourage a daughter to become a religious, should never color the mind of a Catholic father or mother. Remember, too, your children will be alive long after you are dead, and if you love them truly, you will want them happy in the life of their own choosing, rather than frustrated in an existence which they realize too late was not intended for them. For the same reason, parents should be careful not to exercise undue pressure on their children in the direction of religion, when there is no discernible calling from God for that life.

Furthermore, you will find it easier to provide your child's sex education within the proper framework when he attends a Catholic school. Public, nonsectarian schools often teach the fundamentals of sex to impressionable children in coeducational classes. Such classes often completely disregard the spiritual aspect of the sexual act and have often proved to be incitements to immorality. Youngsters obtain intimate facts about sex without the spiritual guidance they need to resist temptation. They are encouraged to regard the beautiful act of married love not as one with its primary basis in the heart but rather as one that begins and ends in the flesh. Out of such an environment comes the increasingly prevalent view that the act of intercourse can be separated not only from morality, but also from marriage itself.

In instructing your child in this subject, you should impress upon him that the gift of procreation is one which God reserved for married persons to be used in accordance with His plans. Your approach to sex should be both realistic and reverent. Your child should realize that the organs of reproduction are necessary for the fulfillment of God's plans for mankind; that their use in marriage is an inspiring, noble act, and not a degrading one; and that his respect for God, for parenthood, and for himself makes it necessary that sex be used only within the sacramental framework of marriage. The teaching your child receives at a Catholic school emphasizes the same principles, hence reinforces your own teaching.

By enrolling your child in Catholic institutions, you will also make it easier for him to marry within the Faith and to avoid the dangers of mixed marriages, for a high percentage of partners in mixed marriages first met and dated in coeducational, public high schools. In a typical case, the dating started without serious intentions. The Protestant boy and the Catholic girl were good dancers and enjoyed each other's company. On their first date, they would have ridiculed any suggestion that they might marry some day; like most young people, they overlooked the fact that marriages usually develop from just such innocent dates. Soon, however, the young man and woman were "in love." In their view now, no barrier was important enough to stand between them. After graduation, they were married; after a few years of endless conflict over religious differences, they were divorced. This permanent blight upon the lives of both young persons—the non-Catholic and the Catholic—might have been avoided if the girl had attended a Catholic school and, following custom, had cultivated friendships among boys of her own religion.

In directing your child to a life of right conduct, you must use discipline. Your authority over your child is most wisely exercised when you direct him firmly, but with love. Some instructions on training of the mind and the character have been given by Pope Pius XII. Speaking before a Concourse of Women of Catholic Action in 1941, the Pontiff said:

"Train the character of your children. Correct their faults, encourage and cultivate their good qualities and coordinate them with that stability which will make for resolution in after life. Your children, conscious as they grow up and as they begin to think and will, that they are guided by a good paternal will, constant and strong, free from violence and anger, not subject to weakness or inconsistency, will learn in time to see therein the interpreter of another and higher will, the will of God, and so they will plant in their souls the seeds of those moral habits which fashion and sustain a character, train it to self-control in moments of crises and to courage in the face of conflict or sacrifice, and imbue it with a deep sense of Christian duty."

Children need security. They achieve it best in a home governed by rules which tell them what they may and may not do. Many acts of misconduct are simply a child's way of trying to determine the limits of acceptable behavior. If he knows the rules, and realizes that you will enforce them, he will be much less inclined to behave incorrectly.

To discipline your child properly, you must be consistent. Many troubles with children stem from the inability of parents to follow a standard, expectable pattern. One day the children race through the house, yelling as loud as they can. Mother smiles indulgently. The next day, her mood has changed. When the children raise their voices, she screams at them to stop. The little minds are unable to grasp why an act tolerated one day provokes anger the next. They are confused and insecure. They have no consistent standards to guide them.

Your discipline should also be constructive. Its purpose must always be to instill proper behavior in your child—not to enable you to vent your anger. If a child makes a mistake, you should criticize his action, explaining precisely why it is important for him to correct his conduct. The purpose of discipline is to instruct; and since most childish offenses result from thoughtlessness rather than malice, you can best improve his conduct by telling him why his actions are wrong. You may find it necessary sometimes to punish your child physically to impress a lesson upon him, but you should try to make him understand clearly why you do so.

A major point to remember is that youngsters respond better to praise for good behavior than to constant criticism. Be appreciative of your child's efforts to improve himself. Remember that progress comes slowly, and that the mannerisms that annoy you today probably will be gone tomorrow. Your child will more easily achieve the standards you set if you inspire him by your affectionate guidance.

Your role as a father: The following incident actually happened in New York. A businessman had devoted all his life to building a profitable textile company. His work took him to all parts of the country and the world. Even when he was not traveling, he seldom saw his wife and son, for he devoted his evenings to office conferences. On weekends, he could usually be found entertaining customers on the golf course. He was an excellent provider, however. On the rare occasions when he spoke to his son, he stressed the importance of material success and emphasized the luxuries which his application to work made possible.

One morning, the man suffered a heart attack at his office. He was rushed to the hospital, where he died. His wife was at home when a business associate phoned to tell her the news. The woman put down the phone and went into the next room to inform the son.

The boy was stunned. Finally, after a moment's silence, he managed to speak. "Mother," he said, "does this mean we'll have to give up the Cadillac?"

This story typifies the role played by many twentieth-century American fathers. They are probably the world's most conscientious breadwinners. They work long hours and suffer ulcers bravely as the badge of their ambition to provide the "good things of life" for their wives and children. Unfortunately, they are often horrible fathers. For example, a group of 300 elementary-school boys was asked to keep accurate check on the amount of time their fathers spent exclusively with them. Records were maintained for two weeks, then tabulated. Results: each week, the average father had spent seven and one-half minutes alone with his son. Another significant study made at Catholic University, in Washington, uncovered the fact that only two freshmen in five understood the kind of work their fathers were doing.

Have fathers given up their traditional role as heads of the family and instead become mere boarders who provide the money for the family's luxuries? Evidence strongly suggests that the answer, in many cases at least, is yes. The typical American mother undeniably exerts more influence over her family today than at any time in our history. Often she is the undisputed boss—the person who makes major policy decisions for the family, who disciplines the children and establishes rules for their behavior, who always says the final word in household discussions. Too often, Father is exactly as he is depicted on television programs—the good-natured oaf who turns over his salary each pay period and relinquishes his rights over the children for the doubtful privilege of being allowed to read his newspaper in peace.

The power of the American father is declining at a time when juvenile delinquency is rising. This is more than a coincidence. Samuel S. Leibowitz, senior judge of Brooklyn's highest criminal court, has long watched with dismay the terrible trend in which more and more teen-agers are represented on the criminal dockets. Writing in *This Week* magazine, Judge Leibowitz stated that it seemed that something basic must have gone from our way of life to cause so many young people to revolt against society. So he decided to visit the country with the lowest rate of juvenile delinquency. That country is Italy, where only two per cent of all sex crimes and one-half of one per cent of all homicides are committed by children eighteen years old and younger. In the United States, corresponding figures are thirteen per cent and nine per cent. Judge Leibowitz toured Italian cities for several weeks, asking officials how they explained the difference. Everywhere he received one answer: youngsters in Italy respect authority.

"I went into Italian homes to see for myself," Judge Leibowitz wrote. "I found that even in the poorest families the father is respected by the wife and children as its head. He rules with various degrees of love and tenderness and firmness. His household has rules to live by, and the child who disobeys them is punished. Thus I found the nine-word principle that I think can do more for us than all the committees, ordinances, and multimillion-dollar programs combined: *Put father back at the head of the family.*"

You cannot do a proper job as a father unless you are the head of your house. As the begetter of the child, the protector of his mother and the provider of the household, you possess authority in a special way. God has given you a basically dominant nature, and your wife a basically submissive one; she wants you to rule and your children need your leadership, too, because you alone serve as their ambassador to the outside world.

More than that, you are God's representative before your family. You believe that God the Father is wise, just and merciful; in a human way, you must try to assume those qualities before your children. In their spiritual life, they know that they can always rely on their eternal Father; on a human level, they also need a father to whom they can look with confidence in his steady, unfailing guidance.

You will be a good father—one who brings his children to a happy, well-adjusted adulthood—if you focus on four fundamental principles.

1. *Make your children a part of your life.* Many modern husbands feel that their job is completed when they provide their children with material comforts. After commuting to and from work and striving for competitive advantage all day, they return home tense and weary. In many a home, the children are fed and put to bed early so that they will not disturb Daddy at the end of his day. He may leave for work before they arise in the morning and therefore may not see them for many days at a time.

In other generations, the children usually were aware of Father's headship, whether he was present or not. He was emotionally prepared to be a true father, because he had a clear idea of what a man should be; advanced, liberal thinkers preaching a false doctrine of exact equality of the sexes had not chipped away the foundations of his position. Moreover, he knew that he had to make sacrifices of time and energy to rear his children properly. This concept of personal duty to children has been diluted. It is not that today's fathers are less conscientious; in fact, in their desire to be good providers, to give their wives and children a good home environment and the comforts of modern living, they may be even more conscientious than their grandfathers. But their perspective has changed. They must relearn what parents of other generations knew: that fathers must give *themselves* to their children. Your personal presence, guidance and example are more important to your youngsters than any material gifts you can provide.

If you could visit a large and successful toy shop on Fifth Avenue, New York, you would see heart-wrenching evidence of this fact. Obviously well-to-do fathers patronize this shop with the little strangers who are their children. Cost is no deterrent as the youngsters choose huge dolls or Teddy bears. One might think that they would be supremely happy with their gifts. But they sense that they are being bribed to compensate for the fact that their fathers are normally too busy to give them personal love and attention. Compare this scene with one at the park, where a father teaches his boys to play football. Here there is genuine happiness, guidance and affection.

You can ask yourself many simple questions to help you judge whether you really make your children a part of your life. Do you spend time with each one, not as a stern judge but as a helpful, constructive teacher and friend? Do you recognize that laughter is as sunshine to a child and do you help yours to be happy in your presence? Do you treat them as individuals with personal feelings to be respected? Do you appear before them in a human light—do you ever admit that you too make mistakes? Do you show enough interest in their welfare to review their school lessons with them? Do you know and treat their friends with courteous respect? Do you take them on family trips? Do you encourage them to discuss their problems with you by listening with sympathy and understanding?

By living intimately with your children, you will gain new pride and pleasure at every stage of their growth. You will learn the age-old truth that the joys of true fatherhood far surpass any which success in the business world might bring.

2. *Inspire by example.* Your son will take a job some day,

perhaps marry and have children. He will face hundreds of problems which you handle in a routine way every day. He will have attitudes about his work, his boss, his companions in his shop or office. He will have ideas about the importance of religion, about disciplining of children and respect for authority. He may like certain foods and refuse to eat others. He may have a Christian respect for all races of men or he may not. He will literally have thousands of attitudes about every aspect of life.

Your daughter likewise will grow to womanhood. She will have definite ideas of what a husband should be; how he should display affection; the part he should play in maintaining the home; how he should discipline the children.

Your children have only one person from whom they can get those necessary ideas. That person is you.

Children are born imitators. One father always gestures with his hands when he talks; his eight-year-old does likewise. Another dad struts when he walks; behind him you invariably see a strutting youngster. A father talks from the side of his mouth and sprinkles every sentence with profanity; his son does likewise in talking to his friends in the fourth grade. It is no coincidence that the doctor's son often chooses medicine for a career, that the restaurant owner's son is so often eager to follow in his dad's footsteps, that the professor's son wants to be a teacher—or that the criminal's son so often becomes a juvenile delinquent. You cannot escape the enormous implications of the adage, "like father, like son."

3. *Do your part in disciplining the children.* Not all of the duties of parenthood are pleasant ones. At times your children must be corrected—perhaps even punished severely—to prevent the development of bad habits. Someone may have to force them to do their homework when they would rather look at television. Someone must see to it that they get to bed on time so as to be well rested for school the next day. Someone must prevent Brother from pulling Sister's hair or from raiding the refrigerator before dinner to eat the custard that was planned as the family's dessert.

That "someone" should be you at least part of the time, for your child is as much yours as he is your wife's. You must share equally in his discipline. Moreover, you and your wife must work together. Sometimes children play one parent against the other. If Mother says Johnny cannot watch television, he runs to Father; the latter then undermines her authority by telling Johnny he may watch. You and your wife should agree on the disciplinary action you will take; once you agree, it should be a joint act. The children must know that what Mother does has your complete support, and that your actions have her approval.

You should never seek to win first place in your child's affections by giving him things that his mother denies him. You should never refuse to shoulder authority by sending your youngsters to their mother for permission to do what they should not be allowed to do. And if you disagree with how your wife handles a disciplinary situation, never belittle her in the child's presence. If you have different ideas, thrash them out with her privately. Never let your child see anything but complete unity in your discipline.

4. *Be a leader, not a dictator.* In most cases, the father's loss of power in our modern society is an unfortunate condition which causes many grave social problems. In one respect, however, the increasing influence of mothers has been all to the good. The tyrannical father, the autocrat whose word was law and who permitted no disagreement from his wife or children is now going out of fashion.

Some Stalin-like fathers remain, however. They pound the table, set up laws for the family without consulting anyone, and demand rigid adherence to their rules with the threat of severe punishment for those who disobey. Their children literally live in terror of their wrath. The brutal, unyielding father often succeeds in breaking the spirit of his youngsters; they grow up cowed and submissive. Or they may react by rebelling against all authority.

As we have seen, children need their father's firm guidance. They need direction and discipline. But you should exercise your authority wisely. Have tolerance and compassion for your children, who are struggling to learn acceptable ways of behavior. Make your discipline reasonable; give your youngsters reasons why they are expected to act in certain ways. If they fail to conform, make certain that their punishment fits the offense; don't "make a federal case" out of a trivial shortcoming. Above all remember that the best way to win acceptable conduct from your child is through your patient, loving and kind explanation of why he should not do certain things.

Your role as a mother: Just as the husband is the head of the home, the wife is the heart. It is she who must make the main emotional contribution to her children and must supply the unfailing diet of love upon which they thrive.

Many modern women underestimate the importance of their job. Beguiled by the idea of their equality with men—if not their superiority to them—they have busied themselves with developing masculine characteristics. As we have seen, they have taken over many of the traditional duties of fathers and in doing so they have tended to dilute the emotional contribution they could make. Instead of the gentle, warmhearted, self-sacrificing mother of a few generations ago, we now often see a brisk, businesslike, semi-masculine woman who handles her children with much greater efficiency, perhaps, but with a corresponding lack of warm motherly qualities.

These qualities are more important to a child than any other. He may be given great intelligence; without the ability to love he will lead a life of bitterness and emptiness. On the other hand, he may be born with physical defects or may be below normal mentally—but if he is taught to love, he can lead a full and happy life.

How does a child learn to love? Most of all, he learns it in his mother's arms. The early years of a child's life, so important in every respect, are crucial as regards the development of his capacity to love. Psychologists tell us that the infant who is held tenderly and often, fed when he is hungry, and shown in other ways that he is loved, develops a feeling of confidence and trust in other people—the sense of security that is the foundation of love. On the other hand, children neglected in infancy may often acquire an unsureness—and a feeling of suspicion of others—that may last throughout their lifetimes.

Not many years ago, with the advent of formula feeding, there was fostered the myth that too much loving given to a young child might "spoil" him. We now know that the only child who is ever really spoiled is one whose mother hovers over him habitually, who is disappointed in him because he is not quite what she expected, or who continually worries because she is not a perfect mother.

The good mother accepts her child as he is. Perhaps she has dreamed that he will be brilliant and handsome, and he is merely ordinary; but she accepts him with gratitude. She knows that this is the child God intended her to have. She might have preferred one who sat quietly, never disturbed the household with his noise nor dragged mud onto her floors from the street. But she knows she must bestow equal love upon the nervous youngster who cannot sit still and who makes constant demands upon her.

Many mothers worry excessively over whether they are doing the "right thing" for their child. They usually try to do too much. When they fail to obtain perfect results either from themselves or the child, they accuse themselves of failure and assume a hopeless attitude. Remember that it is human to err. Your parents made mistakes in your upbringing, no doubt, and their parents did not achieve perfection either. Rather than permit yourself to be filled with remorse after your mistakes, ask for God's grace to enable you to discover where your action was wrong and what you can do to prevent a recurrence.

The greatest danger you risk as a mother is that of overprotecting your child. At first thought, your love would seem to impel you from preventing any harm, however slight, from coming to him. Because you love him, you might assume that you should prevent him from running with other youngsters, lest he fall and injure himself; that you should buy whatever toys he desires, lest he cry from frustration; that you should not discipline him for fear that his personality might thus be damaged. On second thought, however, you will realize that your love should direct you to prepare him in the best possible way for adulthood. And to act as a mature adult, he must sometimes be hurt; he must not always have his own way; he must be prepared to pay a penalty if he does not abide by society's rules.

Overprotection sometimes results when there is too much contact between mother and child—when the child is the only one in the family, for example, or when the father is dead or away from home much of the time. It usually exerts a deadly effect. The boy or girl reaches adulthood and finds it difficult to make normal decisions without help; there is often a pathetic inability to meet the ordinary problems of life; selfishness and lack of courtesy and consideration are marked character defects.

Some mothers often will do a better job if they can rid themselves of another common fault—repression. The repressed mother is usually the one who herself has been denied love by her parents. She finds it difficult to express herself emotionally. She would like to pet and fondle her child and to display affection in other ways. But her own childhood home had such a Spartan atmosphere that such manifestations were not permitted; she has never learned to express the love she feels. Children need physical expressions of their parents' love for them; they tend to express themselves with complete candor, and if their parents do not reply in kind, they may feel a sense of rejection. Sometimes it requires courage for a parent who has spent a lifetime of keeping her feelings repressed to let herself go and to express her love. She may express herself awkwardly at first but gradually her rigidity will disappear. And she will have destroyed a barrier that could always stand between her and her children.

Recently a middle-aged woman in New York took her aging father to a railroad station. He boarded a train for Louisiana, where he would live with another daughter and her husband. The New York woman returned home and burst into tears. "All my life he was aloof from me and although I know he loved me, he never told me so," she said. "I probably will never see him alive again and I wanted to kiss him goodbye. But I couldn't." And the tragedy is that because of her training, this woman is equally aloof from her own children.

16

Religion in Your Home

YOUR power of example as a parent is never more forcibly demonstrated than in the religious observances of your home. If your home is one in which your belief in God is constantly evident, and one in which you practice the principles of your faith, you can be sure that your children will develop a love of Christ and His Church. On the other hand, if your daily practices fail to give evidence of your religious beliefs, this lack will be reflected in the shallowness of your children's religious training.

You can teach your children to know and love God from infancy. For example, in your child's first year, you can sprinkle his bed with holy water and sign him with the Sign of the Cross. By the middle of his second year, he can learn to sing little hymns and to recognize pictures of Baby Jesus. In his third year, you can teach him that God made the universe and help him to see the Creator in flowers, birds, and other living things.

When your child is four, he is old enough to attend Mass with you and to sit quietly. When he sees you pray, he will understand that people go to church because God is nearer to people there than elsewhere. He may learn prayers which he will say throughout his lifetime—prayers at bedtime, the Lord's Prayer, the Hail Mary. In his fifth year he can begin to say morning and evening prayers as a regular procedure. Now he can be taught the difference between moral right and wrong—for example, he can understand why he should not steal. In his sixth year, before he attends elementary school, he should be able to make the Sign of the Cross and to bless himself with holy water. He will do these things as a matter of course if he sees you doing them.

You can impress the importance of religious values upon your child in many ways. Pictures of Our Lord and the Blessed Lady on your walls will excite his curiosity, encourage him to learn what they represent, and give him a feeling that Christ is truly present in your home. You need not feel that your standards of art are degraded by showing sacred pictures in your living room. Many of the greatest artists of all time spent their lives portraying events in the life of Our Lord. Faithful reproductions of these art masterpieces which would enhance the attractiveness of any home can be bought at reasonable prices. Many excellent, illustrated books are also available at low cost to help you teach your child the principles of religion in a way he can understand.

Family religious observances: From his earliest days, your child should observe your family in prayer together. As soon as he is able, he should join the prayers. "The family that prays together stays together," and the child who grows to adulthood in a home where his parents pray with him, carries deep, warm memories. What are suitable prayers for the family? Grace before and after meals can be learned easily. You or your mate may kneel with your youngster as he says his morning or evening prayers. Many families recite the Rosary together every night.

You can give your child a sense of close relationship to God and his patron saint by celebrating his Baptismal Day and his Name Day. You celebrate his birthday. Why not also observe the anniversary of his Baptismal Day—the day when he became a member of the Faith? In many countries, touching and symbolic customs have grown up around the observance of this anniversary. Some European parents provide the candle which is used in the baptismal ceremony and then take the candle home after the ceremony and preserve it in a place of honor. On each anniversary, it is relit for a few minutes while the child prayerfully thanks God for the gift of faith and renews his baptismal vows. The candle may also be used on great religious occasions of his life: when he receives his First Communion, when he is married, even when he receives the last rites. Sometimes the remains of the candle are burned during his wake.

Name Days are celebrated on the day of the saint after whom the child has been named and are often more festive than birthdays. The family may attend Mass and receive Communion together; there may be special meals and presents. During the main meal the father may read a brief story of the saint's life, emphasizing the qualities of character for which he was noted, and thus encourage the child to imitate these virtues. Psychologists say that one of the sweetest sounds to any person is that of his own name; one of the sweetest spiritual bonds is that which can be developed between a young person and his patron saint. The major saints' days are usually listed on religious calendars.

The great feast days of the Church afford excellent opportunities to instill religious values in your children. The foremost of these days is Christmas, of course. Your child will miss its magnificent beauty and symbolism if it is considered in a secular way as a time for Santa Claus, presents and parties, without any real mention of the birth of Christ. Children everywhere respond warmly to the spiritual observance of Christmas. Even three-year-olds can grasp the simple thought that you are preparing for the birth of Jesus; they will enthusiastically help you prepare a simple straw manger and a stable with its farm animals to await the Babe. As another delightful custom, popular in France, the children receive a supply of straw as Advent begins. When they perform good work or say their morning and evening prayers, they are permitted to add some straw to the manger. The comfort of the bed upon which the Christ Child will lie on Christmas Day therefore depends upon the good deeds your youngster performs.

Many families use an Advent wreath to symbolize their preparations for Christmas. This wreath is usually made of evergreens—laurel, yew, or fir. You start with a sturdy wood or wire hoop and firmly attach four holders for candles. Wind the evergreens around the hoop and insert the candles so they will be rigid and upright when you use the wreath as a centerpiece on your dining-room table. Light one candle on the first Sunday evening of Advent. It makes a truly impressive ceremony if the entire family is present and all other lights are extinguished. The candle is symbolic of the coming light of Christ. As it casts its glow over the room, prayers in honor of the Saviour are said. It is lit for the evening meals during the week—a gentle reminder of the season. One additional candle is lighted each succeeding Sunday. Younger family members may be given the honor of lighting the new candles. On the few days preceding Christmas, all four candles are ablaze, a fitting reminder of the Messiah who enlightens them that sit in darkness.

Children also sense the true meaning of Christmas through the singing of appropriate hymns. The treasury of the Church is so rich with beautiful hymns—"*Adeste Fideles*" and "Silent Night," for example—that there is no reason to sing ditties from Tin Pan Alley at family gatherings at this time. Children gain great pleasure from family singing; it creates memories of Christmas that are never forgotten. When your Christmas music is in keeping with the spirit of the season, you create a reverence for the feast that will be transmitted from generation to generation.

Appropriate practices for the home also may be developed for other seasons. For example, during Lent the entire family may abstain from popular desserts, like ice cream or cake. When parents and children alike share in the common sacrifice, a feeling of religious unity is created in the family. Other excellent suggestions for seasonal religious services are available in booklets listed in the Appendix.

The importance of good reading matter: Many newspapers

and magazines are edited from viewpoints which are un-Catholic, if not anti-Catholic. Your efforts to develop spiritual attitudes and habits in your children will meet added resistance if the children are exposed to secular magazines which promote ideas opposed to your own. For example, many publications foster attitudes regarding birth control that are contrary to Catholic thinking. Many consistently feature stories in which immorality thrives; others publish detailed information about the sex act and sex problems which it is improper for minors to be familiar with.

In protecting your children from the influence of undesirable reading matter, you necessarily will be "negative." There are certain publications which you should properly forbid them to read. Which publications will depend upon your children's ages and their ability to resist the unsuitable influences involved.

Your approach to this problem should also be positive, however. Support publications which encourage them to lead the kind of lives you wish for them. Many Catholic monthly magazines are available. They contain light, informative articles of interest to youngsters and adults alike, and exert an inspiring influence which reinforces your teaching and example. Subscribe to your diocesan newspaper. It gives you helpful information about your parish and diocesan activities and also contains special articles of practical value to everyone in the family.

To insure proper spiritual attitudes in your children and to protect them against bad influences, you should also supervise their reading of books, viewing of television programs and attendance at movie theaters. Many of the most widely publicized popular novels discuss scenes and use language which are not appropriate for young persons. Movies sometimes offend in this regard also, as do television programs (particularly those shown at late hours). Catholic publications contain reviews of books, movies, television programs and other entertainment to help you judge whether they are suitable for your children. The cause of decency in literature and entertainment will be best served if you and your family enthusiastically support the good with as much energy as you denounce the bad.

Furnishings for the sickroom: In addition to religious pictures, crucifixes, holy water, possibly a home altar and other religious reminders in your home, you should have available those articles necessary for the priest's visit in time of sickness. When he calls to hear the sick person's confession, to administer Holy Eucharist or to perform the last rites, the following furnishings should be in place: a small table, covered with a white cloth; a crucifix, with lighted, blessed candles on each side; a glass of water with a spoon; and several clean napkins. If the patient is to be anointed with holy oils, a small amount of cotton should be available for the priest's use, and also a dish with a small amount of salt, a small slice of lemon, and some bread crumbs.

If possible, a male member of the family should meet the priest at the door, holding a lighted candle, and should lead the way to the sickroom. All members of the family should interrupt their normal activities and kneel reverently when the Blessed Sacrament is administered. All members of the family should leave the room if a confession is to be heard. A small bell may be sounded to summon them again while the Holy Eucharist or Extreme Unction is administered.

The importance of checkups: So that he never forgets the true purpose of his vocation and the high ideals of his state in life, every priest must participate in a spiritual retreat at least once a year. During that time, he reconsiders his objective in life, weighs his spiritual progress during the preceding year, determines which defects he should strive to remove and which virtues to strengthen.

Those in other vocations also conduct annual checkups. The doctor who does not attend his medical society's annual convention or does not carefully read reports of it soon lags behind other physicians. Through his failure to keep informed of the latest medical advances, he becomes less proficient in his work of healing the sick. The lawyer who does not keep pace with legal developments cannot properly represent his clients in court, for he does not know of the latest ruling upon which to base his arguments. Manufacturers of automobiles, garbage disposal units, women's dresses, or any other item, who ignore all developments in their industry will certainly soon be candidates for bankruptcy.

In your great vocation as a married person and a parent, you too should make frequent checkups—checkups that may give you new perspectives on your state in life, encourage you to remove habits which may be blocking your path to heaven, and help you develop attitudes to strengthen your own sanctity and that of your mate and children. If the period of annual stocktaking is important for the business and professional man, how much more important is it for you, whose salvation depends upon how you do your job as husband and father or wife and mother.

Cana Conferences: One of the best ways to reappraise your life's work is by regular attendance at Cana Conferences. These conferences are named, of course, for the wedding feast at which Our Lord performed his first miracle. They are now regularly conducted in about one hundred dioceses throughout the United States. They have helped hundreds of thousands of couples to gain new insights into the harmony and sanctity it is possible for them to achieve together.

Just as medical conventions are not intended for doctors who have lost all touch with scientific progress, Cana Conferences are not for "problem Catholics." They have not been established to offset divorce, contraception or juvenile delinquency. If you grasp the opportunity to attend a Cana Conference in your community, you will find that it will make a happy marriage happier; or, if your marriage is Christian in name only, that it will stimulate you to make it Christian in fact. Couples of every description—mixed couples, invalidly married couples, non-Catholic couples—are invited to attend.

Conferences usually are organized by a few couples in the parish, working with a parish priest. They can be scheduled for any time; the most popular periods are Sunday afternoons and evenings during Advent and Lent. They are made as informal as possible and are usually held in a small hall where smoking is permitted and light refreshments are served.

At a typical conference, there are two talks by the priest-leader. He discusses common problems in marriage—perhaps difficulties that arise over in-laws, money matters, physical relations, and the bearing and caring for children. Your down-to-earth problems, with which you may have grappled for months, are considered in a realistic way. When they are analyzed and discussed against the background of the true, spiritual meaning of your marriage, their solutions often become clear.

After the second talk, there is a half-hour break for simple refreshments. During this time, you have a chance to talk with couples like yourself. The third session usually consists of a question-and-answer period; without identifying yourself, you can submit written questions about problems or questions which you want clarified. These are discussed by the priest in a friendly, relaxed way. Discussion by other members of the conference is always invited. The typical conference ends with a renewal of the marriage vows and benediction.

Among couples attending Cana Conferences, you will surely find many with problems similar to your own. These conferences are attended by newlyweds; by men and women who have celebrated their golden wedding anniversaries; by couples with unpaid milk bills, jobs that seem to have no future, cranky landlords, and in-laws who do not understand them. You will meet couples striving to overcome weaknesses similar to your own, who lack patience with their children, who have forgotten the importance of saying a kind word to their mates, who have fallen before materialistic pressures and perhaps have allowed themselves to forget the true reasons why they live. You will also meet those couples who, hand in hand, are leading lives of true sanctity. Regardless of your background as you attend a Cana Conference, you will find that this is a unique way to gain a new feeling of reverence, respect and enthusiasm for your vocation.

The Christian Family Movement: Many couples who have attended Cana Conferences have recognized the tremendous potentialities that exist when they work together with other couples throughout the community, state and nation. Members of the Christian Family Movement in any parish are true leaders who demonstrate the many ways in which it is possible to introduce Christian concepts into activities of daily life.

C.F.M. was formed in Chicago in February 1943. Today twenty thousand couples in ten different countries and one hundred dioceses of the United States use the C.F.M. technique.

The basic unit of C.F.M. is parochial: a small group of couples from the same parish meets every two weeks with a parish priest. The discussion is an attempt to know Christ. Couples study how He reacted to various situations to find out how they should react to similar situations today.

The C.F.M. strives in its actions to create a Christian climate throughout the nation. Monsignor Reynold Hillenbrand of Chicago has described members of the Christian Family Movement as follows:

"We are the hands of Christ in the most noble sense; where we work, Christ works. We are the feet of Christ in the most noble sense; wherever we go, Christ goes. We are the lips of Christ; whenever we speak, we speak for Christ. We are the heart of Christ; wherever we are, the love of Christ is alive."

Until recent years there had been no way for a married couple to identify as a couple with their parish. The C.F.M., as the most popular married couples' organization in the American Church, is a response by lay people to the demands of their own conscience. Amid a sea of secularism they have found that they must band together to protect Christian family traditions. The C.F.M. thus becomes a powerful force for bringing the American culture back to Christ.

By associating yourself with this movement, you will achieve the true purpose of marriage-salvation for yourselves and the reconsecration of families everywhere with Christian ideals. In 1948, the American hierarchy summed up the duties of your vocation in this way:

"It is not enough to profess the Christian truths of the stability and sanctity of the marriage bond and to keep in mind the purpose of marriage. The Christian must make his home holy. It remained for modern history to record the first experiment in secularizing the home: an experiment which is at the root of so many of our greatest social evils. The Christian home must realize the Christian ideal. The whole atmosphere of the home must be impregnated with genuine Christian living. The domestic virtues must be practiced, and family prayer made a daily exercise. It is in the home that the children learn their responsibility to God and in this responsibility their duty to others. The home is the child's first school, in which he is taught to make the vision of Christian truth the inspiration of all living."

Appendix

THE MASS ON THE DAY OF MARRIAGE

(Couples married without a Mass may obtain the nuptial blessing any time after marriage, e.g., on the occasion of a wedding anniversary.)

INSTRUCTION BEFORE MARRIAGE

Dear friends in Christ: As you know, you are about to enter into a union which is most sacred and most serious, most sacred because established by God Himself, most serious because it will bind you together for life in a relationship so close and so intimate that it will profoundly influence your whole future. That future, with its hopes and disappointments, its successes and its failures, it pleasures and its pains, its joys and its sorrows, is hidden from your eyes. You know that these elements are mingled in every life, and are to be expected in your own. And so, not knowing what is before you, you take each other for better or for worse, for richer or for poorer, in sickness and in health, until death.

Truly, then, these words are most serious. It is a beautiful tribute to your undoubted faith in each other, that recognizing their full import, you are nevertheless so willing and ready to pronounce them. And because these words involve such solemn obligations, it is most fitting that you rest the security of your wedded life upon the great principle of self-sacrifice. And so you begin your married life by the voluntary and complete surrender of your individual lives in the interest of that deeper and wider life which you are to have in common. Henceforth you belong entirely to each other; you will be one in mind, one in heart, and one in affections. And whatever sacrifices you may hereafter be required to make to preserve this common life, always make them generously. Sacrifice is usually difficult and irksome. Only love can make it easy; and perfect love can make it a joy. We are willing to give in proportion as we love. And when love is perfect, the sacrifice is complete. God so loved the world that He gave His only begotten Son; and the Son so loved us that He gave Himself for our salvation. "Greater love than this no man hath, that a man lay down his life for his friends."

No greater blessing can come to your married life than pure conjugal love, loyal and true to the end. May, then, this love with which you join your hands and hearts today, never fail, but grow deeper and stronger as the years go on. And if true love and the unselfish spirit of perfect sacrifice guide your every action, you can expect the greatest measure of earthly happiness that may be allotted to man in this vale of tears. The rest is in the hands of God. Nor will God be wanting to your needs; He will pledge you the lifelong support of His graces in the Holy Sacrament which you are now going to receive.

THE MARRIAGE CEREMONY

The Priest asks the Bridegroom (*Stand*):

N., will you take N., here present, for your lawful wife according to the rite of our holy Mother, the Church?

Response: I will.

Then the Priest asks the Bride:

N., will you take N., here present, for your lawful husband according to the rite of our holy Mother, the Church?

Response: I will.

The consent of one is not sufficient; it must be expressed in some sensible sign by both. After obtaining their mutual consent, the Priest bids the man and woman join their right hands.

The man says after the Priest:

I, N.N., take you, N.N., for my lawful wife, to have and to hold, from this day forward, for better, for worse, for richer, for poorer, in sickness and in health, until death do us part.

Then the woman says after the Priest:

I, N.N., take you, N.N., for my lawful husband, to have and to hold, from this day forward, for better, for worse, for richer, for poorer, in sickness and in health, until death do us part.

The Bridegroom and Bride may kneel, and the Priest says:

I join you together in marriage, in the name of the Father, and of the Son, and of the Holy Spirit. Amen.

He then sprinkles them with holy water. This done, the Priest blesses the ring(s), saying:

Versicle: Our help is in the name of the Lord.

Response: Who made heaven and earth.

V.: O Lord, hear my prayer.

R.: And let my cry come unto Thee.

V.: The Lord be with you.

R.: And with your spirit.

Let us pray. Bless, O Lord, this ring, which we bless in Thy name, so that she who is to wear it, keeping true faith with her husband, may abide in Thy peace and obedience to Thy will, and ever live in mutual love. Through Christ our Lord.

R.: Amen.

The Priest sprinkles the ring(s).

The Groom, having received the ring from the hand of the Priest puts it on the third finger of the left hand of the Bride and repeats after the Priest: "With this ring I thee wed, and plight unto thee my troth."

The Priest then says:

In the name of the Father, and of the Son, and of the Holy Ghost.

Confirm, O God, this work which you have begun in us.

From Your holy temple, which is in Jerusalem.

V.: Lord, have mercy.
R.: Christ, have mercy.
Our Father (*silently*)
V.: And lead us not into temptation.
R.: But deliver us from evil.
V.: Grant salvation to Thy servants.
R.: For their hope, O my God, is in Thee.
V.: Send them aid, O Lord, from Thy holy place.
R.: And watch over them from Sion.
V.: O Lord, hear my prayer.
R.: And let my cry come unto Thee.
V.: The Lord be with you.
R.: And with your spirit.

Let us pray. Look down, we beseech Thee, O Lord, upon these Thy servants, and graciously protect Thy institutions, whereby Thou has provided for the propagation of mankind; that those who are joined together by Thine authority may be preserved by Thy help. Through Christ our Lord. Amen.

The Mass follows.

After the "Our Father" the Priest interrupts the usual sequence of the Mass, and turning to the bridal couple who kneel before the altar, confers the Nuptial Blessing upon them.

Let us pray. Listen with favor, O Lord, to our prayers; and in Thy goodness maintain the ways which Thou hast established for the continuation of the human race, so that the union which has been founded by Thy authority may be preserved by Thy aid. Through our Lord Jesus Christ, Thy Son, Who lives and reigns with Thee in the unity of the Holy Spirit, God, world without end.

R.: Amen.

Let us pray. O God, Who by Thy mighty power hast made all things where before there was nothing; Who, having put in order the beginnings of the universe, didst form for man, made to Thy image, an inseparable helpmate, woman, so that Thou didst give woman's body its origin from man's flesh and teach that it is never right to separate her from the one being whence it has pleased Thee to take her:

O God, Who has consecrated the union of marriage making

it a sign so profound as to prefigure in the marriage covenant the mystery of Christ and the Church:

O God, Who dost join woman to man, and give to that society, the first to be established, the blessing which alone was not taken away in punishment for original sin nor in the doom of the Flood:

Look with kindness on this Thy servant who is now to be joined to her husband in the companionship of marriage and who seeks to be made secure by Thy protection.

May this yoke that she is taking on herself be one of love and peace. May she be faithful and chaste, marrying in Christ, and may she always imitate the holy women. May she be the beloved of her husband, as was Rachel; wise, as was Rebecca, longlived and loyal, as was Sarah.

May the author of sin have no mastery over her because of her acts. May she hold firm to the Faith and the commandments. Faithful to one embrace, may she flee from unlawful companionship. By firm discipline may she fortify herself against her weakness. May she be grave in her modesty, honorable in her chastity, learned in the teachings of heaven.

May she be rich in children, prove worthy and blameless, and may she attain in the end to the peace of the blessed, the Kingdom of heaven.

May she and her husband together see their children's children to the third and fourth generation and enjoy the long life they desire. Through our Lord Jesus Christ Thy Son, Who lives and reigns with Thee in the unity of the Holy Spirit, God, for ever and ever.

R.: Amen.

Before the last blessing of the Mass, the Priest once more turns to the bridal couple and gives the final blessing of the Church, after which he sprinkles them with holy water.

May the God of Abraham, the God of Isaac, the God of Jacob be with you, and may He fulfill in you His blessing; so that you may see your children's children to the third and fourth generation and afterwards possess everlasting and boundless life. Through the help of our Lord Jesus Christ, Who with the Father and the Holy Spirit lives and reigns; God, forever and ever. Amen.

BLESSING OF AN EXPECTANT MOTHER

V. Our help is in the name of the Lord.
R. Who made heaven and earth.

V. Save Thy servant, Lord.
R. For she puts her hope, O God, in Thee.

V. Be a tower of strength for her, O Lord.
R. Against Enemy attack.

V. Let not the Enemy have power against her.
R. Nor the son of evil come near to harm her.

V. O Lord, send her aid from Thy holy place.
R. And guard her from Sion.

V. The Lord be with you.
R. And with your spirit.

Let us pray.

Almighty, everlasting God, Thou hast granted Thy servants in the profession of the true Faith, to show forth the glory of the eternal Trinity and to adore Its Unity in the power of Its majesty. We ask that Thy servant, N., by her constancy in that Faith, may ever be safeguarded against all adversity. Through Christ our Lord.

R. Amen.

Let us pray.

O Lord God, Creator of all, Thou art mighty and awe-inspiring, just and merciful; Thou alone art kind and loving and didst set Israel free from every evil, making our fathers Thy chosen people. Thou didst sanctify them by the power of Thy Spirit and by the co-working of the Holy Ghost, didst prepare the body and soul of the glorious Virgin Mary to become a worthy home for Thy Son. Thou didst fill John the Baptist with the Holy Ghost, making him leap with joy in his mother's womb. Accept now the offering of the contrite heart and the ardent desire of Thy servant, N., who humbly petitions Thee for the welfare of the child which Thou didst grant her to conceive. Protect the work which is Thine and guard it from all the deceit and harm of our bitter Enemy. May the hand of Thy mercy assist her delivery, and may her child see the light of day without harm; may it be kept safe for the holy rebirth of Baptism, serve Thee always in all things, and thereby merit everlasting life. Through the same Christ our Lord.

R. Amen.

The priest then sprinkles the woman with holy water, and prays:

Psalm 66

May God have pity on us and bless us;
  may He let His face shine upon us.
So may Your way be known upon the earth;
  among all nations, Your salvation.
May the peoples praise You, O God;
  may all the peoples praise You!
May the nations be glad and exult
  because You rule the peoples in equity;
  the nations on the earth You guide.
May the peoples praise You, O God;
  may all the peoples praise You.
The earth has yielded its fruits;
  God, our God, has blessed us.
May God bless us,
  and may all the ends of the earth fear Him!
Glory be to the Father, and to the Son,
  and to the Holy Spirit.
As it was in the beginning, is now, and ever
    shall be,
  world without end. Amen.

V.: Let us praise the Father and the Son with the Holy Spirit.
R.: Let us praise and glorify Him forever.

V.: To His angels God has given charge over you.
R.: To guard you in all your ways.

V.: O Lord, hear my prayer.
R.: And let my cry come unto Thee.

V.: The Lord be with you.
R.: And with your spirit.

Let us pray.

Visit this dwelling we beg Thee, O Lord, and drive far from it and from this Thy servant, N., all the snares of the Enemy. May Thy holy angels dwell here to preserve her and her child in peace, and may Thy blessing be ever upon her. Save them, O Almighty God, and bestow upon them Thy unfailing light. Through Christ our Lord.

R.: Amen.

May the blessing of Almighty God, the Father, the Son, and Holy Spirit, come down upon you and your child, and remain forever.

R.: Amen.

BLESSING OF A MOTHER AFTER CHILDBIRTH

Vested in surplice and white stole, the priest with his server proceeds to the entrance of the church where the mother with her baptized child awaits him, holding a lighted candle. He sprinkles them and all the others present with holy water, saying:

V.: Our help is in the name of the Lord.
R.: Who made heaven and earth.
ANT.: She shall receive.

Psalm 23

The Lord's are the earth and its fullness;
the world and those who dwell in it.
For He founded it upon the seas
and established it upon the rivers.

Who can ascend the mountain of the Lord?
or who may stand in His holy place?
He whose hands are sinless, whose heart is clean,
who desires not what is vain,
nor swears deceitfully to his neighbor.
He shall receive a blessing from the Lord,
a reward from God his Savior.

Such is the race that seeks for him,
  that seeks the face of the God of Jacob.

Lift up, O gates, your lintels;
  reach up, you ancient portals,
  that the king of glory may come in!
Who is this king of glory?
The Lord, strong and mighty,
  the Lord, mighty in battle.

Lift up, O gates, your lintels;
  reach up, you ancient portals,
  that the king of glory may come in!

Who is this king of glory?
  The Lord of Hosts; He is the king of glory.
Glory be to the Father, and to the Son,
  and to the Holy Spirit.
As it was in the beginning, is now, and ever shall be,
  world without end. Amen.

ANT.: She shall receive the Lord's blessing, and mercy from God, her Savior, because she is of the generation who seek the Lord.

The priest puts the end of his stole in the woman's hand and leads her toward the altar, saying:

Enter God's temple. Adore the Son of the Blessed Virgin Mary who has given you fruitfulness of offspring.

The mother kneels on the altar step and is grateful to God.

V.: Lord, have mercy.
R.: Christ, have mercy. Lord, have mercy.
V.: Our Father (*silently*).
And lead us not into temptation.
R.: But deliver us from evil.
V.: Save Thy servant, Lord.
R.: For she puts her hope, O God, in Thee,
V.: O Lord, send her aid from Thy holy place.
R.: And guard over her from Sion.
V.: Let not the Enemy have power against her.
R.: Nor the son of evil come near to harm her.

V.: O Lord, hear my prayer.
R.: And let my cry come unto Thee.
V.: The Lord be with you.
R.: And with your spirit.

Let us pray.

PRAYERS FOR ONE'S FAMILY

O God of goodness and mercy! We commend our family and all that is ours to Thy fatherly protection; we confide all to Thy love. Do Thou fill our house with Thy blessings, even as Thou didst fill the holy house of Nazareth with Thy presence. Before all else, keep sin far from it. Do Thou alone reign by Thy law, by Thy most holy love and by the exercise of every Christian virtue. Let each of us obey Thee, love Thee and study how to copy in his own life, Thine example, that of Mary, Thy Mother and our Mother most loving, and that of Thy blameless guardian, Saint Joseph.

Keep far from us and our house all evils and misfortunes, but grant that we may be ever resigned to Thy divine will, even in the sorrows which thou shalt be pleased to send to us. Finally, grant unto us all grace to live in perfect harmony and in the fullness of charity toward our neighbor. Grant that every one of us may deserve by a holy life the comfort of Thy holy sacraments at the hour of death. O Jesus! Bless and protect us.

O Mary, Mother of grace and of mercy! Protect us against the wicked spirit; reconcile us with Thy Son; commend us to Him, that so we may be made worthy of His promises.

Saint Joseph, foster father of our Savior, guardian of His holy Mother, head of the holy Family! Be our intercessor; bless us and defend our homes at all times.

Saint Michael! Guard us against all the wicked wiles of hell.
Saint Gabriel! Make us understand the holy will of God.
Saint Raphael! Preserve us from all sickness and all danger to our lives.

Our holy Guardian Angels! Keep our feet on the path of salvation both day and night.

Our holy Patrons! Pray for us before the throne of God.

Yea, bless this house, O God the Father who hast created us; O God the Son who hast suffered for us upon the Holy Cross; and Thou, O God the Holy Spirit who hast sanctified us in holy Baptism. May the one God in three divine Persons preserve our bodies, purify our minds, direct our hearts and bring us all to everlasting life.

Glory be to the Father, glory be to the Son, glory be to the Holy Ghost! Amen.

Indulgence: 500 days, once a day.

—Cardinal Spellman's Prayer Book

PRAYER FOR VOCATIONS TO THE PRIESTHOOD AND RELIGIOUS LIFE

Lord Jesus Christ, Savior of the world! We humbly beg of Thee to manifest in Thy Church the Spirit Whom Thou didst so abundantly bestow upon Thy Apostles. Call, we pray Thee, very many to Thy priesthood and to the religious life. And may zeal for Thy glory and the salvation of souls inflame those whom Thou hast chosen; may they be saints in Thy likeness, and may Thy Spirit strengthen them. O Jesus, give us priests and religious according to Thine own Heart!

Indulgence: 7 years.

O Mary, Mother of Jesus! Obtain for fervent souls the grace to hear and the courage to follow Thy divine Son in the path of religious perfection.

Queen of Apostles, pray for us.
Queen of Virgins, pray for us.

A plenary indulgence.

—Cardinal Spellman's Prayer Book

A DECALOGUE FOR PARENTS

Thou shalt honor no other gods but God, steadfastly, refusing to make the child a minor deity in the household;

Thou shalt make no promises that are broken, whether these be promises of pleasure or promises of punishment; for unless the child learns to respect *the word,* he will not respect any person;

Thou shalt teach the child by example, and not by precept; for a parent who teaches a child religion and morality, and yet lives by greed, passion, and hypocrisy must expect his conduct to be followed and his counsel ignored;

Thou shalt worship on the Sabbath communally, with thy family, and not seek solitary pleasures, which plunge each member of the family into social and spiritual isolation when they should be most together;

Thou shalt instill no anxious fears into thy child, but rather impress upon him that love casteth out fear; and that he who commits no wrongs because of fear is merely weak, whereas he who pursueth righteousness because of love is truly strong;

Thou shalt help the child accept the variety of mankind with joy and wonder in God's creative originality; and not breed in him that terrible false pride of superiority, which stunts and twists the personality of man;

Thou shalt not be too much a parent, allowing the child freely to make his own mistakes, and not protecting him unduly from the painful consequences of his errors;

Thou shalt not expect nor demand love from the child simply because thou art his parent; but thou shalt try to win his respect as a person by justice, humor and understanding;

Thou shalt not force the child to develop in thine own image, but assist him in becoming the best kind of person his own nature requires;

Thou shalt look daily into thine own heart and examine there the motives; for when the motives are impure, love curdles into possessiveness, and the child is no longer a creature of God but an instrument of man's misguided passion.

FAMILY PRAYER CARD

Published by the Family Life Bureau, Archdiocese of New York, 451 Madison Avenue, N. Y. 22, N. Y.

Every family should pray together. The time for prayer should be convenient to parents and children, perhaps shortly after the evening meal. It is suggested that prayer be led by the father of the family.

*

In the Name of the Father and of the Son and of the Holy Ghost. Amen.

Our Father. Hail Mary. Gloria. Apostles' Creed.

THE CONFITEOR

I confess to Almighty God, to Blessed Mary, ever Virgin, to Blessed Michael the Archangel, to Blessed John the Baptist, to the Holy Apostles Peter and Paul, and to all the Saints, that I have sinned exceedingly in thought, word and deed. (*Strike breast three times, saying:*) Through my fault, through my fault, through my most grievous fault. Therefore I beseech Blessed Mary, ever Virgin, Blessed Michael the Archangel, Blessed John the Baptist, the Holy Apostles Peter and Paul, and all the Saints, to pray to the Lord our God for me.

May the Almighty God have mercy on us, forgive us our sins, and bring us to life everlasting.

May the Almighty and Merciful Lord grant us pardon, absolution, and remission of all our sins. Amen.

Make an Act of Contrition.

PRAYER FOR THE HOME

Visit, we beseech Thee, O Lord, this home, and drive far from it all snares of the Enemy; let Thy holy Angels dwell herein to preserve us in peace and let Thy blessing always be upon us. Through Christ, our Lord. Amen.

PARENTS' PRAYER FOR CHILDREN

Lord God! Thou hast called us to the holy state of matrimony and hast been pleased to make us parents. We recommend to Thee our dear children. We entrust them to Thy fatherly care. May they be a source of consolation, not only to us, but chiefly to Thee Who are their Creator. Be watchful, O Lord; help and defend them.

Grant us the grace to guide them in the way of Thy commandments. This we will do by our own perfect observance of Thy holy law and that of our holy Mother, the Church. Make us conscious of our grave obligation to You and bless our efforts to serve You. We humbly ask this blessing from the bottom of our hearts, for ourselves and for the children whom Thou hast been pleased to give us.

We dedicate them to Thee, O Lord. Do Thou keep them as the apple of Thy eye and protect them under the shadow of Thy wings. Make us worthy to come, at last, to heaven, together with them giving thanks unto Thee, our Father, for the loving care Thou hast had of our entire family and praising Thee together through endless ages. Amen.

CHILDREN'S PRAYER FOR THEIR PARENTS

Dear Lord! Fill our parents with Thy choicest blessings; enrich their souls with Thy holy grace; grant that they may faithfully and constantly guard that likeness to Thy union with Thy Church, which thou didst imprint upon them on their wedding day. Fill them with Thy spirit of holy fear, which is the beginning of wisdom; inspire them to impart it to their children. May they ever walk in the way of Thy commandments, and may we their children be their joy on earth and their crown of glory in heaven. Finally, Lord God, grant that both our father and mother may attain to extreme old age and enjoy continuous health in mind and body. May they give Thee abundant thanks because Thou hast bestowed upon them the great gift of parenthood. Amen.

PRAYER FOR A SICK PERSON

Almighty and Eternal God, the everlasting health of those who believe; hear us for Thy sick servant (*name inserted here*) for whom we implore the aid of Thy tender mercy, that, being restored to bodily health, he (or she) may give thanks to Thee in Thy Church. Through Christ our Lord. Amen.

BLESSING ON SLEEP

Jesus Christ, my God! I adore Thee and thank Thee for all the graces Thou hast given me this day. I offer to Thee my sleep and all the moments of this night, and I beseech Thee to keep me without sin. Wherefore, I put myself within Thy Sacred Side and under the mantle of our Lady, my Mother. Let Thy holy angels stand about me and keep me in peace; and let Thy blessing be upon me.

PRAYER FOR THE DEAD

May the souls of the faithful departed through the mercy of God rest in peace. Amen.

Additional Readings on Marriage

Many excellent books and pamphlets are available for the lay reader on the subject of Catholic marriage. Some of the many books include:

BOOKS

BANAHAN, JOHN S. *Instructions for Mixed Marriages.* Milwaukee: Bruce, 1957.

CAFFAREL, H. *Marriage Is Holy.* Chicago: Fides, 1957.

CARNEY, F. W. *The Purposes of Christian Marriage.* Washington, D. C.: Catholic University of America Press, 1950.

CLARK, WILLIAM R., O. P. *One in Mind, One in Heart, One in Affection.* Providence, R. I.: Providence College Press, 1952.

CLEMENS, ALPHONSE H. *Marriage and the Family.* New York: Prentice-Hall, 1957.

DE BLANC, IRVING and SCAVILLA, NORMA. *Sanctity and Success in Marriage.* Washington, D. C.: N. C. W. C. Family Life Bureau, 1956.

DOYLE, CHARLES H. *Cana Is Forever.* Tarrytown, N. Y.: The Nugent Press, 1949.

FIRKEL, EVA. *Woman in the Modern World.* Chicago: Fides, 1956.

FOERSTER, F. W., M. D. *Marriage and the Sex Problem.* Philadelphia: Lippincott, 1936.

HEALY, EDWIN. *Marriage Guidance.* Chicago: Loyola University Press, 1948.

HOPE, WINGFIELD. *Life Together.* New York: Sheed and Ward, 1943.

IMBIORSKI, WALTER (ed.). *The New Cana Manual.* Chicago: Delaney, 1957.

KANE, JOHN J. *Marriage and the Family.* New York: The Dryden Press, 1952.

———. *Together in Marriage.* Chicago: Fides, 1957.

KEENAN, ALAN, O. F. M., and RYAN, JOHN, M. D. *Marriage, a Medical and Sacramental Study.* New York: Sheed and Ward, 1955.

KINSELLA, LEO J. *The Wife Desired.* Techny, Ill.: Divine Word Missionary Pub., 1953.

———. *The Man for Her.* Oak Park, Ill.: Valiant Publications, 1957.

KNOX, RONALD. *Bridegroom and Bride.* New York: Sheed and Ward, 1957.

LE CLERCQ, JACQUES. *Marriage, a Great Sacrament.* Dublin: Clonmore and Reynolds, 1951.

LORD, DANIEL A., S. J. *The Guidance of Parents.* St. Louis: The Queen's Work, 1944.

MAGNER, JAMES A. *The Art of Happy Marriage.* Milwaukee: Bruce, 1947.

MESSENGER, E. C. *Two in One Flesh.* Westminster: The Newman Press, 1950.

MIHANOVICH, CLEMENT S., SCHNEPP, GERALD J., S. M., and THOMAS, JOHN L., S. J. *A Guide to Catholic Marriage.* Milwaukee: Bruce, 1955.

MOORE, EDWARD. *The Case Against Birth Control.* New York: Century, 1931.

O'BRIEN, JOHN A. *Happy Marriage: Guidance Before and After.* Garden City, N. Y.: Hanover House, 1956.

PERKINS, MARY. *Beginning at Home.* Collegeville, Minn.: Liturgical Press, 1955.

REED, GRANTLY DICK, M. D. *Childbirth Without Fear.* New York: Harpers, 1944.

SHEEN, BISHOP FULTON J. *Three to Get Married.* New York: Sheed and Ward, 1951.

THIBON, GUSTAVE. *What God Has Joined Together.* Chicago: Henry Regnery Co., 1952.

THOMAS, JOHN L., S. J. *The American Catholic Family.* Englewood Cliffs, N. J.: Prentice-Hall, 1956.

———. *Marriage and Rhythm.* Westminster: The Newman Press, 1957.

VON GAGERN, BARON FREDERICK, M. D. *The Meaning of Life and Marriage.* Translated from the German. Westminster: The Newman Press, 1954.

WARD, MAISIE (ed.). *Be Not Solicitous.* New York: Sheed and Ward, 1953.

ZIMMERMAN, CARLE C., and CERVANTES, LUCIUS F., S. J. *Marriage and the Family.* Chicago: Regnery, 1956.

PAMPHLETS

Many hundreds of pamphlets dealing with different phases of Catholic marriage have been published. They may be purchased from racks in the rear of churches, from Catholic bookshops or information centers, or obtained by mail from the publishers or from organizations such as the International Catholic Truth Society, 405 Bergen Street, Brooklyn 17, New York. When ordering by mail, include the price of pamphlets plus postage.

MARRIAGE IS A SACRED VOCATION

CONNELL, FRANCIS J., C. SS. R. *Marriage—Human or Divine?* New York: The Paulist Press. 10 cents.

COX, REV. IGNATIUS W., S. J. *The Divine Romance of Marriage.* New York: The Paulist Press. 10 cents.

MCCOWN, J. H., S. J. *Man, Woman and God.* St. Louis, Mo.: The Queen's Work. 10 cents.

NOLL, BISHOP JOHN F. *Seven Instructions Before Marriage.* Huntington, Ind.: Our Sunday Visitor Press. 30 cents.

O'BRIEN, JOHN A. *Marriage a Vocation.* Notre Dame, Ind.: Ave Maria Press. 10 cents.

PIUS XI, POPE. *Encyclical Letter on Christian Marriage (Casti Connubii).* New York: America Press, 1936. 25 cents.

POWER, RICHARD E. *Marriage in Christ: the Rite of Marriage.* Collegeville, Minn.: The Liturgical Press. 10 cents.

VANN, GERALD, O. P. *Christian Married Love.* Collegeville, Minn.: The Liturgical Press. 10 cents.

THE KEYS TO MUTUAL LOVE

HYNES, EMERSON. *Seven Keys to a Christian Home.* Washington, D. C.: National Catholic Welfare Conference. 25 cents.

LOVASIK, LAWRENCE, G., S. V. D. *Making Marriage Click.* St. Paul, Minn.: Radio Replies Press. 15 cents.

MILLER, DONALD F., C. SS. R. *How to Be a Good Husband.* Ligouri, Mo.: Ligourian Pamphlet Office. 5 cents.

———. *How to Be a Good Wife.* Ligouri, Mo.: Ligourian Pamphlet Office. 5 cents.

O'BRIEN, JOHN A. *Ideal Marriage: How to Achieve It.* New York: The Paulist Press. 10 cents.

A CATHOLIC DOCTOR LOOKS AT MARRIAGE

CONWAY, MONS. J. D. *What They Ask About Marriage.* Notre Dame, Ind.: Ave Maria Press. 10 cents.

DOLAN, ALBERT H. *All the Answers About Marriage and Birth Control.* Chicago: Carmelite Press. 15 cents.

MEYER, FULGENCE, O. F. M. *Plain Talks on Marriage.* Cincinnati, Ohio: St. Francis Book Shop. 40 cents.

PIUS XII, POPE. *Moral Questions Affecting Married Life.* Washington, D. C.: National Catholic Welfare Conference. 20 cents.

SHEED, F. J. *Marriage and the Family.* New York: Sheed and Ward. 75 cents.

THOMAS, JOHN L., S. J. *Beginning Your Marriage.* Oak Park, Ill.: Delaney, 1956. 50 cents.

VANN, GERALD, O. P. *Christian Married Love.* Collegeville, Minn.: The Liturgical Press. 10 cents.

BIRTH CONTROL AND THE RHYTHM METHOD

CAWLEY, THOMAS. *Letter to an Unborn Child and His Answer.* Scranton, Penn.: Catholic Light Publishing Co. 5 cents.

CONWAY, MONS. J. D. *What They Ask About Birth Control.* Notre Dame, Ind.: Ave Maria Press. 10 cents.

———. *What They Ask About the Rhythm.* Notre Dame, Ind.: Ave Maria Press. 10 cents.

LORD, DANIEL A., S. J. *A Mother Looks at Birth Control.* St. Louis: The Queen's Work. 10 cents.

MILLER, DONALD F., C. SS. R. *For Wives and Husbands Only.* Ligouri, Mo.: Ligourian Pamphlet Office. 25 cents.

———. *What's Your Reason for Birth Control?* Ligouri, Mo.: Ligourian Pamphlet Office. 5 cents.

PIUS XII, POPE. *Moral Questions Affecting Married Life.* Washington, D. C.: National Catholic Welfare Conference. 20 cents.

Planned Parenthood: An Answer. Washington, D. C.: National Catholic Welfare Conference. 10 cents.

RYAN, JOHN, M. D. *Family Limitation.* New York: Sheed and Ward. 50 cents.

THE MIRACLE OF BIRTH

FRANCIS, BARBARA. *Childbirth Is Natural.* Notre Dame, Ind.: Ave Maria Press. 10 cents.

Godparents at Baptism. Yonkers, N. Y.: The Cowl Press. 5 cents.

LORD, DANIEL A., S. J. *Let's Pick a Name for Baby.* St. Louis, Mo.: The Queen's Work. 10 cents.

LORD, DANIEL A., S. J. *Attention, Godparents!* St. Louis, Mo.: The Queen's Work. 10 cents.

PLACE, MARGARET. *Sanctifying Pregnancy.* Collegeville, Minn.: The Liturgical Press. 15 cents.

REGAN, JOHN J. *Mothers with Empty Arms: Is Miscarriage a Misfortune?* St. Louis, Mo.: The Queen's Work. 10 cents.

ROHMAN, MRS. W. F. *The Office of Sponsors.* Washington, D. C.: National Catholic Welfare Conference. 5 cents.

DANGER SIGNS IN MARRIAGE

HAUNGS, EDWIN C., S. J. *An Examination of Conscience for Married Couples.* St. Louis, Mo.: The Queen's Work. 10 cents.

LOVER, JAMES F., C. SS. R. *Is Your Marriage on the Rocks?* New York: The Paulist Press. 10 cents.

MILLER, DONALD F., C. SS. R. *How to Check Your Anger.* Ligouri, Mo.: Ligourian Pamphlet Office. 10 cents.

O'BRIEN, JOHN A. *Why Marriages Fail.* Notre Dame, Ind.: Ave Maria Press. 10 cents.

MONEY VALUES IN MARRIAGE

CORLEY, FRANCIS J. *Family Allowances,* St. Louis, Mo.: Institute of Social Order. 12 cents.

DUNN, MARGARET M. *Careers Do Not Make the Woman.* Washington, D. C.: National Catholic Welfare Conference. 5 cents.

LORD, DANIEL A., S. J. *Money Runs or Ruins the Home.* St. Louis, Mo.: The Queen's Work. 10 cents.

SENSER, BOB. *Should Wives Work?* Notre Dame, Ind.: Ave Maria Press. 10 cents.

THE IN-LAW PROBLEM

LORD, DANIEL A., S. J. *In-Laws Aren't Funny.* St. Louis: The Queen's Work. 10 cents.

MILLER, DONALD F., C. SS. R. *How to Honor Your Father and Mother.* Ligouri, Mo.: Ligourian Pamphlet Office. 10 cents.

PROBLEM OF ALCOHOLISM

ALCOHOLICS ANONYMOUS. Free pamphlets describing the purposes and methods of this organization are available by writing Alcoholics Anonymous, Box 459, Grand Central Annex, New York 17, N. Y.

FORD, JOHN C., S. J. *Shall I Start to Drink?* St. Louis, Mo.: The Queen's Work. 10 cents.

O'BRIEN, JOHN A. *Why Drink?* New York: The Paulist Press. 10 cents.

RILEY, FRANK A. *Alcoholics Anonymous: An Interview with Edward Dowling, S. J.* St. Louis, Mo.: The Queen's Work. 10 cents.

"UNTIL DEATH DO YOU PART"

CONWAY, MONS. J. D. *What They Ask About Divorce.* Notre Dame, Ind.: Ave Maria Press. 10 cents.

———. *What They Ask About Marriage Cases.* Notre Dame, Ind.: Ave Maria Press. 10 cents.

LORD, DANIEL A., S. J. *About Divorce.* St. Louis: Queen's Work, 1946. 10 cents.

MILLER, DONALD F., C. SS. R. *When May Husband and Wife Separate?* Ligouri, Mo.: Ligourian Pamphlet Office. 10 cents.

O'BRIEN, JOHN A. *Why Not Get a Divorce?* New York: The Paulist Press. 10 cents.

IF YOUR MATE IS NOT A CATHOLIC

CARROL, THOMAS. *Mixing Your Marriage.* Collegeville, Minn.: Liturgical Press. 5 cents.

CONWAY, MONS. J. D. *What They Ask About Mixed Marriages.* Notre Dame, Ind.: Ave Maria Press. 10 cents.

LILLY, WARREN, S. J. *The Mixed Marriage Prenuptial Contract.* New York: The Catholic Information Society. 5 cents.

MILLER, DONALD F., C. SS. R. *Program for Catholics in a Mixed Marriage.* Ligouri, Mo.: Ligourian Pamphlet Office. 10 cents.

RUMBLE AND CARTY, FATHERS. *Six Pre-Marriage Instructions for Catholics and Non-Catholics.* St. Paul, Minn.: Radio Replies Press. 15 cents.

YOUR PRIVILEGE OF PARENTHOOD

ARNOLD, OREN. *Love Enough to Go Around.* Reprinted from *Better Homes and Gardens.* Notre Dame, Ind.: Ave Maria Press. 10 cents.

D'ORSONNENS, J. I., S. J. *Choosing Your Career!* New York: The Paulist Press. 10 cents.

Father, the Head of the Home. Washington, D. C.: National Catholic Welfare Conference. $1.50

GANSS, GEORGE E., S. J. *On Thinking Out Vocations to Four States of Life.* St. Louis, Mo.: The Queen's Work. 10 cents.

KELLY, GERALD L. *Modern Youth and Chastity.* St. Louis: The Queen's Work, 1941. 25 cents.

KIRSCH, FELIX M., O. M. Cap. *The Sex Problem: A Challenge and an Opportunity.* New York: The Paulist Press. 10 cents.

KRIEGER, B. J. *How to Recognize a Vocation.* Ligouri, Mo.: Ligourian Pamphlet Office. 10 cents.

LORD, DANIEL A., S. J. *Questions People Ask About Their Children.* St. Louis: The Queen's Work. 25 cents.

MILLER, DONALD F., C. SS. R., *How to Be a Good Father.* Ligouri, Mo.: Ligourian Pamphlet Office. 5 cents.

———. *Questions Parents Ask About Raising Children.* Ligouri, Mo.: Ligourian Pamphlet Office. 25 cents.

The Parent-Educator Series in five volumes: "Parental Responsibility," "Teaching Prayer in the Home," "Teaching Obedience in the Home," "Teaching Honesty in the Home" and "Teaching Citizenship in the Home." Washington, D. C.: The Confraternity of Christian Doctrine. 20 cents each.

SCHMIEDELER, EDGAR, O. S. B. *Parent and Child.* New York: The Paulist Press. 10 cents.

———. *Your Child's World.* New York: The Paulist Press. 50 cents.

———. *Your Home: A Church in Miniature.* Washington, D. C.: National Catholic Welfare Conference. 25 cents.

Towards a Better Family Life. Washington, D. C.: National Catholic Welfare Conference. 35 cents.

RELIGION IN THE HOME

BRODERICK, MONS. EDWIN B. *TV and Your Child.* New York: The Paulist Press. 15 cents.

BUSCH, WILLIAM. *Family Prayers.* Collegeville, Minn.: The Liturgical Press. 5 cents.

BYLES, KATHERINE DELMONICO. *Religion in the Home for Elementary School Children.* New York: The Paulist Press. 15 cents.

———. *Religion in the Home for the Pre-School Child.* New York: The Paulist Press. 15 cents.

FARRELL, JOHN and EILEEN. *This Is Cana.* St. Meinrad, Ind.: The Grail. 10 cents.

For Happier Families. Chicago, Ill.: Coordinating Committee of the Christian Family Movement. 75 cents.

MCLOUGHLIN, HELEN. *Family Advent Customs.* Collegeville, Minn.: The Liturgical Press. 15 cents.

MUELLER, THERESA. *Family Life in Christ.* Collegeville, Minn.: The Liturgical Press. 20 cents.

STOKES, BERNWARD, O. F. M. *How to Make Your House a Home.* Washington, D. C.: National Catholic Welfare Conference. 50 cents.

Weiser, Francis X., S. J. *Religious Customs in the Family.* Collegeville, Minn.: The Liturgical Press. 25 cents.

MAGAZINES AND NEWSPAPERS

MAGAZINES SPECIALIZING IN MARRIAGE AND FAMILY LIFE

Family Digest. Monthly reprint magazine of articles appearing elsewhere in the Catholic press with stress on family information and entertainment. Address: 41 E. Park Drive, Huntington, Indiana. Subscription: $3 a year.

The Grail, The Magazine of Catholic Marriage. Monthly magazine of articles on marriage and family life with stress on relationships between husband and wife, parent and child, the family and society, and the family and God. Address: St. Meinrad, Indiana. Subscription: $3 a year.

Act. Official publication of the Christian Family Movement. Monthly newsletter stressing news of C.F.M. activities, reprints of pertinent talks, and articles on family life. Address: 100 W. Monroe St., Chicago 3, Illinois. Subscription: $1 a year.

Family Life News and Comment. Quarterly publication of NCWC Family Life Bureau. Address: 1312 Massachusetts Ave. N.W., Washington 5, D. C. Subscription: $2 a year.

GENERAL MAGAZINES PUBLISHING MATERIAL OF FAMILY INTEREST

Catholic Digest. General interest digest of popular articles, including family human interest. Address: 2959 N. Hamline Ave., St. Paul, Minnesota. $3 a year.

America. Catholic weekly review featuring occasional articles of family interest. 70 East 45th St., New York 17, New York. Subscription: $8 a year.

Ave Maria. Catholic family weekly featuring occasional articles on family life, both serious and human interest. Address: Notre Dame, Indiana. Subscription: $5 a year.

Crosier. Catholic family monthly featuring occasional articles on marriage and family life. Address: Onamia, Minnesota. Subscription: $3 a year.

Information. Catholic family monthly stressing role of Church in the United States and featuring occasional articles on family life. Address: 401 W. 59th St., New York 19, New York. Subscription: $3 a year.

Jubilee. Catholic pictorial monthly, featuring occasional picture and text articles on family life. Address: 377 Fourth Ave., New York 16, New York. Subscription: $4 a year.

The Ligourian. Catholic monthly featuring occasional articles on moral problems of dating, courtship, and marriage. Address: 1 Ligouri Rd., Ligouri, Missouri. Subscription: $2 a year.

The Sign. Catholic family monthly, featuring occasional articles and picture stories on family life in the United States and foreign countries and on marriage and family problems. Address: Monastery Place, Union City, New Jersey. Subscription: $3 a year.

SPECIALIZED PUBLICATIONS OF INTEREST TO FAMILY LIFE

Altar and Home. Liturgical Review for the Laity, featuring occasional articles on liturgy and the family. Address: Conception Abbey, Conception, Missouri. Subscription: $1 a year.

Social Order. Monthly (except July and August) magazine on social problems, featuring occasional sociological studies of family problems. Address: Institute of Social Order, 3908 Westminster Place, St. Louis 8, Missouri. Subscription: $4 a year.

Spiritual Life. Quarterly review of spirituality for the laity, featuring occasional articles on marriage and lay spirituality. Address: 514 Warren St., Brookline, Massachusetts. Subscription: $3 a year.

NEWSPAPERS OF INTEREST TO FAMILIES

Our Sunday Visitor. National Catholic weekly newspaper featuring two-page section for articles on marriage and family life, produced by arrangement with Fides Publishers. Address: 41 East Park Drive, Huntington, Indiana. Subscription: $3 a year.

Work. Monthly newspaper for "all who work for a living," featuring articles on economic and social influences on family life. Address: Catholic Council on Working Life, 21 West Superior St., Chicago 10, Illinois. Subscription: $2 a year.

INDEX

Date Due

FEB 15	FEB 20		
FEB 29	NOV 24		
APR 11	MAY 8		
APR 25	AUG 1		
7/3	NOV 24		
7/17			
July 18			
7/21			
7/28			
Aug 1			
NOV 7			
JAN 16			

Kelly, George Anthony, Father.
The Catholic marriage manual.